THREE'S COMPANY

A History of No.3 (Fighter) Squadron RAF

THREE'S COMPANY

A History of No.3 (Fighter) Squadron RAF

JACK T. C. LONG

Pen & Sword
AVIATION

First published in Great Britain in 2005 by
Pen & Sword Military an imprint of
Pen & Sword Books Ltd
47 Church Street
Barnsley
South Yorkshire
S70 2AS

ISBN 1 84415 158 1

A CIP catalogue record for this book is
available from the British Library

Printed and bound in England
by CPI UK

Pen & Sword Books Ltd incorporates the Imprints of Pen & Sword Aviation, Pen
& Sword Maritime, Pen & Sword Military, Wharncliffe Local History, Pen and
Sword Select, Pen and Sword Military Classics and Leo Cooper.

For a complete list of Pen & Sword titles please contact
PEN & SWORD BOOKS LIMITED
47 Church Street, Barnsley, South Yorkshire, S70 2AS, England
E-mail: enquiries@pen-and-sword.co.uk
Website: www.pen-and-sword.co.uk

FOREWORD

AIR CHIEF MARSHAL SIR RICHARD JOHNS GCB CBE LVO FRAeS

JACK LONG, a self-confessed Aeronautical Anoraksic, has produced a Squadron history that is a true labour of love and unique in both its style and presentation. The many photographs and the accompanying text, with its rich mixture of anecdote and comment, paints a vivid picture of a Squadron that was, and remains, very special to everyone who has enjoyed the privilege and pleasure of serving within its ranks.

The (F) stands, of course, for fighter but to my mind it represents much more. Any reference to the development of air power in the first hundred years of powered flight will invariably include the word Flexible. How appropriately can this (F) word be applied to No.3 Squadron, which has operated some fifty types of aircraft since its formation in 1912, from the pioneering Aeroplane Company and in a variety of roles which include day fighter, night/all weather fighter, light bomber and ground attack, even a short spell as the Eyes of the Fleet. That's real flexibility of employment and there can be few other Squadrons in the entire history of the RAF which can compete with that record.

My second (F) is for fighting because the Squadron's operational history has within it a golden thread of courage, skill and devotion to duty that is second to none. Some of the stories in Jack Long's book are breathtaking and will stand as enduring testament to the fighting spirit of a Squadron that has always lived up to its motto of Tertius Primus Erit and how appropriate that the Stop Press to this book should record the citation for Wing Commander Stuart Atha's DSO in recognition of his leadership and courage during the second Gulf War.

My third and final (F) stands for Friendship. When I look back on my time as CO of 3 (F), I recall an intensely busy three years. The Harrier Concept of operations was continuing to evolve and we still had much to learn as we faced the challenges of Tactical Evaluation (TACEVAL) on and off base while coping with the forward deployment of the whole Harrier Force from RAF Wildenrath to RAF Gutersloh. And then, just as our future seemed settled for the next year, I was tasked to form and lead an eight-pilot Squadron Display Team for HM The Queen's Review of the Royal Air Force as part of the Silver Jubilee Celebrations. This involved two detachments, each of a month's duration, to RAF Finningley in 1977. At that time, sacking Squadron Commanders who were suspected of failing to cut the mustard was much in vogue. Now, and indeed then, I know I could not have survived the pooh-bah traps within these various activities without the full support of a quite outstanding bunch of people for whom I retain affection and respect in equal measure. No surprise then, that my wife and I remember with much pleasure the enduring friendships we made at that time throughout the ranks of a superb Squadron. Friendships that we can still well remember and celebrate at the Annual Meeting of the Squadron Association, a thriving enterprise that owes so much to the leadership, energy and determination of Alan East.

In his introduction Jack Long quotes Dr J Bronowski as writing 'History is not events but people.' Given my 3 (F)s, not surprisingly I say 'Amen to that' confident in my belief that readers of Jack's distinctive history will find much to enjoy and to admire.

CONTENTS

INTRODUCTION

THIS COLLECTION is the result of forty years' labour of love, starting in 1963 at RAF Geilenkirchen in Germany. Originally intended as sixty pages of text for a booklet, the only problem was what to leave out and therefore who would be upset. To cover ninety years meant approximately two-thirds of a page per year; to cover fifty types of aeroplane meant just over a page each; but 3 Squadron had operated the Canberra for eleven years out of ninety, therefore requiring eight pages, and the Harrier for twenty-eight years, needing nineteen! Much of the material has appeared in our No. 3(F) Squadron Association Magazine *Three's Company*, or is intended for it in the near future. Many were written to accompany my Model Moments, a type-by-type series, or as a response to it.

If you are looking for an alphabetical or chronological list, they are available elsewhere though prone to error in the first decade. So I 'cop out' by quoting Dr J. Bronowski in *The Ascent of Man* 'History is not events, but people. And it is not just people remembering, it is people acting and living their past in the present. History is the pilot's instant act of decision, which crystallises all the knowledge, all the science, all that has been learned since man began.'

Later I quote Santayana and I hope you agree with my choices and get the feel of the Squadron. You may ask: 'What is so special about a squadron?' Chaz Bowyer expressed it well in *Fighter Command 1936-1968*:

> To don a flying overall carrying the cloth badge of a particular fighter squadron was an honour akin to admittance to a masonic enclave. Such an honour had to be 'earned' worthily and upheld in all matters. Unwritten codes of conduct were strictly observed, even at the expense, occasionally, of the written 'rules' laid down in King's Regulations. The squadron came first – indeed, was first in all considerations. Such attitudes were virtually an extension of the British public school system of conduct. Such an attitude is almost wholly associated with maturing adolescence; akin to the muscle-testing capers of young cubs in any pride of lions, daring their elders and savouring the sheer joy of unknown danger in the maturing process.

Therefore I use some of the personal anecdotes and notes of the people who wrote this history for me to present as the text to accompany many illustrations. Throughout, any opinions not in quotation marks or italics are mine, based on sixty years of aeronautical 'Anoraksia' and twenty-two years in the Royal Air Force (eighteen as a service pilot) followed by twenty-seven as a civilian pilot.

Many of the books I have used are long out of print – and sometimes reprint! – but they can be found. The photographs were collected over forty years and, partly due to the loss of two files, the original source cannot always be quoted; especially those which have been copied and recopied and are then claimed as belonging to various archives or collections. I am thinking particularly of the original John Yoxall, Charles Sims and Charles E. Brown pictures of aeroplanes which appeared in the weekly *Flight* and *Aeroplane*, as well as the fortnightly *Aeroplane Spotter,* and may be seen in published volumes. Partly because of this, for each copy of this book sold, I intend to pay 50 pence each – i.e. £1 in total – to both the Soldiers, Sailors and Airmens Families Association and the Royal Air Force Benevolent Fund, to honour 'the debt we owe'. Particular thanks is owed to the J. M. Bruce/G. S. Leslie collection – which is now owned by the Fleet Air Arm Museum, Yeovilton – for the early period. Jack Bruce and Bruce Robertson both died during this project, two historians I am proud to have known and count as friends, on whom I depended for advice and encouragement – so I hope I got it right!

I believe in the two sayings: 'Freedom is cheap until you lose it' and 'It's always politicians who lose the peace and the people who have to regain it.' Beware weasel words such as those of Clausewitz: 'War is an extension of policy.' Who promotes policy? Politicians. Who dies in war? People. So this is mostly about people and their primary equipment – aeroplanes – and therefore about pilots, although we are the first to admit our dependence on others, particularly the ladies who are rarely rewarded or praised.

I dedicate this work to:

'The First of the Many',
Lieutenant Reginald Archibald Cammell, Royal Engineers (1886–1911), the first
British, Commonwealth and Empire aviator who was detailed to learn to fly the first
British service owned aeroplane and also the first to die in an aviation incident on duty.
Also to the many air and ground personnel who followed his superb example; at the
time of writing, the latest are the crew of a No. 9 Squadron Tornado, downed by a
'friendly fire' Patriot missile.

Went the day well?
we died and never knew,
but well or ill,
Freedom we died for you.
ANON

'The First of the Many', Lieutenant Reginald Archibald Cammell, Royal Engineers, 1886 – 1911, in the cockpit of his own Blériot XXI. (The woollen Balaclava being a prototype flying helmet). *(Ron Ledwidge)*

CHAPTER ONE

The Air Company

THE TITLE OF THIS CHAPTER properly reflects the fact that the direct antecedent of No. 3 Squadron (NOT No. 2 Squadron, as is so often written) is Britain's first independent aviation unit – No. 2 (Aeroplane) Company, the Air Battalion, Royal Engineers, known to many, then and now, as 'the Air Company'; No.1 (Airship) Company was 'the Gas Company'.

There is a saying, 'If the Army was meant to fly the sky would be brown.' This is an insult to those pioneers of service aeronautical endeavour who began in 1878 as aeronauts and by 1918 were aviators. My concern is only with the latter, and only with the so-called 'professionals' who began as self-financing amateurs to gain their brevets.

The Air Battalion was formed on 1 April 1911, with No. 2 Company commanded by Captain J.D.B. Fulton RFA (Royal Field Artillery) at Larkhill; just prior to the formation of the Royal Flying Corps and the creation of the Central Flying School. He was posted there, first as an instructor in charge of the workshops and then to the Aeronautical Inspection Department. He died in November 1915, and few past or present air and ground crew, both service and civil, know the debt they owe him.

His place was taken by Captain H.R.M. Brooke-Popham, (Oxfordshire & Buckinghamshire Light Infantry) who in a letter to John Yoxall of *Flight*, when the latter was researching a short series of squadron histories, stated: 'On or about 13 April [1912] I took over the Aeroplane Company at Larkhill and in May this became No. 3 Squadron, Royal Flying Corps (subsequently 3 RAF), still at Larkhill'. This was published in *Flight*, but the information had been available since 1922 when Volume 1 of *The War In The Air* by Sir Walter Raleigh was published.

Although both Fulton and Brooke-Popham foresaw the probability of aerial fighting, bombing and the need for countermeasures to such 'ungentlemanly behaviour', the primary duty of aviators at this time was reconnaissance, until then the *raison d'etre* of the élite cavalry regiments and squadrons. Before then the flyers had been operating as a battalion split into companies, the smallest units that could be allowed to operate independently by those that got their hands dirty. Then the 'cream' realised that there could be a future in the air lark, as well as being fun.

The first three squadrons (of a proposed total of seven) date from 13 May 1912. Raleigh says: 'Towards the end of April Captain H.R.M. Brooke-Popham took over from Captain Fulton the command of the old aeroplane company on Salisbury Plain, and on 13th of May, when the Royal Flying Corps was formed, this company became No. 3 Squadron of the new formation. No. 2 Squadron was formed from the nucleus of aeroplane pilots at Farnborough, and was placed under the command of Captain C.J. Burke.' Later, he says: 'Major Brooke-Popham's squadron on Salisbury Plain was the first to get to work. In its origin, as has been told, it was the old aeroplane company of the Air Battalion, so that it was free from some of the difficulties which attend the creation of a new unit.'

What has history to do with today? In the foreword to *The Rise and Fall of the Third Reich* by William L. Shirer, one of four quotes is from George Santayana, the philosopher: 'Those who do not remember the past are condemned to relive it.'

All squadrons, stations, groups and commands have badges which are always Crown Copyright, and they are worthy of a book to themselves. No. 1 got away with a red upright monolith, with wings, which looks like the number 1, although numbers should not be used, to avoid confusion in battle, supposedly. The grant of No. 3's was delayed because the first submission consisted of five monoliths erected as a Roman III with the eagle and crown superimposed. The one that was granted is a cockatrice above a single prone grey monolith.

It is interesting to note that, to mark the fiftieth anniversary of the School of Artillery, Wiltshire County Council granted it the privilege of using the county badge, a circle depicting a bustard against eight alternate green and silver bars. It is no coincidence that the cockatrice of No. 3's badge is posed similarly upon a monolith. Squadron mottoes are also interesting: No. 1's is *In Omnibus Princeps* (first in all things) and No. 3's is *Tertius Primus Erit* (the third shall be first).

The Wiltshire County Badge, from which the 'Cock on a Rock' was hatched. (Larkhill)

An ivory simulation of the original badge presented by Squadron Leader Martyn. (3 Squadron)

The Approved Badge: Authority King George VI, September, 1937 - 'On a monolith a cockatrice'. (Crown Copywright)

CHAPTER TWO

The Conception of Air Power

L ARKHILL IS FOUR MILES NORTH-WEST OF AMESBURY on Salisbury
Plain. Chris Ashworth, in *Action Stations* says:

Larkhill – one of the oldest and most revered names in British aviation – and also one of the most difficult airfields to locate. Several sites in the Salisbury Plain area have carried the name, and this has caused much confusion.

The first Larkhill was on Durrington Down, a stretch of rough land south of the Packway, known locally as the Hill of Larks. Horatio Barber obtained permission from the War Office to use this ground for aeronautical experiments and erected a shed there in 1909. He was joined by G.B. Cockburn and Captain J.D.B. Fulton of the Royal Artillery, Bulford Barracks, the following year when the War Office offered free use of the area for flying and encouraged the development of the Bristol School of Aviation on the site.

The first Army experiments in aerial reconnaissance followed when Captain Bertram Dickson of the Air Battalion, Royal Engineers, used a Bristol Boxkite at Larkhill to observe a mock battle. In the spring of 1911 No. 2 (Aeroplane) Company was formed and housed their amazing selection of aeroplanes in sheds on the Down while the personnel lived at Bulford Camp. They became 3 Squadron when the Royal Flying Corps was formed in April 1912, and while a new aerodrome was being prepared for them at Netheravon, tents were provided on the site of the present Packway Church for the men, while the officers used the Bustard Inn as their mess.

In August 1912 Larkhill was the venue for the first military aircraft trials, but with the development of Upavon and Netheravon War Office interest in the original aerodrome waned. The Bristol School was finally closed in June 1914 after training 129 pupils at Larkhill, and with the outbreak of war the airfield site was soon covered with hundreds of corrugated iron huts as the barracks expanded.

Horatio Barber formed the Aeronautical Syndicate Limited (ASL) to build aeroplanes – believing that they had a key role to play in any future war, in particular for reconnaissance. The first design was flying by March 1910 and by 5 September his fifth design, Valkyrie I, was airborne, powered by a 35 hp Green engine. In that month the ASL moved to Hendon, where Valkyrie I was flying again by 1 October. We will return to Barber's Valkyrie and Hendon shortly.

The little flying that was done at Larkhill had not gone unnoticed, however, for Captain 'Bertie' Fulton was stationed at Bulford camp when Blériot crossed the

A Henry Farman III piloted by Claude Graham White seen at Blackpool in 1910. Note the early stick and rudder bar, plus a Burberry flying coverall advertised by him in magazines. (Alan East)

Channel and was inspired first to build his own monoplane, then to purchase from Claude Grahame-White a 28 hp Anzani-powered Blériot monoplane with which he taught himself to fly. This aeroplane lasted until after the spring of 1912, when it was being re-erected and tuned up. Never officially an Air Company mount, it was not allotted a number, but it was flown by Captain Eustace B. Loraine as late as 14 June 1912 – after the formation of the RFC.

In the autumn of 1909, Captain Dickson learned to fly in France after purchasing a Henry Farman biplane. He returned to Salisbury Plain and the following year joined the British & Colonial Aeroplane Company. Thus began his association with their Boxkite, two of which he and the actor/manager Robert Loraine flew during manoeuvres in September 1910, when Lieutenant Gibbs also flew his own 'racing' Farman with 'clipped-wings' and Robert Loraine successfully transmitted wireless signals while airborne. The results of these semi-official trials had far-reaching effects. Up to this time the War Office had spent little and been told to spend no more, but even the dinosaurs of Whitehall looked up and were forced to act.

The little money they had spent had gone to Dunne's attempts to produce an automatically stable aeroplane to enable the crew to perform other tasks and Cody's attempts to produce reliable flight: the first by scientific means, deduction and calculation, the second empirically, adding bits to improve performance and control, removing them if they had no or adverse effect. After funds had been curtailed, the Hon. C.S. Rolls offered to train Army officers. He turned down Farnborough as a suitable flying area, but approved of the Plain, and the War Office erected an aeroplane shed there for him. He died on 12 July 1910 during the Bournemouth flying meeting; his place was then taken by G.B. Cockburn and the shed was then allocated to Captain Fulton. Thus began a long association, with both working together then serving in the Aeronautical Inspection Department.

It should be remembered that at this time it was an achievement to leave the ground and to return without either injury or breakage. Aviation was an expensive hobby and those early pioneers had not only to design, build, test and demonstrate their brainchildren, but promote them as best they could. This led to mutual recrimination, partisan alliances, reporting of doubtful authenticity and the self-interested presentation of sometimes doubtful equipment and performance figures. Such a case can be made for the first aeroplane to belong officially to any British armed service.

In June 1910 a second-hand Blériot XII was purchased by the Duke of Westminster and Colonel Laycock, a director of the ENV Engine Company. This Blériot type already had a questionable reputation and was powered by a 60 hp ENV engine. It was presented to the War Office, which officially had no aviators. Therefore Lieutenant R.A. Cammell, RE, was directed to go to France, examine this present, become familiar with the construction and learn to fly it. He went to

This Blériot XII is believed to be the aircraft presented to the War Office by the Duke of Westminster and Colonel Laycock in June 1910. (JMB/GSL)

Etampes on 28 June 1910, learned to fly on the Blériot XI, then flew the XII. The engine was badly out of tune, the flights were not considered successful and damage sustained on 1 July led to repairs. This gave him time to visit the Rheims aviation meeting and report on what he saw there, which would have influenced the report he made to Fulton early the following year, which was forwarded to the War Office. This report laid the foundations of the Air Battalion, RFC and RAF – can any other junior officer lay such claim to fame, or have been so ignored and eventually vilified?

This aeroplane was accepted on 3 August 1910 and taken to Amesbury by rail, then to Larkhill. It was next flown on 9 October, but again flights proved disappointing. However on 27 November Cammell 'flew eight circuits each about 4 miles [6.5 km] in circumference before landing with a broken wire'. Repaired, he then set off for Aldershot (49 miles/78.5 km) but strong winds at 1,000 ft (300 metres) forced him to land at North Waltham (21 miles/33.5 km). This seems abysmal, but the top speed recorded for the XII was 60 mph (96 kph) and winter winds at that height frequently exceed 50 mph (80 kph). Remember also that most meteorological studies at that time took place at sea level for the Admiralty, who cared little for wind speeds at heights above the crow's nest. By 29 December it was in the Balloon Factory for repair and although stated to be one of five aeroplanes 'available for Army work' seems not to have flown again, the engine probably being used in the SE1. Again, remember that any engine was a rare commodity at this time, even one of doubtful reliability. It was probably intended to carry the early number B1, but it does not seem to have been applied, either to the craft itself or to relevant paperwork.

Cammell's experiences at the Blériot aerodrome at Etampes and of the XI probably led to his purchase of the XXI which was powered by a 70 hp Gnome rotary engine. It was flying with the Air Battalion by May 1911. The side-by-side seating was probably conducive to the number of experiments carried out with it by enabling an observer to assist and note the actions of the pilot – remember that there was no intercom and it was necessary to shout over the engine and 'wind' noise. At least two different types of compass, an air speed indicator and an altimeter were tried, and a 100 ft (30 metre) wireless aerial carried on a drum and fed back through rings to the tail. It would be interesting to know if an oft-repeated mistake started on this type? Namely-the failure, prior to landing or simulated combat, to wind it in! I recall being frightened once when attacking a Lincoln with a Meteor in the fifties; but Ernest K. Gann found it a good substitute for a low-level radio altimeter when 'attacking' Iceland in the early forties. Did the XXI have any 'arrested' landings?

But we are slightly ahead of ourselves. Before this the purchase of a Farman Militaire and a Paulhan were authorised. Captain C.J. Burke, Royal Irish Regiment, who had learned to fly Farmans in France, was assigned to the former, which became available in November 1910. The Paulhan, a month later, was to be Fulton's mount. He was accompanied to France to collect it by Cockburn, who described the Paulhan as 'weird'. It was not a success – any description pales beside a photograph. But it did carry the number F2 and a 50 hp Gnome, as did the Farman which was F1. This was not only the first reference to a numbering system but the recipient of the first form of certification ever applied to an aircraft in Britain:

CERTIFICATE NO.1

This is to certify that Aeroplane No. F1 has been tested by me in flights of
5 to 7 miles without wing extension, both with a 14-stone passenger and
without a passenger, and in two flights of 5 to 7 miles with wing extension,
with a 14-stone and a 12-stone passenger respectively.

Weather calm with slight gusts.

It was subsequently examined and showed no defect.

(signed) Mervyn O'Gorman

Superintendent Balloon Factory

16 March 1911

In Cammell's report of 19 January he recommended the purchase of aeroplanes for
training and experimentation. For the former, both biplane and monoplane, he
suggested the Boxkite and Blériot XI; for the latter the Farman Militaire and Paulhan
biplanes (which were already available by then), a Blériot - whether the XII which
was available or his XXI is uncertain, Antoinette and Valkyrie monoplanes, and

Cody and Dunne
biplanes. His choice of the
Valkyrie is ironic as it was
in one of these craft that
he was killed (see Chapter
3). It is interesting to
speculate what the future
would have been for him
and the Company's
descendants had he lived
– would they have
remained in khaki (with
dress blues and spurs),
with the Air Ministry at
Chatham?

The War Office took

*Farman III the first
known markings of
ownership and serial
number.   (JMB/GSL)*

*Paulhan biplane at
Farnborough
showing unusual
construction of flying
surfaces. (JMB/GSL)*

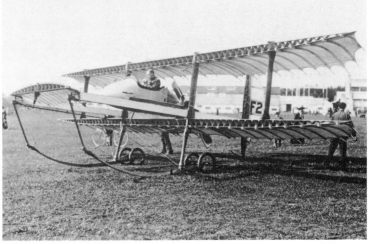

note of Cammell's report, endorsed by Fulton, and placed the first order for a mass-produced aeroplane. These were to equip the first independent British service unit to operate aerodynamic apparatus that could navigate the atmosphere without physical connection to the ground, such as kites and static balloons.

1910 Bristol Boxkite

The accompanying pages from *War in the Air, Vol. 1* by Sir Walter Raleigh show the importance of the Bristol Boxkite to the Company. It was the first to gain a production order, trained more than any other prior to the First World War, and achieved the first successful vertical landing! Its wing loading was only 2 lbs/sq ft (9.8 kg/sq m). Between 1910 and 1914 a total of seventy-six were built, and two were exported to Germany, nine to Russia, three to South Africa and two to Spain.

ROYAL ENGINEERS, BALLOON SECTION PREPARING FOR AN ASCENT WITH BALLOON 10,000 FEET CAPACITY,

Copyrigh

A balloon plus support transport of what became No.1 (Airship) Company (hence Gas Company), the No.1 Squadron R.F.C./R.A.F. (JMB/GSL)

The airframe was made of ash and silver spruce, with cast aluminium or steel fabricated joints. Harald Penrose, in *British Aviation: The Pioneer Years*, describes the covering,

> *Doping the wings was the latest step towards perfection. Soggy fabric*

had always been a source of trouble. The earliest practice with the Boxkites had been to use cotton cloth and souse it with sago, kept simmering in a bucket of water for twenty-four hours and then strained through muslin until it emerged as a glutinous mass. This was pasted on the wings, which became taut when the mixture was dry, but if it rained or there was dew the whole fabric became soggy again. By the beginning of 1911 there had been brief popularity for the patent material called Pegamoid, smelling strongly of camphor, which was impervious to the air, but however tightly stretched when new, it soon slackened off. Rubberised fabrics were popular

A Bristol Boxkite F4 outside RFC sheds, further downhill are the sheds of the Bristol Flying School. (JMB/GSL)

for a time, and lasted somewhat better than Pegamoid. Then in mid-1911 came Emaillite from France which, like the British-produced Cellon, was derived from the chemical research work in Berlin of Dr Eishengrun on cellulose acetates. Aircraft constructors soon switched to these new transparent solutions, and were delighted to find that not only did they tighten the fabric and render it impervious to humidity and extremes of temperature but also this 'dope' enabled fabric surfaces to be joined as easily and firmly as though held by the rubber solution used to join the rubberised fabrics. At this stage of aircraft development cellulose dope was an even more important invention than duralumin.'

This aeroplane was built by someone as unsung as the aeroplane: Sir George White,

Bt. He was the first Chairman and Managing Director of the British & Colonial Aeroplane Co. as well as many important transport undertakings. A Chair of Aeronautics, Bristol University is endowed in his name. Penrose explained:

> It was decided to scrap the Zodiac, and further construction of the production series was suspended at Filton . . . However, George Challenger, in the light of his practical experience in constructing the Filton Zodiacs, insisted it would be easy to make a British replica of the Farman, as the design had not been patented and full constructional details with dimensions of scantlings had been published in the world's aeronautical press.

> 'Do it,' decided Sir George.

> Within a couple of days Challenger had sketched the design details, and by using much of the original structure of a production Zodiac, the first Boxkite was completed within three weeks.

> It was taken to the high, smooth expanse of Larkhill alongside the Packway road, about a mile from Amesbury, where Bertram Dickson kept his Farman close by the Royal Artillery Camp. The War Office, with a knowledgeable eye to the future, offered free use of this splendid and unencumbered area to any serious flying experimenter, so Sir George White had no difficulty in securing permission to erect three large sheds on its northern brow – where they remain to this day, hidden behind recent buildings. From the great sliding doorways a broad view extended across the Plain, with the dark circle of Stonehenge like a lodestar in the middle distance southward. . .

> By the end of July [1910] the Boxkite had been erected, and the Darracq from the discarded Zodiac installed . . . rather than trust the groping efforts of Sydney Smith to fly, Sir George obtained the services of a French pilot, Maurice Edmond, who was expert with Farmans. In the still of early morning he made the first flight (30 July 1910) and reported the handling was perfect but engine power deficient.

> Sir George immediately instructed Challenger to lay down a batch of twenty Boxkites at Filton, where floor space was ample to erect four or five simultaneously. Through Stern's efforts in France a 50 hp Gnome was secured for immediate delivery, despite the waiting list, and installed in the prototype.

Subsequently *The Aero* reported:

> On Tuesday, September 6th, at the Flying School of the British and Colonial Aeroplane Company Limited at Larkhill, Salisbury Plain, some trials were carried out by Captain Bertram Dickson with the Bristol biplane he will use in the forthcoming Army manoeuvres. The machine was specially built for the purpose at the Filton Works and was only commenced on the 17th August, but was delivered complete in seventeen days on Salisbury Plain, on Saturday, which is probably a record in aeroplane construction.

CHAPTER THREE

The Gestation of Air Power

THE GESTATION PROCESS commenced with the formation of the Air Battalion on 1 April 1911 and ended with its renaming with effect from 13 May 1912 – at just over one year, longer than the norm but speedily for Whitehall committee work! The decision to form the battalion was promulgated in an Army Order dated 28 February 1911 and it 'opened for business' on All Fool's Day, ostensibly with seven aircraft bought and paid for at £6,303 – not all available – plus the Blériot XII, Rolls' Wright and the FE1. However, in late 1910 the XII was subject to reconstruction and transmogrified into the SE1! Moreover, if the Paulhan (F2) was one of the seven, it only appears to have flown at Farnborough and disappeared into the Army Aircraft Factory on 3 February 1912 never to reappear! Also Rolls sold his Wright to the War Office on 15 March 1910 for £1,000! So was that sum included in, or should it be added to, the £6,303? If the latter, then was it actually one of the seven or should it be added to that total and also deleted from the extras, leaving only the FE1? Or should the SE1 be added to that?

Of the Air Battalion only No. 2 (Aeroplane) Company is relevant to this brief history. Their commander was Captain Fulton, with Burke plus Lieutenants B.H. Barrington-Kennett, Grenadier Guards (B-K), Cammell and D.G. Conner, Royal Artillery. They were shortly joined by Captain E.B. Loraine, Grenadier Guards, Lieutenants G.B. Hynes, of the Royal Garrison Artillery and H.R.P. Reynolds of the Royal Engineers, and later by Captain Henry Robert Moore Brooke-Popham ('Brookham'), Oxfordshire & Buckinghamshire Light Infantry, one of many who foresaw air combat and, upon taking over as CO of the Air Company prior to the formation of the RFC, soon put his ideas to the test. The relevance of Regiment of origin will become, to the reader that is, apparent after August 1914 (pages 43 & 51 refer), particularly for Burke and Barrington-Kennett.

Four Boxkites were ordered in March 1911 but none were available until May, so Cammell's Blériot XXI, plus Fulton's G-W Blériot and Cockburn's Farman formed a 'private air force', nominally with Rolls' Wright, which never appeared, and an ENV powered [!] Howard Wright F3 which became the BE2: BE5/205, which was purchased from Captain Maitland but withdrawn from service after a month in July 1911. Maitland is reported by Raleigh as flying this machine at Larkhill when only two other machines were there, Fulton's Blériot and the first Bristol biplane, but he crashed and broke both ankles on 1 August 1910. He subsequently took command of the Gas Company and leaves our story. His was a distinguished career, both before and after his brief flirtation with aviation. Strangely, the following year his brother, H.M. Maitland, stalled and crashed from 100 ft (30 metres) while attempting a right-hand turn in a Bristol. Not only did he impact at virtually the same spot with the same injuries but that aircraft was also powered by an ENV!

Cammell 'looks to the future' as future 'Company men' of the Royal Engineers consider how to retrieve the Blériot XII. Probably December 1910. (Royal Engineers Museum)

The only accommodation at Larkhill was tented until the onset of winter when quarters were arranged in Royal Artillery Barracks at Bulford – a 3 mile (4.8 km) march. An old army dictum was, 'Look after the horses, then your men, and only then yourself.' Unsurprisingly, some men of the Air Company chose to 'sleep with the horses' in their wooden sheds.

The Boxkites (B7 and F4–8), an additional four having arrived in the summer, achieved much, albeit basically as training machines, but every take-off then was a learning and therefore training flight. Continued requests for more modern and, in particular, faster types led to the procurement of a Breguet tractor biplane with a 60 hp Renault engine (B3/202), a Nieuport monoplane with a 50 hp Gnome engine (B4/253) and Deperdussin with a 60 hp Anzani engine (B5/252). If the fact that control of the Air Company was vested in the Royal Engineers, is understood, then obtaining a diversity of aeroplane and engine types – apparently more advanced than home products – enabling study of their assembly and construction, was eminently sensible.

The Farman 'Militaire' (F1) had crashed in January and virtually only the tail was left, but the Factory rebuilt it. After a preliminary test flight at Laffan's Plain (Farnborough), Burke took off for a longer test. Soon after take-off the biplane tilted, dug the right wing into the ground and nosed over, smashing itself to pieces and severely injuring Burke.

With their limited resources the Company soon got to work. Early in June it was reported that four machines got away from Amesbury at short intervals, heading for Aldershot, Burke in the Farman, Fulton and B-K in Bristols and Cammell in a Blériot. All four landed safely about one and a half hours after the first had left. Cockburn, among others, was full of praise. This was a practice for the next big event; manoeuvres at Cambridge in August.

Before that, starting on 22 July, was the *Daily Mail* Round Britain Race for a prize of £10,000 – about £10 per mile – on a circuit with nominated stops and certain compulsory conditions. The company was represented by Cammell in a Blériot and Reynolds in a Howard Wright. The departure of the latter was delayed until 6 p.m. by the ENV motor and between Brooklands and Hendon engine trouble forced Cammell to land on Hounslow Heath. Both arrived at Hendon for the night. The next day Cammell suffered a slight delay on the line, then on the way to Edinburgh via Harrogate and Newcastle the Blériot burst a cylinder at Wakefield. Owing to an even more delayed start, caused by further engine problems, Reynolds landed at Doncaster for the night. Incidently, seven other competitors out of thirty failed to reach Harrogate. Upon arriving at Harrogate, Reynolds found he was so far behind the leaders that he opted to retire.

Because of drought conditions the summer manoeuvres were cancelled, but the company was not dismayed. Another cross country was not to be denied them, reported as a "massed flight of Bristols – five machines". Yet 'Brookham', who was attached from Staff College at the time, records setting off with Burke on the old Farman – only four were, therefore, Bristols – most probably the first Bristol order. They flew from Larkhill to Oxford, which they reached the following morning, having spent the night at Wantage owing to a head wind and a slow speed of 30 mph (48 kph) in a calm. B-K, with a mechanic, made it as far as Burford where a forced landing necessitated assistance, which was provided by 'Brookham' and Lieutenant Hynes in the only motor vehicle possessed by The Company. Lieutenant Conner crashed on high ground at West Ilsley, fortunately without injury and possibly because he was using a map torn from a Bradshaw Railway Guide – no aeronautical charts with contours etc., only spot heights if anything and a railway would only mark summits such as Shap.

Support tools and equipment had all gone ahead to Cambridge so, when Burke and 'Brookham' had engine failure 10 miles (16 km) out of Oxford, repairs were

In 1911 Reynolds and Cammel flew the Howard Wright F3, entered by The Company in the Daily Mail *Round Britain Race. (JMB/GSL)*

effected by a coachbuilder in the city. They sustained more serious damage shortly into the next flight, however. Captain Massy had engine trouble 50 yards out and the machine was wrecked, again without injury. Next to suffer was Lieutenant Reynolds. In his own words:

> That evening, soon after seven o'clock, I started again, it was warm and fine but rather suggestive of thunder; the air was perfectly still. I scarcely had occasion to move the control lever at all until I got to Bletchley, where it began to get rather bumpy; at first I thought nothing of this, but suddenly it got much worse, and I came to the conclusion it was time to descend. A big black thunder-cloud was coming up on my right front; it did not look reassuring, and there was good landing ground below. At this time I was flying about 1,700 ft [520 metres] altitude by my aneroid, which had been set at Oxford in the morning [it was now evening and pressure can change in such a length of time by a considerable amount – obvious now but not then]. I began a glide, but almost directly I had switched off the tail was suddenly wrenched upwards as if it had been hit from below, and I saw the elevator go down perpendicularly below me. I was not strapped in, and I suppose I caught hold of the uprights [struts] at my side, for the next thing I realised was that I was lying in a heap on what ordinarily is the undersurface of the top plane. The machine in fact was upside down. I stood up, held on, and waited. The machine just floated about, gliding from side to side like a piece of paper falling. Then it over-swung itself, so to speak, and went down more or less vertically sideways until it righted itself momentarily the right way up.
>
> Then it went down tail first, turned over upside down again, and restarted the old floating motion. We were still some way from the ground, and took what seemed like a long time reaching it. I looked round somewhat hurriedly; the tail was still there, and I could see nothing wrong. As we got close to the ground the machine was doing long swings from side to side, and I made up my mind that the only thing to do was to try and jump clear of the wreckage before the crash. In the last swing we slid down, I think, about 30 ft [9 metres], and hit the ground pretty hard. Fortunately I hung on practically to the end, and, according to those who were looking on, I did not jump till about 10 ft [3 metres] from the ground.
>
> Those who were looking on were two men, stark naked, who had been bathing nearby. About fifty or sixty people soon collected, and some time passed before it occurred to anyone to remark that these two men had no clothes on.

Knowing what we do about both the Boxkite and its builder, we are better placed to understand why it was chosen for the initial basic flying training role, to the chagrin of other pioneer aviation experimenters, who – as we have seen – did not possess similar resources.

B-K and Cammell got to Cambridge with the only remaining two servicable aeroplanes, the latter having been delayed at Larkhill and flown via London. Many valuable lessons had been learned and were put into effect for the following year, but

A Valkyrie, with The Aeronautical Syndicate Limited sheds behind. This company presented one to the War Office, in which Lieutenant. R.A. Cammell, RE, became the first of many service men to die on duty in an aviation incident, at Hendon on 17 September 1911. (JMB/GSL)

by then five companions had paid the ultimate price, starting with Cammell.

At Hendon, Horatio Barber was barred from participating in the May 1911 Parliamentary Aerial Defence Committee display. On the 25th Mr B.G. Benson, a pupil at his Valkyrie School, was killed attempting a first gliding descent from 200 ft (60 metres), when, at 40 ft (12 metres) he stalled and crashed. Barber offered four of his Valkyrie monoplanes to the services and two used models with engines went to Lieutenant Samson at Eastchurch. One new two-seat model was accepted by the War Office in August but they had to provide the engine. Cammell supervised the installation by company men of a 50 hp Gnome and on 17 September he took it up on a trial flight, later intending to fly it to Farnborough. He slid inwards during a steep turn and the crash killed him. It was suggested that he may have forgotten to use the forward elevator – control surfaces and levers were yet to become standardised – but a number of sources claim he was overconfident.

Of a later accident Joubert de la Ferte says, in his book *The Fated Sky*, 'I am inclined to think, fully equipped as I am with hindsight, that this accident was caused by reversed controls. Owing to the steep angle of turn (bank), the rudder had become the elevator and the elevator the rudder. Misuse of the controls in such circumstances very often produced a crash, particularly at low altitude.' Consider also the lack of a seat belt or safety harness and only having controls or the airframe to hold on to. If the turn is unbalanced, the body will obey centrifugal or centripetal force and slide outwards or inwards, the 'clutching hand' over or miscontrolling.

Note also that on 28 September Samson reported that his Valkyries were unusable and appear to have vanished into storage at Shorts Brothers. They were not new and were said to have been sold to gain cheap publicity. Even the engines, which were also 'gifted', Samson declared to be inherently unreliable. Barber is recorded as being the first in Britain to fit dual controls, but this tends to be overlooked, which is unfortunate.

Criticism is easy but the author, R. Dallas Brett, says, 'The Air Battalion was equipped with seventeen aeroplanes of eleven different types, most of them useless.' But earlier he had said, 'Machines were built or repaired at Brooklands with wood stripped from old packing cases. There were instances of constructors covering their wing surfaces with stout paper because they could not afford to buy canvas or linen.' This was hardly likely to instil the confidence to buy and operate such machines, so Fulton, Sykes and B-K went to Rheims and witnessed the military aviation trials, leading to later trials on Salisbury Plain. Among the specifications laid down was dual control! These also closely followed the performance of the de Havilland designed and Factory-built BE1, which led to more criticism. Yet if this was the best performance known to the Factory for military purposes, can they be blamed for aiming at parity and hoping for superior achievement from competitors?

The Government had purchased three more aeroplanes: a Breguet B3/202, Nieuport B4/253 and a Deperdussin B5/252; Fulton's memo of 8 September had recommended the purchase of these and Sommer aeroplanes. Testing these machines required a winter skeleton staff to remain at Larkhill, but the majority were expected to return to barracks and 'do some proper soldiering', which meant drill and 'spit and polish', an aspect of service life that always caused conflict, particularly when it was found that all the white, bright and shiny equipment made observation from the air during exercises easy.

The Nieuport was the first to arrive, having been purchased in September. B-K was to achieve fame but not fortune on this type. Hynes was nominated for the Breguet L1 and was sent to Douai to learn to fly it. It arrived in England in October and on the 14th it was tested by de Havilland, who found the top speed to be 49 mph (78.5 kph). Cockburn said of it: 'It was a most unwholesome beast, with flexible wings, steel spars, and wheel control . . . It required enormous strength to steer it, and was perseveringly and valorously flown by Lieutenant Hynes.' He is believed to have taken up three passengers on at least one occasion. On 1 April 1912 it was dismantled, overhauled at the Factory in June, and was flying again on the 20th. It remained at Farnborough. It was to be overhauled at the British Breguet works at Hendon that summer. It was then flown to Farnborough on 7 March 1913, and was totally wrecked on landing, still marked B3 although it had been allotted 202 the previous autumn. The Deperdussin arrived in January 1912.

A Breguet L1 B3 [later allotted 202 but never carried] flown by Lieutenants G.B. Hynes [once with 3 passengers] and A.G. Fox. The aeroplane was nicknamed 'The Tin Whistle'. (JMB/GSL)

CHAPTER FOUR
The Birth of Air Power

T HE YEAR 1912 was extremely important in British aviation history, and it has therefore been well covered elsewhere. Here I shall dwell only on those aspects that affected The Air Company and its 'mounts'.

The first Deperdussin, which was purchased by the War Office in January, had a 60 hp Anzani radial engine and was numbered B5, later 252. It was soon joined by a similar aeroplane in June, after the new system was imposed, which therefore immediately became 257. This aircraft was owned by Captain Patrick W. Hamilton, who brought it with him to Farnborough on secondment.

Two more were purchased after the military trials: number 26, French built, became 258, and number 21, British built, 259. The former was involved in the first of a series of fatal crashes which led to the so-called 'monoplane ban', which affected 260 and 279, both powered by 70 hp Gnomes. Numbers 252, 257, 258, 259 and 260 were all on charge to No. 3 Squadron, RFC although some did little flying – 259 was described as 'design bad' and 'unsafe to fly' at different periods of its grounding, subsequent to the suspension of all monoplane flights.

In January occurred a very significant first flight, that of the BE1; designed by de

The Royal Aircraft Factory BE1 [allotted B7, later 201] delivered to The Aeroplane Company 11 March. Its Wolseley engine was water cooled with radiator, tank and plumbing; on 18 June it was replaced by an air-cooled Renault with improvement in performance. (JMB/GSL)

The R.A.F. BE2 [later 205] Renault-powered model, proved superior to all official entrants in the Military Trials in August 1912. (JMB/GSL)

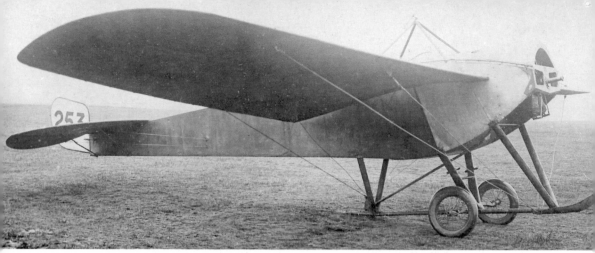

The Nieuport IVG 253 [ex B4] flown by Lt. B.H. Barrington-Kennett for 4 hours and 51minutes covering 249 miles & 840 yards on 14 Feb 1912 to win the Mortimer Singer £500 prize. (Author)

An R.A.F. BE.3 204 [ex BE4], delivered on 31 July 1912, being observed by King George V at Farnborough during the Royal Review. The aircraft crashed on 11 March 1914 killing Capt. C.R.W. Allen & Lt. J.E.G. Burroughs. (JMB/GSL)

Havilland and built at the Factory it met all the requirements of military aviation of the moment. In the same month, on the 29th, Barrington-Kennett (B-K) flew 111 miles (177.05 km) non-stop in an attempt to win the Army share, £500, of a prize put up by Mortimer Singer. However, this was short of the 129 miles (206.5 km) which won the Naval prize the previous August. So he set out again sixteen days later with Corporal Ridd, RE, as passenger in the Gnome Nieuport, and flew 249 miles 840 yards (399.16 km) to set the new world's distance record in a closed circuit – marked out on Salisbury Plain – and in so doing set a new British duration record of 4 hours 32 minutes; he was then awarded the Army prize. His younger brother, V.A., passed his test for the Royal Aeronautical Club Certificate (No.190) at Eastchurch on a Short on 5 March.

The pace was increasing and even before the trials the War Office ordered three two-seater Avro biplanes, to be powered by 50 hp Gnome engines. A 'prototype' with a 60 hp ENV engine had large flat radiators either side of the passenger which might have kept him warm but would definitely have restricted observation. In the Army Estimates it was disclosed that thirty-six new aircraft, of which eighteen were British, had been ordered to supplement the sixteen machines already owned by the Army. Of the total of £320,000 allotted to the War Office to develop military aviation, £90,000 was to be spent on a new aerodrome on Salisbury Plain, and the Royal Flying Corps was to be created.

There were to be seven squadrons each with twelve aeroplanes, thirteen officers and thirteen NCOs, all of whom were to be qualified pilots – two and a half years later little over half this target was available to go to France. Flying training was to take place at the new Central Flying School (CFS) and the Royal Aircraft Factory was to train air mechanics, rebuild aeroplanes, test new aircraft and engines – British or foreign – and repair the equipment of both the Military and Naval Wings. This work must have been hindered by an early visit by the King. R. Dallas Brett observes:

> *Following on the Naval Review H.M. King George V visited Farnborough and inspected the Military Wing of the RFC. He was received by Major F. H. Sykes of the 15th Hussars, who had been appointed to command the Military Wing, and witnessed flights by Captains Burke and Loraine, and Lieutenants Fox, Reynolds, and Barrington-Kennett. The aircraft flown before His Majesty were three examples of the BE type, built at the Royal Aircraft Factory, a Nieuport and a Deperdussin. The new Avro biplane, which had been built to a War Office order, was paraded but not flown.*
>
> *Mr. Geoffrey de Havilland flew the latest edition of his BE biplane and dived it from 2,500 ft to 100 ft to demonstrate its strength. This machine [BE3/203] differed from his first two models [BE1/201 and 2/202] in having staggered wings, a longer fuselage, and a four-bladed airscrew which was driven by a 50 hp Gnome engine.*
>
> *Corporal Frank Ridd, who had accompanied Lieutenant B.H. Barrington-Kennett on his world's record flight for the Mortimer Singer prize, was the first NCO of the RFC to secure his brevet (No.228)* [NB: in Appendix E of Brett's book this number is given for Lieutenant L. Dawes, 4 June, Bristol (Br.) Salisbury Plain; preceded by No.227 2nd Corporal Frank Ridd 4 June Bristol (CFS) Salisbury Plain; both of these number/name combinations are confirmed in 'Jane's All the World's Aircraft' 1913], *and he was followed a few days later by Staff-Sergeant R.H.V. Wilson* [No. 232, 18 June Bristol (CFS) Salisbury Plain: both sources agree]. *Both men received their instruction on Bristol biplanes* [Boxkites] *from officer pilots of the CFS at Salisbury Plain.* [At this time Salisbury Plain was actually still Larkhill, not Upavon or CFS].
>
> *A double tragedy occurred at the CFS Salisbury Plain on 5 July. Captain E.B. Loraine, who was one of the most capable and experienced pilots of*

The parade to witness the unveiling of The Airmen's Cross, 5 July 1913. This was erected in memory of Captain Loraine and Sgt. Wilson.   *(JMB /GSL)*

the RFC, and who had learned to fly on a Valkyrie monoplane at Hendon [No.154, 7 November, 1911], was flying a Nieuport monoplane (Gnome) with Staff-Sergeant Wilson in the passenger's seat. Soon after taking off the pilot attempted a sharp turn, but the machine side-slipped inwards, and then the nose dropped and she dived vertically into the ground from 400 ft. Both occupants were killed.

Evidence was given at the inquest by Corporal Ridd to the effect that he had flown as passenger with Captain Loraine on a flight immediately preceding the fatal one and a similar incident had then occurred, the machine slipping out of a steep turn and diving towards the ground. On that occasion the turn was begun at 1,000 ft and the pilot managed to pull out of the dive with height to spare [this became known as a spiral dive, almost as deadly then as a spin].

It is obvious that Captain Loraine was suffering severely from over-confidence, and it is difficult to justify his action in repeating a manoeuvre which he knew from such recent experience to be dangerous without first attaining a safe height. This accident once more emphasised in no uncertain manner the vital necessity for gaining plenty of height when about to attempt unusual evolutions.

At this point it is worth returning to the death of Cammell, as recorded by Dallas Brett:

The Army pilot who was detailed to take delivery of the first of the two Valkyrie pusher monoplanes, which had been presented to the War Office by Mr Barber, was Lieutenant R.A. Cammell. No doubt he was chosen as he had had much more experience with monoplanes than any other officer. He arrived at Hendon to execute his commission on 17 September, and it was arranged that he should have thirty minutes practice round Hendon aerodrome before he attempted to fly across country to Farnborough.

Apparently he was over-confident, and, instead of waiting until he had become familiar with the peculiar controls of the Valkyrie, [forward fixed stabiliser with separate elevator, instead of rear tailplane with elevator which became standard, as in Blériots] *he began to execute steep turns, such as he was accustomed to perform on his own Blériot, as soon as he had got it into the air.*

After a few minutes of this, he was seen to cut off his engine and attempt a gliding turn. He overbanked and the machine side-slipped inwards to the ground.

Lieutenant Cammell, who was thrown out on to his head and killed, had taken his R.Ae.C. certificate [No.45] on December 31st, 1910, on a Bristol biplane. He was an accomplished Blériot pilot and his death was a great loss to the Air Battalion.

Rereading the above reports, with their comments based on 100 per cent accurate hindsight, and also remembering Joubert's comment on apparent cross-controlling, I am reminded of the dangers of making well-considered judgements, after consulting a multitude of sources, about a split-second decision. Consider again Bronowski and Santayana.

It is also worth stressing again that CFS Salisbury Plain still meant Larkhill – the new aerodrome at Upavon was preparing for the first course throughout June and July. But because of the delay some pupils received ground instruction at Farnborough and flying instruction continued at Larkhill even after the official start date of 17 August – which was weeks after the official, 19 June, opening of Upavon! – when seventeen pupils commenced the first course.

At the end of July at Larkhill preparations were well under way for the start of the military trials. The Bristol school temporarily vacated their sheds, relocating most of their machines to their school at Brooklands. A passage from Dallas Brett is interesting:

One of the conditions of the trials required each competitor to demonstrate before the judges that his aircraft was stable in flight, and capable of flying in a wind averaging 25 mph without undue risk to the pilot. Eleven machines flew in gusts above the minimum, but only in five cases was the average wind velocity above 25 mph throughout the flight.

A splendid feat was performed by Howard Pixton in connection with this test. The wind had been rising steadily for an hour and was becoming more and more squally when, to the amazement of the other competitors, he brought out his Bristol monoplane for the required demonstration. Captain Patrick Hamilton, RFC, bravely volunteered to fly with him as observer.

Pixton fought the gusts, which varied between 17 and 44 mph for fifteen minutes, whilst the little monoplane was tossed violently about the sky. On many occasions during this grand flight the control column was jerked forcibly out of the pilot's hand.

This was No.15 in the trials, becoming No.262, as No.14 became 263, both being taken on charge by No.3.

What was the Air Company up to, meanwhile? According to R. Dallas Brett:

1912 Bristol Prier 256 flew and crashed frequently with 3 until grounded with all monoplanes in mid-April. (JMB/GSL)

About two hundred members of Parliament came down to Salisbury Plain on the 8th of August to witness the competition of the aeroplanes in the Military Trials. The wind was judged to be too tempestuous for flying, and the flights were limited to a few short circuits round the aerodrome in the afternoon. On the morning of that same day a brigade of territorials, training at Wareham, asked for a couple of military machines to co-operate with them. Major Brooke-Popham and Lieutenant Porter started off in an Avro [E/500 Gnome], and, a little later, Captain Hamilton followed in his Deperdussin. The wind was so strong that Captain Hamilton could make no headway, and was obliged to turn back. Major Brooke-Popham and Lieutenant Porter battled their way to Wareham, but could not get farther to co-operate with the troops, and flew back to the plain in the afternoon. On their arrival there they found that the wind had abated a little, and that flying had just begun in the trials. The next day the newspapers published long accounts of the exhibition flying over the aerodrome, with a single line at the end recording that 'military airmen also flew'.

In the early days of September No. 3 Squadron co-operated in the cavalry divisional training, but without much success. The weather was bad, and the cavalry, being preoccupied with their own work, had not much attention to spare for the aeroplanes. In France, a year earlier, aeroplanes had been systematically practised with cavalry, sometimes to direct a forced march, sometimes to detect dummy field works, prepared to deceive the cavalry and to lead them into a trap.

Avro Es [later designated Avro 502] 290. All five went from 3 to help form 5 Squadron. (JMB/GSL)

CHAPTER FIVE

The Growing Pains
of Air Power

Raleigh gives the following account of No. 3 Squadron's work with the military:

> But if their co-operation with the cavalry was imperfect and
> disappointing, the work done by aeroplanes a few days later, during the
> army manoeuvres, was a complete vindication of the Flying Corps. There
> were two divisions on each side; the attacking force, under Sir Douglas
> Haig, advanced from the east; the defending force was commanded by
> General Grierson. . . . The fatal accidents of the summer and the
> consequent prohibition of monoplanes diminished the available force of
> aeroplanes, but a squadron of seven was allotted to each side. Major
> Burke's squadron [No 2], with its headquarters at Thetford, operated with
> the attacking force; Major Brooke-Popham was with the defence at
> Cambridge.

The first fatals referred to were on 6 September, Captain Patrick Hamilton with
Lieutenant Athole Wyness-Stuart, flying a 100 hp Deperdussin (No 258). While on
reconnaissance for cavalry divisional training they crashed at Graveley near Hitchin.
Four days later Lieutenants E. Hotchkiss and C.A. Bettington, flying an 80 hp
Bristol (Coanda No 263) from Larkhill to Cambridge, crashed at Wolvercote near
Oxford. This caused the plan to allocate a force of monoplanes to one force and
another of biplanes to the other to be nullified.

> No. 3 Squadron, nevertheless, assembled near Cambridge in such
> strength as it could muster; there were Major Brooke-Popham, Captain
> Fox, and Second Lieutenant G. de Havilland of the squadron [the latter
> was in the RFC Reserve]; these were joined by Mr. Cody, who came as a
> civilian with his own machine, and by officers of the Naval Air Service,
> who flew Short biplanes.

A frequently miscaptioned and occasionally cropped photo was corrected for *Flight*
by 'Brookham' in 1949:

The location is given as '*Cambridge Hotel yd 1912 Man.*', Charteris' anno-
tation '*chicken farming*' and the word '*Wadham*', are both in pencil.

It is captioned in *The Sky Their Battlefield* as: 'A group of pre-war aviators
at Eastchurch in 1912' and B-K is identified as his younger brother
V.A., Gregory as Gordon, looking at the uniform, this is Captain R. Gordon,
RMLI (Royal Marine Light Infantry) RAeC 166 – given as 161 in 1913 Janes –
6 December 1911: Lieutenant R. Gregory, RN, would have been wearing the

Back Row: *Captain G.W.P. 'Father' Dawes, Wadham, Lieutenant P.H.L. Playfair, Charteris, Ashton, Lestrange Malone, Spenser Grey, Fox.*
Front Row: *Second Lieutenant de Havilland, Captain Gregory, Majors Brooke-Popham and Sykes, Commander Samson, Lieutenant Barrington Kennett.*

1912 Bristol Coanda monoplane 14 (There was also a Coanda biplane in the Military Trials) which became 263, and crashed 10 September killing Lieutenants C.A. Bettington and E. Hotchkiss. (JMB/GSL)

Third Squadron machines on manoeuvres, Mr. Rothschild's estate 1913 : Joubert's caption in his album. It shows three Blériot XI, a B.E.2a 226 and an H.F. 20 on the right. (Joubert)

same uniform as Commander S.C. Samson, RN, who commanded the Eastchurch, Sheppey, Navy flying school (hence the confusion?) and Lieutenants C. L'Estrange-Malone, RN and Spencer Grey. This agrees with the naval contingent listed by Dallas Brett. It would appear that these were the defenders, with reinforcements or replacements for the fatals. Sykes was boss of the RFC Military Wing and B-K the Adjutant – 'He made a vow that the corps should combine the smartness of the Guards with the efficiency of the Sappers'.

A full description of these manoeuvres, entitled 'The Royal Flying Corps' First Field Exercise' by Bruce Robertson, appeared in *Aviation News* 1992, including the visit by the King, who popped down by train from Balmoral for a two-day visit.

Dallas Brett has little to say of the manoeuvres but reports more on the crashes:

> *Each of the opposing forces in the Army's autumn manoeuvres was provided with one squadron of aeroplanes [eight machines] of which twelve aircraft were provided by the Military and four by the Naval Wing of the RFC.*
>
> *The results obtained by the RFC were kept secret, but it is known that in spite of very bad weather a number of magnificent flights were made, notably by Com. Samson, Capt. Raleigh, and Lieuts. Fox and Mackworth. The weather and engine troubles caused innumerable forced landings and the RFC paid a terrible price for its first official co-operation with the Army.*
>
> *On Friday, 6 September, Capt. Patrick Hamilton, accompanied by Lieut. Wyness-Stuart, was on reconnaissance in a Deperdussin monoplane [Gnome] at a height of 2,500 ft above Graveley, near Hitchin. Witnesses saw the machine wobble violently following a loud report, and the whole aircraft collapsed and broke into several pieces. Both officers were killed instantaneously.*
>
> *Heer Fritz Koolhaven, the designer of the machine, gave evidence at the inquest to the effect that the probable cause of the disaster was that some part of the rotary engine had come off, burst through the cowling and cut one of the flying wires. This theory was corroborated by Major Brooke-*

Popham, who had been flying in company with the Deperdussin just prior to the accident. The Accidents Committee of the RAeC came to the conclusion that the airscrew had burst and the consequent vibration had caused the engine, which was not supported by the extra front bearing recommended by the makers, to foul the cowling. This would have broken the cabane to which the landing wires were attached.

Captain Patrick Hamilton was a pilot of great experience who had learned to fly at the Blériot school at Hendon, and had subsequently toured the United States and Mexico in company with Mr G.M. Dyott.

Earlier Dallas Brett says: A daring experiment in night flying was conducted at the Nassau aerodrome, New York, by the two English pilots, Mr G.M. Dyott and Capt. Patrick Hamilton, who had both qualified during August [1911] at the Blériot school at Hendon. Dyott went to the Deperdussin factory in France and watched the construction of two monoplanes with which he and Capt. Hamilton proposed to tour the USA and Mexico, giving exhibition flights.

One of these machines had been fitted with a powerful searchlight, and Dyott flew it successfully on a pitch black night without any ground lighting of any kind. Capt. Hamilton accompanied him and operated the searchlight, picking up the aerodrome from a height of 300 ft, after a short flight across the surrounding countryside.

He was the most accomplished Deperdussin pilot in the RFC [brevet 194, 12 March 1912, Deperdussin, Brooklands]. Lieutenant Wyness-Stuart was a pupil of the Bristol school.

Four days later, on September 10th, another double fatality occurred. This time the victims were Lieut. E. Hotchkiss, who was noted as the

Deperdussin 26 in the Military Trials became 258. It broke up in mid air over Graveley, killing Captain Patrick Hamilton and Lieutenant Wyness-Stuart. (JMB/GSL)

1913 R.A.F. B.E.2 267, 18 March 1913, wrecked in what appears to be a landing accident at Larkhill on top of H.F.20 No. 268 (JMB/GSL)

Bristol Company's brilliant chief instructor at their Brooklands school, with Lieut. C. Bettington.

Lieutentant Hotchkiss was flying a Bristol monoplane [80 hp Gnome] from Larkhill, Salisbury Plain, to Cambridge, with Lieut. Bettington as observer. The machine was one of two [Bristol Coanda] which had competed in the Military Trials.

The aircraft was seen at 2,000 ft [600 metres] above Port Meadow, Oxford, and it began to glide down as if the pilot had decided to land. It descended normally to 500 ft [150 metres] but at that point it began to dive steeply. At 200 ft [60 metres] the fabric tore off the right wing and the aircraft crashed vertically into the ground. Both the occupants were killed instantaneously. Lieut. Hotchkiss was the first officer of the RFC Reserve to meet his death while on Military duties.

The RAeC inquiry established beyond reasonable doubt that a quick-release catch, which was secured to a perforated steel strap screwed to the bottom of the fuselage had opened. The flying wires were anchored to the ends of this strap, which had been torn from its fastenings by the heavy strain thrown upon them by the opening of the catch. A piece of flying metal had evidently punctured the wing and the fabric had ripped and torn off.

Faced with the break-up of two monoplanes of different types whilst flying normally in reasonable weather conditions, Col. Seely, Secretary of State for War, issued an edict banning the flying of all monoplanes by pilots of the Military Wing, RFC.

This ill-considered decision was not followed by Mr Winston Churchill, First Lord of the Admiralty, so that the peculiar position arose of officers of the same corps working under quite different conditions. The spectacle of pilots owing allegiance to the Navy happily flying their fast monoplanes, whilst they themselves were confined to slower biplane types, infuriated the military officers of the RFC, and this unfortunate affair hastened the inevitable split between the two sections of the service.

The ban was also a deadly blow at the more enterprising manufacturers, and was responsible in large measure for the unfair facilities which were accorded to the Royal Aircraft Factory to enter into direct subsidised competition with private constructors.

This official stupidity was to continue for five months, the ban not being finally removed until February 1913.

However, there was no sudden rash of monoplanes or other superior types offered to the service following the end of the ban. It had been able to maintain firm control – and continued to do so – over the construction of aeroplanes for military use with the aid of the Aeronautical Inspection Department headed by

R.A.F. B.E.2a [note extended upper wing] taken on charge 26 March 1913. It went to No.2 Squadron to be flown to Montrose by Captain J.H.W. Becke 19-21 May. (Author)

Fulton. He would not have tolerated the 'packing case and brown paper' apparently favoured by Dallas Brett. Moreover, he refers to 'The ancestor of the Moth, Mr Geoffrey de Havilland's brilliant design, the BE2A' which was both designed and built at the RAF! So why should the RFC buy from private manufacturers? They did in fact subcontract construction of this 'brilliant design' to private firms, thus enabling them to learn what was expected. Raleigh says:

> Operations started at six o'clock on the morning of Monday, the 16th of September. At a conference on Sunday afternoon, General Briggs, who commanded the cavalry on the side of the defence, told General Grierson that the forces were far apart, and he could not hope to bring in any definite information until Tuesday. General Grierson was reminded by his chief staff officer that he had some aeroplanes. 'Do you think the aeroplanes could do anything?' he asked of Major Brooke-Popham, and on hearing that they could, ordered them to get out, 'and if you see anything, let us know'. Monday morning was fine and clear; the aeroplanes started at six o'clock; soon after nine o'clock they supplied General Grierson with complete, accurate and detailed information concerning the disposition of all the enemy troops. During the rest of the manoeuvres he based his plans on information from the air. On his left flank there were only two roads by which the enemy could advance; he left this flank entirely unguarded, keeping one aeroplane in continual observation above the two roads, and so was able to concentrate the whole of his forces at the decisive point. In the course of a few days the aeroplanes rose into such esteem that they were asked to verify information which had been brought in by the cavalry.
>
> After the manoeuvres No. 3 Squadron returned to Larkhill, to do battle all the winter with the old difficulties. The officers were accommodated at an inn called the 'Bustard', about two and a half miles [4 km] to the west of Larkhill sheds; the men were at Bulford camp, three miles [5 km] to the east of the sheds. After a time the men were shifted to the cavalry school at Netheravon, which, though it was a little farther off, gave better quarters. Meantime a new aerodrome was being made, with sheds complete, at Netheravon, for the use of the squadron. The winter was passed in the old exercise of co-operation with the artillery and in new experiments. At Easter a 'fly-past' of aeroplanes took place at a review of a territorial brigade on Perham Down. General Smith-Dorrien, who reviewed the troops, took the salute from the aeroplanes. There was a cross-wind, so that the symmetry of the spectacle was a little marred by the crab-like motion of the aeroplanes, which had to keep their noses some points into the wind to allow for drift.

Dallas Brett reports:

> On May 9th [1913], No. 3 Squadron of the Military Wing, RFC, flew from Salisbury Plain to Farnborough as a unit. Sqdrn-Cdr Brooke-Popham tested the air and then gave orders for the nine aircraft to take-off at five-minute intervals.

Henry Farman 20 284 flown by Lieutenant G.I. Carmichael in June 1913. In August he took it with him to form No. 5 Squadron along with 3s five Avro Es/502s.
(Chaz Bowyer)

Major G.I. Carmichael when he became the CO of No.5 Squadron.
(Chaz Bowyer)

Capt. Allen and Lieut. Wadham of 'A' Flight led the way on BE2 tractor biplanes [70 hp Renaults], *followed at the appropriate intervals by Lieuts. Cholmondley, Carmichael, and Allen, and Maj. Higgins of 'B' Flight on their Henry Farman pusher biplanes [70 hp Gnomes]. The last-named pilot was forced down by engine trouble shortly after taking off, but this was put right in twenty minutes, and he continued to Farnborough. 'C' Flight, represented by Sergt Frank Ridd, Lieut Ashton, and Capt. Connor, brought up the rear on their Maurice Farman pusher biplanes [70 hp Renaults]. Sergt. Ridd was* the only pilot who failed to complete the course, as he had to make a forced landing near Andover with serious engine trouble.

On June 3rd, a great review was held on Laffan's Plain in honour of the King's birthday, which was attended by His Majesty in person. The Royal Flying Corps was represented by six Maurice Farman biplanes, four BE2 *tractor biplanes, two Henry Farman pusher biplanes, and one Blériot monoplane. These machines first taxied past in line ahead at fifty yards intervals, and later took-off and flew past at 150 feet [45 metres]. As each machine came to the saluting base the pilot dived and pulled up again to the regulation height. This was the first occasion on which this now-established form of ceremonial salute from the air was carried out.*

Dallas Brett gives details of The Great War Office Scandal; but here a summary will suffice:

On 19 March, Colonel Seely, the War Minister, stated categorically: 'We have in our possession 101 aeroplanes capable of flying.' After much angry argument in the house, on June 4th he stated that he had '126 aeroplanes,

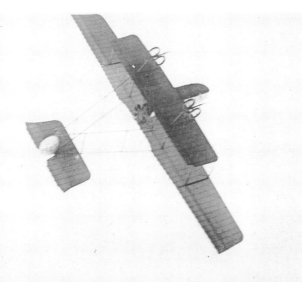

Biplane Looping the loop at Aldershot 31.

A Henry Farman 20 352. The photograph was probably printed upside down to cash in on looping the loop popularity. Its regular pilots were Lieutenants T. O'Brien Hubbard and R. Cholmondley. (JMB/GSL)

Henry Farman 20 274 in shed at Netheravon on 19 August 1913. It was taken on charge on 31 March, went to France and was wrecked on 19 September 1914. (Joubert)

of which thirty-one were in various stages of repair'. Further discussion and request brought forth a written tally of 120 machines, stated to be in first-class order. On investigation this was whittled down to fifty-two, of which 'No. 3 Squadron at Larkhill had ten machines in all, two of which were under repair. The proper equipment of each squadron had been fixed at eighteen machines, so that No. 3 was eight aeroplanes deficient, and of the ten machines on hand, two were unsuitable for active service. The two Blériots were understood to be in transit between Farnborough and Larkhill.'

Of the 120 listed only fifteen were monoplanes; all had been at Farnborough with a strange split: four were under repair there and at the Royal Aircraft Factory there were two under repair and nine under reconstruction. If it is assumed that the two under repair were the two Blériots said to be en route to Larkhill, then the other thirteen were probably all those grounded under the 'monoplane ban'- which had been lifted in February!

Dallas Brett goes on:

On visiting Farnborough the investigators found such a muddle that they were unable to distinguish between the equipment of No. 4 Squadron, then in embryo form [just split off from No. 2, which was not listed, only mentioned as 'Montrose'; 3 were mentioned as 'Larkhill'], and that of the Royal Aircraft Factory . . . The investigators found forty-four aeroplanes actually capable of flight and at the disposal of the officers of the RFC . . . a large proportion of which were school machines . . . after eighteen months of preparation.

In *Fifty Years Fly Past*, Geoffrey Dorman states:

Col. Seely [who died as Lord Mottistone] *had succeeded Haldane as War Minister. Mr. Joynson-Hicks, MP, nicknamed 'Jix'* [afterwards Lord Brentford], *who, as a rising young politician had taken an interest in the RFC, accused Seely of not providing sufficient aeroplanes for the Corps. Seely claimed that the Military Wing possessed 101. Jix claimed that there were not half that number, and demanded to be taken on a tour of inspection. The War Office, Jix alleged at the time, tried to fool him, flying aeroplanes from a station he had already inspected to the next one, so that he could count them again* [The RAF did it during a Russian visit to the UK early in the Cold War]. *The second Lord Brentford [Dicky] who went on the inspection with his father has recently told me that his father did not know much about aircraft recognition, but that he, Dicky, was the keen young type, who would in more modern times have been an Air Training Corps cadet with Proficiency badge. He had noted numbers on rudders, and points such as that, and was able to tell his father what was happening.*

Raleigh says:

As early as September,1912, a part of Major Burke's squadron [2], stationed at Farnborough, was detached, and became the basis of No. 4

Squadron, commanded by Major G.H.Raleigh, of the Essex Regiment, who had joined the Air Battalion before the birth of the Royal Flying Corps. In August 1913 a single flight of Major Brooke-Popham's squadron became the basis of No. 5 Squadron, under Major J.F.A. Higgins.

Dallas Brett refers to:

'The first [November, 1913] *of the Scout Class: the revolutionary Sopwith Tabloid* [80 hp gnome] *which set new standards of design . . . the best aeroplane of the year'* – [which conveniently forgets the Royal Aircraft Factory's Blériot Scout No. 1, also known as the SE2, which had flown almost a year earlier!] – and, albeit with passenger, turned in 80.9/ 43 mph and 1,000 ft (300 metres) in 1minute 45 seconds. Compare this with the figures given later for the de Havilland/Royal Aircraft Factory design.

Raleigh continues:

Several officers joined during the winter, and the squadron began to be better supplied with machines. For the manoeuvres of 1913 it was made up to war strength both in aeroplanes and transport. These manoeuvres, however, did not give much opportunity to aeroplanes; the idea was that

R.A.F. B.E.3 203 [ex BE3] delivered 13 May 1912 and fitted with a wireless on 24 August, seen on manoeuvres during the autumn of 1913 with Lieutenants Allen and Birch talking to the CO, Major Brooke-Popham. (JMB/GSL)

four divisions, and with them No. 3 Squadron, should operate against a skeleton army. The squadron had next to nothing to observe, but could not get full value out of their skeleton force. The tactics of the air had hardly reached the point at which a theoretical trial of this kind might have been of value. Yet a good deal was learnt by the Flying Corps from these manoeuvres. Major Brooke-Popham drew up a very full report on them, and in the following winter Lieutenant Barrington-Kennett, under the title 'What I Learnt on Manoeuvres, 1913', brought together the information he had obtained as adjutant from the talk and written statements of those who took part in them. Both reports show a relentless attention to detail, and an unfailing imagination for the realities of war. The squadron had twelve machines at work during the manoeuvres. Of these one was wrecked. Two had to be brought home by road, one for lack of spare parts, the other because it had been taken over with a damaged engine – both avoidable accidents. The one wrecked machine, Major Brooke-Popham remarks, does not represent the loss that would have occurred on a campaign. Four machines had to land, and would have been captured in war. That is to say, the loss amounted to five machines in four days, or one-tenth of the force every day.

There is far more here than can be recorded in a relatively small book but, in view of later events, the following extract is important:

Lieutenant Barrington-Kennett's essay well illustrates his keenness and foresight in preparing the corps for the ordeal of 1914. He was a great disciplinarian, he knew every officer and man individually, he was universally liked, and he did more perhaps than anyone else to hold the corps together and to train it in an efficient routine. He knew – no one better – that the corps, though it did its work in the air, had to live on the

1913 Henry Farman 20 with a Vickers .303 machine gun seen in 1913. The aircraft is believed to be 352 seen at Farnborough. (JMB/GSL)

ground, and that its efficiency depended on a hundred important details.

In 1916, now a Major, he returned to the Grenadier Guards who had lost many officers – leadership can only be from the front – and was killed in action near Festubert. In the following year Colonel Burke rejoined the Royal Irish Regiment, being killed on the first day of the Arras offensive, 9th April 1917.

The work of Major Brooke-Popham's squadron, during these years of preparation, included a great diversity of experiment. With the progress of flight it began to be realized that fighting in the air was, sooner or later, inevitable, and in the winter of 1913 a series of experiments was carried out at Hythe, by a single flight of No. 3 Squadron, under Captain P.L.W. Herbert, to determine the most suitable kind of machine-gun for use in aeroplanes. A large number of types were tested, and the Lewis gun was at last chosen, with the proviso that it should go through a series of tests on the ground. These took a long time, and it was not till September 1914 that the first machines fitted with Lewis guns reached the Flying Corps in France.

From the beginning of 1914 onwards, No. 3 Squadron also began a whole series of experiments in photography; Government funds were scanty, and the officers bought their own cameras. There was no skilled photographer among them, but they set themselves to learn. They devised the type of camera which was used in the air service until 1915, when Messrs. J.T.C. Moore-Brabazon and C.D.M. Campbell brought out their first camera. They would develop negatives in the air, and, after a reconnaissance would land with the negatives ready to print. In one day, at a height of five thousand feet [1,500 metres] and over, they took a complete series of photographs of the defences of the Isle of Wight and Solent.

The squadron still has an album of Joubert's photographs; descriptions of some of his flights are in his books.

From time to time there were a good many adventures by members of the squadron outside the daily routine. The first night flight by any officer of the Military Wing was made on 16 April, 1913, by Lieutenant Cholmondley, who flew a Maurice Farman [an MF 7] machine by moonlight from the camp at Larkhill to the Central Flying School at

The Squadron's first Maurice Farman MF7 Longhorn.   (JMB/GSL)

Upavon, and back again . . . During the month of July 1913 Lieutenants R. Cholmondley and G.I. Carmichael became evangelists for the Flying Corps; they went on a recruiting tour to Colchester, and gave free passenger trips to all likely converts among the officers of the garrison there. Long before this, in 1912, the squadron had begun to train non-commissioned officers to fly. The first of these to get his certificate was Sergeant F. Ridd. He had originally been a bricklayer, but after joining the Air Battalion had developed an extraordinary talent for rigging, and became an all-round accomplished airman. Others who were taught to fly soon after were W.T.J. McCudden, the eldest of the four brothers of that name, and W.V. Strugnell who, later on, became a flight commander in France. The most famous of the McCuddens, James Byford McCudden, VC, who brought down over fifty enemy aeroplanes, joined the squadron as a mechanic in 1913, and became a pilot in the second year of the war. In his book, Five Years with the Royal Flying Corps (1918), he says, 'I often look back and think what a splendid Squadron No. 3 was. We had a magnificent set of officers, and the NCOs and men were as one family.'

An interesting observation, at Netheravon in April 1914, appears in this latter book:

In the same shed in which this Farman [Maurice] was housed was an SE, which for some unknown reason was not flown except one afternoon when Major Higgins arrived from Farnboro' to fly the machine back there. This was the SE2/2a No. 609, then known as the BS1, to which we will return – after its second reconstruction in 1914 – with Salmond's deep recce in 1915.

In his autobiography Geoffrey de Havilland says:

The R.A.F. BE4 [later 204] at Farnborough with airship sheds in the background, did much flying with 203 in 1913 during autumn Manoeuvres. (JMB/GSL)

The aeroplane was the BS1, a small single-seater scout, the first of its type . . . This machine has since been referred to as the prototype of all single-seat fighters . . . But I think I most appreciated a book by H.G. Wells, which he gave me. On the title page was written: 'To Geoffrey de Havilland from Mervyn O'Gorman. In memory of an aeroplane 92–50–900.' The figures referred to the performance we had measured: 92 mph [147 kph] top speed, 50 mph [80 kph] slow speed, and 900 ft [275 metres] per minute climb. The climb was phenomenal for those days. I appreciated the words on the title page more than the contents of the book.

With a nominal 100 hp 14-cylinder Gnome rotary in 1913 it set an astonishing target. Bruce states that the actual output was about 82 bhp which established figures of 91.7/51 mph and 900 ft/minute initial rate of climb. The engine mounting was designed to take a 140 hp Gnome! Imagine squadrons of these escorting flights of BE2a's in 1914 – it would all have been over by Christmas.

Dallas Brett says:

The second disaster, which occurred on the following day [11 March 1914], was definitely due to the breaking of the rudder post of an old BE [80 hp Gnome] which had been built at the Royal Aircraft Factory in June 1912.

Capt. C.R.W. Allen of No. 3 Squadron, RFC, was flying the machine,

R.A.F. B.E.4 204, seen during autumn Manoeuvres, strict security with two riflemen and a civilian bobby – note spectator at rear! The aircraft crashed on 11 March 1914. (JMB/GSL)

with Lieut. J.E.G. Burroughs as passenger. They took off from Netheravon in a perfect calm and began to circle the aerodrome. After flying for five minutes, and having nearly completed a circuit, the whole rudder fell off the machine at a height of 350 feet. The biplane flicked into a spin and both occupants were killed instantaneously as it hit the ground.

The pilot was a most experienced officer who had taken his certificate [No.159] as long ago as November 14th, 1911 [Bristol, Brooklands], and his passenger was also a pilot, having qualified in France and been awarded his brevet [No. 1213] on January 31st, 1913, by the Aero Club de France.

An investigation showed that the steel tube which formed the rudder post was fractured at the base of the rudder, just below where it passed through the frame of the rudder itself and was welded to it.

The rudder post was examined microscopically at the National Physical Laboratory and the general opinion was that the factor of safety of such a tube was three, and that it was of such design and construction that it should have been capable of withstanding all normal strains in flight. It was thought possible that the material had been weakened by overheating during the welding process and that the flaw thus caused was masked by the fracture itself. This particular machine had been subjected to severe stresses during its life and the Accidents Committee of the RAeC found that it had 'probably been damaged prior to this particular flight'.

No. 3 Squadron is fortunate to have Allen's letters, bound and presented by his

Blériot XI once belonged to the International Correspondence School, who presented it to the War Office. As 219 it joined 3 Squadron in June 1913 and was used on manoeuvres. (M Davis)

Blériot XI 293 collected by its regular pilot Joubert on 26 August 1913, who then flew it during the manoeuvres. It was tested to destruction at Farnborough on 6 November. (JMB/GSL)

sister, ending with a eulogy from the men of the squadron at the time.

Here's Raleigh:

> *The month of June in 1914 was given up to a Concentration Camp at Netheravon. The idea of bringing the squadrons together seems to have originated with Colonel Sykes, whose arrangements were admirable in their detailed forethought and completeness . . . There was a natural rivalry among the squadrons. Major Burke's [2] was reputed to have the best pilots, while the Netheravon squadrons had had more training in co-operation with other arms, and in the diverse uses of aeroplanes in war.*

When civil flying was suspended, Dallas Brett records that 'of the 881 British subjects who had qualified for aviators' certificates at the outbreak of war, 305 were serving as officers and 47 as NCOs or men in the Army or the RFC (Military Wing), and 101 were officers, and 39 petty officers or ratings serving in the Royal Naval Air Services'. That means that over half, 492, were in the fighting services and 389 were civilians.

Before leaving the UK, Fate had one last trick for the Air Company. Raleigh reports:

> *No. 3 Squadron was at Netheravon when war broke out; on the 12th of August the machines flew to Dover and the transport moved off by road to Southampton, where it embarked for Boulogne. The squadron suffered a loss at Netheravon. Second Lieutenant Skene, a skilful pilot, with Air*

Blériot XI 221 seen here with the ex Military Trials number 4 seen on the wing and with French pilot Perryon up. It joined 3 in June 1913 to be flown by Captain A.G. Fox and Lt. V.H.N. Wadham; crashed 31 October. (JMB/GSL)

Mechanic R.K. Barlow as passenger, crashed his machine soon after taking off; both pilot and passenger were killed.

Godfrey Negus gives Barlow's initials as R.N. buried at Bulford, Wilts., and R.R. Skene is buried at Send, Surrey. They were the first airmen to have war graves. The aircraft was a two-seat, 80 hp Gnome-powered Blériot XI which Joubert refers to in *The Fated Sky*: 'The flight started with a tragedy as one of our reservists stalled his aircraft – my old friend No. 260 – when taking off, and crashed, killing himself and one of our best engine mechanics.' The number 260 was originally allotted to a Deperdussin monoplane (80 hp Gnome) reallocated No. 419 from C.F.S. number series 401–600 from August 1912, according to *British Military Aircraft Serials* by Bruce Robertson; No. 3 Squadron was allotted 250–300. Like all good theoretical schemes it suffered from the practical needs of the situation pertaining at the time. As to the reasons behind the crash McCudden, in *Five Years in the Royal Flying Corps*, states that Skene returned to the airfield for adjustments to his engine, then after this *second* take-off the engine failed *before* the crash and it was probably overloaded with essentials for overseas war service.

CHAPTER SIX

Baptism of Fire

WHEN THE CORPS WENT TO WAR, it initially operated as one unit. Raleigh describes the departure:

The transport of the squadrons, which proceeded by way of Southampton, was largely made up from motor-cars and commercial vans collected at Regent's Park in London. The ammunition and bomb lorry of No. 5 Squadron had belonged to the proprietors of a famous sauce: it was a brilliant scarlet, with the legend painted in gold letters on its side – The World's Appetiser. It could be seen from some height in the air, and it helped the pilots of the squadron, during the retreat from Mons, to identify their own transport.

The early days are well covered by McCudden in *Five Years in the Royal Flying Corps* and in *Swifter Than Eagles* by John Laffin, a biography of Marshal of the Royal Air Force Sir John M. Salmond, who, as a major on the outbreak of war, had taken over from 'Brookham' when he became Deputy Assistant Quartermaster-General at Headquarters. This led to numerous adverse comments by those who should have known better, one of which implied that he 'chickened out' of the cross-Channel flight. However:

On the same day, Salmond saw off the 'planes of his own squadron –

A 1914 postcard from the front, to mother from a loving son. It depicts a Blériot XI-2, note union flag under wing. (Author)

each aircraft carrying the pilot, his mechanic and his tools, and the kits of both men . . .

Salmond then shepherded the transport to Southampton docks. Normally he would have flown to France with his squadron and he would have much preferred to do so, but he realised that the transport was the weakest link in his command – as it was in any squadron at that time. Salmond knew that if the transport failed his aeroplanes would be short of fuel, tools, spares and some mechanics. In short, his squadron would not be a fighting unit. As it happened, his presence with the transport was providential, for at the docks a staff officer ordered mechanics and vehicles on to different ships.

Major-General Sir W. Salmond had once told his son about a flotilla destined for the Nile in 1881. Rudders had been packed on one ship, which sank, and hulls on another. Remembering this, Salmond protested at the order. When this had no result he refused to move from the docks unless he could take his unit intact.

This had immediate results. There was an urgent exchange of telegrams between Southampton and the War Office and Salmond won the point. Arriving at Boulogne he could find no orders waiting for him, but he sought out the help of Major (later Lord) Ironside who applied his usual energy to the matter and had orders for Salmond by the evening. The squadron slept on the quayside that night and on the next day the transport joined the aircraft and pilots at Amiens.

As we saw in the last chapter, Colonel Seely gave the number of aircraft available in 1913 as 120. In fact, the total strength in the field was sixty-three – and one of those did not last long. Three provided the first victims on active service in France. Raleigh reports:

On Sunday, the 16th of August, the headquarters of the Flying Corps, the aeroplanes of Nos. 2, 3 and 4 Squadrons, and the transport of Nos. 3 and 4 Squadrons moved from Amiens to Maubeuge. Second Lieutenant E.W.C. Perry [another reservist] and his mechanic, H.E. Parfitt, of No. 3 Squadron, who were flying a BE 8 [No.625] machine [familiarly known as a 'bloater'] crashed over the aerodrome at Amiens; the machine caught fire, and both were killed. . . . Three of these machines in all were flown over at the beginning; they had been allotted to the Aircraft Park, and were taken on charge of the squadrons in the field to fill vacancies caused by mishaps.

McCudden refers to this as a BE4, which, with the BE3, was the forerunner of the 8 and known as the 'goldfish'; the major difference is the gap between the top of the lower wing and the bottom of the fuselage, as used on the Bristol F2b Fighter the 8 had no gap.

Raleigh continues:

The first aerial reconnaissances by the Royal Flying Corps were carried out on Wednesday, the 19th of August, by Captain P.B. Joubert de la Ferte of No. 3 Squadron, in a Blériot [XI-2], and Lieutenant G.W. Mappleback in a BE[2]. They started at 9.30 a.m., and flew without observers. [This was the first of many, which saved the BEF from encirclement by von Kluck's Second Corps, but it seems to be ignored by eminent academics and historians in recent TV programmes on World War One].

On the 24th the retreat was in progress. As early as the morning of the 23rd the Royal Flying Corps had begun to shift its quarters from Maubeuge to Le Cateau. The transport and machines of No. 3 Squadron moved southward on that day, and on the 24th headquarters and other squadrons also moved to Le Cateau. 'We slept,' says Major Maurice Baring, 'and when I say we I mean dozens of pilots, fully dressed in a barn, on top of, and underneath, an enormous load of straw . . . . Everybody was quite cheerful, especially the pilots.'

Ten bases in nineteen days, all that peacetime practice had paid off.

. . . The news was not reassuring. Captain H.C. Jackson [retired as General Sir Henry] *as observer with Lieutenant E.L. Conran* [No. 3 Squadron] *went up at 8.30 a.m.* [on the 24th] *and came back at 12.30 pm with information of long enemy columns moving from Grammont through Lessines into La Hamaide and further troops on the Ath–Leuze road. They had flown as far as Ninove and Alost, but found the country there clear. On returning over Lessines at 11.30 a.m. they saw three German aeroplanes on the ground; they dropped a bomb overboard, but missed.*

Another reconnaissance on the 26th – No. 57 – is described in full but the aeroplane is given as 387, which was a *single*-seat Sopwith Tabloid. Since it had a pilot, Lieutenant G.F. Pretyman and an Observer, Major L.B. Boyd-Moss, however, this cannot be it. No. 397 was an Avro 504, but No. 3's only known one was 517 and that did not join the squadron until November, so it was probably 367, a Henry Farman F.20 with an 80 hp Gnome. Whichever machine it was, at the end of the sortie it force-landed and was burnt to prevent capture.

According to Laffin:

Sir John French's infantry was so hard-pressed, so battle-worn and exhausted that Salmond and several other officers asked Sir David Henderson if they could temporarily become soldiers again and help the officer-depleted battalions. Told to report to Sir Charles Ferguson, they found him near Le Cateau – scene of a magnificent rearguard defence. Tired but calm, Ferguson pondered for a minute, then said to Salmond, 'Thank David, will you, but tell him I think I now have almost more officers than men'.

On the way back Lt. W.F. MacNeece [of No. 3 Squadron.], *one of the RFC party, passed the regiment from which he had been seconded* [Royal West Kent]. *Seeing their state he burst into tears and had to be restrained from joining them.* [pages 19 & 53 refer]

Failing to destroy the British, von Kluck eventually wheeled left across the British front, planning to smash the French Army, and walked into a bag with armies on three sides of him. This, the Battle of the Marne, saved the Allies. It was one of the great decisive battles of the world.

All this time the RFC squadrons observed and reported on German movements. Their reports were not always passed on, nor were they always acted upon. Thus for a short time a remarkable situation obtained during the Marne battle. Unbeknown to both sides, the British and Germans were retiring away from each other. From the air Salmond saw three enemy columns, each of eight miles – '24 miles of scuttling Germans', as he expressed it. He landed near a Marne bridge and there met a British Army Brigade-major, E.L. Ellington [later Marshal of the Royal Air Force Sir Edward, Chief of the Air Staff 1933–37], who was supervising the retreat of his own troops across the bridge. After giving Ellington the news, Salmond hurried to HQ 2nd Corps with his report. The high-ranking GSO who received it was incredulous and unenthusiastic, but the report was accurate. Sometimes during this period the Army did not show as much confidence in air reports as it might have done.

Soon, however, the value of air reconnaissance proved itself fully, and Corps commanders began to ask for aircraft to be allotted specifically for their own use. Up till this time all four squadrons had operated with GHQ as one command under Henderson. The British C-in-C decided on decentralisation and as a beginning Salmond was ordered to detach a flight daily to report to Sir Horace Smith-Dorrien, commanding 2nd Corps. In this way the Corps squadrons were born. . .

A machine of Salmond's squadron had an early success. Lt. V.H.N. Wadham and his observer, A.D. ['Bosky'] Borton, forced a German to land within British lines. When Salmond reported this to GHQ the two airmen were congratulated by the C-in-C . . . The squadron was transferred to St Omer as part of a move to protect the Channel ports, and for the rest of the war some part of the RFC was stationed there. Salmond chose a root field near the Chateau de Werrpes and marched his men up and down to flatten the surface. The machines flew in without a casualty. Salmond himself brought in the RFC's only SE2 single-seater scout. During the first winter of the war the country and roads became the yellow, sticky, muddy mush that the troops were to hate. Salmond's squadron laid tons of cinders, brought from gasworks, to keep the airfield serviceable.

Trenchard, now a Colonel, arrived from England in November and by the spring of 1915 the RFC had six squadrons divided into three wings. The 1st Wing, made up of Nos. 2 and 3 Squadrons, and commanded by Trenchard, was with the 1st Army; the 2nd Lt-Col C.J. Burke, and the 3rd Lt-Col B-P ['Brookham'].

At the Chateau de Werrpes [Choques/Gonnehem] No. 3 Squadron pushed on with wireless and photography. Capt. Arthur Barratt developed a Morse signalling lamp and with it ranged the British batteries on the

A Blériot Parasol in 1914 with Lieutenant A.S. 'Ugly' Barratt in the cockpit. Note the Union flag is inboard under the wing and the Aldis lamp for signalling to our artillery batteries. (Joubert)

enemy target. The gunners greatly admired him, for the Germans constantly shot at him while working with the guns.

Capt. C.H. Darley, under Salmond's encouragement, developed Pretyman's photographic ideas and soon No. 3 Squadron was taking far clearer pictures. By the New Year of 1915 Darley had completed an accurate photograph in length of the German trench system in the area of Salmond's squadron and transferred it to a map. Salmond took Darley and his map, the first of its kind, to Corps HQ where it was acclaimed.

Darley's next success was to photograph a long German sap [a communication track from rear bases to the front line, which rapidly became entrenched and camouflaged] *which the Army had not suspected. It was very important to the British and French commanders and it led to the plan of an attack on La Bassee being altered. This was another occasion when the RFC had saved soldiers lives.*

By the middle of March 1915, in preparation for the second Battle of Neuve Chapelle, No. 3 Squadron's cameras had covered the entire relevant front. The squadron's initial job in the battle was to bomb enemy divisional headquarters. Salmond, enthusiastic as always, had visions of throwing the whole enemy defence into confusion by killing the commander and his staff, and took off to do just that. Salmond flew with Eric Conran (on a later occasion Salmond saved his friend's life. One dark night Conran, his mind on other things, was about to walk into a spinning prop when Salmond jerked him to safety), and two other machines, flown by Lts. W.C.K. Birch and D.R. Hanlon, followed. They started at dawn, found the specified house and made sure of it by dropping their 25-lb [11 kg] bombs from 100 feet [30 metres]. The place burned fiercely, but it was such an insignificant place for a German divisional headquarters that Salmond thought some mistake had been made and dosed a large, ornate building with bombs as well. Flying back low over the trench line, the British pilots were strafed by German gunners. Salmond felt a shock in the stomach and put a hand inside his shirt to feel a clammy ooze of blood. But when he pulled his hand out it was clean. A bullet had passed through the fuselage and brushed his clothes and imagination had done the rest.

There follows a number of stories of others' experiences. By this time the squadron was operating Moranes, and was soon to be a single-type unit, when manufacturers, British and French, had geared up for war – but not quite yet.

The SE2a. The only one of its type which was flown by Salmond on his Lille reconnaissance flight. Note holstered .45 revolver (JMB/GSL)

Among the many difficulties the flyers of 1914–18 faced was the prevailing westerly wind. It helped them immensely when they were on their way to enemy territory but they had to fight against it on the return journey. It nearly finished Salmond one day. Corps asked him to send a pilot to have a look at Lille, but as it was a violently windy day which only the SE Scout could cope with Salmond took the duty himself.

[This was, of course, the B.S.1/S.E.2/2a No. 609.]

After running the gauntlet of AA fire on the way, Salmond made his reconnaissance. On the homeward journey he made slow headway against the wind and his petrol was running low. As he had plenty of height, he put the plane's nose down to gain speed and made straight for the AA guns on the direct line home. In spite of violent jinking the guns caught him and badly holed a wing. Rifle fire made several other holes, but he landed safely with his petrol tanks practically dry. He was lucky. That adverse wind was responsible for the death of many an airman.

Much of the foregoing and the bomb incident which follows are covered by McCudden. No. 3 Squadron is also fortunate to have a diary covering the period 12 August to 1 November 1914, kept by Lieutenant W.R. Read, who flew 'B' Flight Henry Farman with Herbert, Shekleton and Fuller and left for France in HF 295 on 12 August. He writes:

19/8. Smith-Barry broke himself up and his machine [BE8, No.625, the second of three which flew to France with the Aircraft Park, leaving No. 377] *on the 16th* [actually the 18th] *near Amiens. His mechanic was killed. Ryley broke his machine up on landing here today – a BE – he was not hurt. If we have all these accidents now, whatever will it be like when we begin to come into action. However the estimate is that not more than 5 per cent of us who have come out with the Corps will go back, so cherry oh* [sic]. . .

26/8. [After a reconnaissance, Read landed at Bertry to report to Headquarters and overturned]. *Jackson was thrown out about 10 yards ahead and I was left in the machine. Neither of us was hurt – only shaken. Good old Henri* [sic], *he did me well and even at the last he would not do me in. There was not time to repair the damage as shells were already falling over the town, so I hurriedly removed all the instruments, guns, maps, etc, and cut off the Union Jack* [believed to have been on the fin with the number] *and so left Henri in his last resting place. When I arrived in the town, everyone was busy getting out of the place as best he could.*

Headquarters, where General Smith-Dorrien was, was busy packing up to go, but they said it was doubtful if we would get out of the town at all as it was thought to be surrounded by the enemy. General Smith-Dorrien spoke to me and asked where I had come from and when I told him that I had broken my machine he was very kind and said 'Well, you must not be left here. You are wanted with the Flying Corps', and then, like the sportsman that he is, found someone to give me a seat in a staff car. I think we got away just in time as shells were bursting all round the town.

Many more excitements followed, including the loss of more machines and efforts to get replacements.

29/8. I received orders early to go to Paris to take over a new Henri Farman. Pretyman, Wellesley, Abercromby and Major Brooke-Popham also came in the same car, the three former to fly back machines . . .

3/9. Reveille 4.30 a.m. A rather disastrous day. Went off first of all with Major Moss as observer to reconnoitre at 5.15 a.m. On coming back I smashed up my new Henri Farman on landing. The engine 'chucked it' at a critical moment when I was near the ground and about to go over some Indian corn. I tried to 'pancake' the machine but it was not successful and as soon as the wheels touched it we did a complete somersault . . . I have broken two machines in a week.

Yesterday [2nd], Spratt on a Sopwith Scout [No. 387 struck off charge (SOC) on the 2nd, 611 SOC on the 3rd; both reported wrecked] *had a narrow escape. He was sent up to give chase to a German machine and did not get back until after dark. In landing, his machine turned completely over and it looked a very nasty accident, but he crawled out unhurt . . .*

5/9. I was told to fly Fuller's old Henri No. 274 to Etampes, and, with mechanics who were sent by car, to take it to pieces and re-cover the planes. It is a big aerodrome with some sheds . . .

9/9. Received orders to go by car to Buc and fly back a new Henri Farman which is ready for delivery from the works. Arrived at Buc at 9 a.m. with Birch and Wellesley, the former to fly back a Blériot and the latter a Henri. Met Valentine at Buc. He and Birch flew away on Blériots after lunch. Wellesley's and my Henri Farmans were not quite ready, so we stay here tonight . . .

10/9. Low flying clouds and rain prevented Wellesley and me getting away until 3 p.m. from Buc. A moderate to strong South West by South wind and having to dodge rain clouds delayed us. Arrived Etampes 4 p.m. Shekleton came here this morning on HF 351 which is to be overhauled. He is taking over the new Henri which I have flown over. My machine, No. 274, is still under repair [it was ready on the evening of 14 September, and flew to Fere en Tardenois on the 15th]. *News that Birch has not arrived at Collomiers . . .*

15/9. . . . Three nights ago a sudden squall got up and turned over five BEs and two Henris. They are all badly smashed up. Shekleton's machine was making love to Fuller's, one was found leaning against the other . . .

17/9. . . . During the afternoon a strong wind sprang up preventing me and three Bleriots, Joubert, Pretyman and Birch getting back [from the landing ground at Muret] *to our camp . . .*

18/9. Reveille 6.30 a.m. after a ripping good night's rest in the barn. Yesterday my machine [which I am flying, but which is really Shekleton's new one] *tipped over on to one wing and damaged itself. Spent part of the morning repairing the wing. Nothing doing for me today. Flew back to camp at 2.30 p.m. Was glad to have a partial bath. Have not had a wash or a shave for four days . . .*

19/9. A day spent in camp as it is Shekleton's and Fuller's turn for reconnaissance. It rained all last night and our bivouac, made out of two Henri Farman wings leaning up against one another, did not altogether keep out the rain. It stopped raining at 7a.m . . .

Today, Fuller, with Allen as passenger, smashed up HF274 – the machine I was rebuilding at Etampes.

21/9. We have now only one Henri in the flight and are waiting for new ones to be ready . . .

23/9. . . . At last we have had a fine day after three weeks of rain and wind and one has had a fine chance of drying damp clothes . . . Shekleton brought back a new Henri from Buc today . . .

24/9. This new Henri I am flying today climbs rippingly and gets up to 5,000 feet [1,500 metres] in under the half hour. It is the one that Shekleton brought over from Buc yesterday . . .

26/9. . . . Yesterday four new RE machines arrived. Today two new Maurice Farmans came fitted with Maxims [machine guns; none were for No. 3 Squadron].

28/9. Cholmondley arrived this evening with a new Bristol Scout [93 miles per hour] [No.633] . . .

1/10. Reveille 4.45 a.m. Started out at 6.15 a.m. with Walker as passenger, to the 5th Division. When a mile from camp Henri began to miss badly and we came down in a field. Soon afterwards Pretyman passed over and landed and he went back to camp to get a spanner and a new plug which he dropped as he flew over again. Went up on a reconnaissance of the enemy's lines at 9 a.m. and again at 2 p.m.

Last night and tonight there was a conference of pilots and observers who have been out, asking us what we thought of the general situation ...

4/10. . . . Nobody seems to know quite where the Indian troops are, although there are rumours that they are at Arras.

However, on 26 October he says:

Met some Sikhs there [Estaires] and had an opportunity of talking some Hindustani to them. They had come from Ambala. And on 27 October: Took ten wounded – 32nd Sikh Pioneers – in the car to a Field Ambulance Hospital. All had been hit in the left hand, some poor devils with all their fingers off. Their left hands being exposed over the top of the trench when firing their rifles would account for this.

11/10. In the morning painted some large Union Jacks 6 feet by 4 feet on Henri's extensions. . .

15/10. . . . This afternoon went down to the town [St Omer] with Shekleton and Fuller to get a bath. Had quite a good one. Forgot to put that down on Monday the 12th, Cholmondley put up a good show against a German machine that flew over. He went off on the Bristol Scout [648] and caught up the German. I watched through glasses; he simply made circles round the German who was all for getting back to his lines. They had a tremendous battle for ten minutes until Cholmondley's ammunition gave out. Neither hit the other. C. came back with four bullet holes in his machine, two being very near to him. Major Higgins [Officer Commanding No. 5 Squadron] *also went after him on the 'other' bullet* [644] *but got lost. I think the German was thoroughly frightened . . .*

16/10. Reveille 6.30 a.m. Orders at 8 a.m. to fly as passenger with Pretyman [in a Blériot] *to Juvisay where our aircraft park is, 180 miles* [290 km] *from here. Both of us to fly back new machines.* [Overnight at St Pol after a forced landing due to mists at 100 feet *(30 metres)*, then lunch in Amiens at Hotel de l'Universe], *where we met all of No. 2 Squadron. Left Amiens at 2 p.m. and arrived at Juvisay about 4 p.m . . . Went into Paris where we put up at the Hotel Ritz, and went on to dinner at Maxims.*

Bad weather then intervened, until:

21/10. Started at 11.30 a.m . . . Landed at Amiens at 1.30 p.m. and took on some petrol and oil. Left Amiens at 1.45 p.m. and landed at St Omer at 3.15 p.m. As soon as I landed, heard that the flight was just going off to Hinges – 25 miles – for a week for reconnaissance flights. So started off for Hinges almost at once with Air Mechanic Glidden as passenger.

Fuller broke his machine by landing too fast and over-shooting the field and hitting a heap of manure or something. Herbert also lost his engine and landed somewhere in another field but without breaking his machine. Everybody is looking very mournful about something – or perhaps it is that I am feeling less mouldy after being in Paris. They have been breaking up a good many machines since I have been away.

No. 6 Squadron – which is detached somewhere up North – broke six out of its total of twelve machines in one day by landing in a field with a dyke running across it. Wilson broke up two Blériots in one day, in one case hitting some trees with one wing. Walker was his passenger and he had his knee badly twisted and has been sent to England. We have billets here at Hinges on the floor on some straw in a cottage which is quite comfortable.

22/10. . . . It took me 40 minutes to climb to 4,000 feet on my brute of a Henri. They are rotten machines. My opinion of Henri goes down daily. It won't climb on some days, and it isn't good enough going over 'Archie' at 4,000 feet [compare with entry for 24/9] *. . . An order has come that Flight Commanders are not to fly.*

27/10. . . . Arrived back at camp at 5 p.m., when it was nearly dark [after taking the Sikhs to hospital]. *Feel dog tired and absolutely fed up tonight. Have done 4.25 hours flying today, and 14.5 hours over the last five days, and tonight I do not feel as if I shall be able to go on for long at this rate without an easy. It isn't that my nerve is going but I feel stale.*

29/10. . . . Yesterday Herbert tried to persuade me to go back to England for a rest for a week or ten days. He is awfully thoughtful in that way but I do not want a rest. Feel as fit as when I came out.

Shekleton went up for a reconnaissance with Jackson in the morning and had to come down feeling unwell. Herbert went up instead. A few days' rest at St Omer will do Shek' good. So far he has scarcely been away from the Squadron for a day since we came out and he has not broken a machine yet. Most of us have.

He went back to St Omer from Hinges and 'Found billets with "A" Flight who are in a very nice furnished chateau which is empty'.

30/11. . . . The great treat came in the afternoon when Shek' and I went off to the town with some clean clothes and had a bath – a real big hot bath. It was a treat and I wanted one rather badly. My socks were really beginning to bark at me, and as for Herbert – well – he owned that he had not had a bath since Moyenville [2½ weeks!], so he wanted one more than I did.

31/10. . . . At 9.30 a.m. went off in a car with Major Salmond to Hinges. A very cold drive. Arrived back at Hinges at 2.30 p.m., having brought Conran back. He is going to Paris to fly back a new Blériot as he has broken up his own . . .

1/11. . . . About 12 machines went off at 2 p.m., including Herbert and Fuller, to drop bombs on the Kaiser who was reported to be at a place called Gewules, about 36 miles by air. Everybody went off bristling with bombs. Herbert lost his way but came back after 3.5 hours, having dropped all his bombs.

Fuller came back with his bombs complete, having been unable to get the detonators into them.

No official information so far that the Kaiser is dead.

NOTE: The next day I stopped one at 5,500 feet with my leg over Courtrai and was invalided to England.

The Sky Their Battlefield dates this as the 3rd, but the observer Robert Loraine, in *Actor, Soldier, Airman*, agrees on the 2nd. He helped land the aeroplane near a casualty station then took-off to complete the recce!

This diary, Laffin's biography of Salmond and McCudden's book give a wonderful picture of the first six months in the air. This record would apply to most squadrons in some degree.

In April Salmond was promoted to brevet Lieutenant-Colonel and transferred to Great Britain to command the RFC wing at Farnborough – he was our first Chief of the Air Staff, and 'Peter' Portal was our next. Jimmy McCudden was posted to England for flying training and later gained the VC, as did Freddie West – although neither did so while with No. 3 Squadron. All four honed their skills with the squadron and all four flew in Morane Parasols.

CHAPTER SEVEN

Flying Moranes

THE MORANE is another unsung yet historically very important aeroplane. Jack Bruce states: 'In general terms, the Morane Saulnier Type L was a not particularly remarkable aeroplane, but in the history of fighter aircraft its place is unique and secure.' The main reason for British interest is 3253, in which Sub-Lieutenant R.A.J. Warneford attacked and destroyed Army Zeppelin LZ 37 over Ghent, Belgium on 7 June 1915, for which he was awarded the Victoria Cross. Bruce continues:

> Nevertheless, it should be remembered that one of the RFC's earliest combat successes was won by 2nd Lt V.H.N. Wadham and his observer Lt A.E. Borton on a Morane Type L of No. 3 Squadron on 5th February 1915 [probably 1848 in which they crashed on 27 February]. Although armed only with a rifle, his sustained fire drove down an Aviatik

Morane Saulnier type L with pilot George Pretyman and observer Hoppy [because of a limp] Cleaver demonstrating our first stripped (no cooling jacket) Lewis on pillar mounting. (3 Squadron)

A Morane Saulnier type LA, 5120 with early streamlining, note that the engine is not fully cowled. (JMB/GSL)

encountered over Merville, the conclusive shots being fired at a range of only 50 feet [15 metres].

Other Ls known to have seen aerial combat with No. 3 are 1849, 1855, 1863, 1870, 1872, 1874, 1875, 5034 and 5055.

The first, 1829, arrived on 2 December 1914 and was wrecked seven days later when Captain Cholmondley side-slipped into the ground. He had brought a Bristol Scout 'B' with an 80 hp Gnome to the squadron in September. By 1 April 1915 No. 3 had on charge fourteen Ls plus one Blériot XI, for instructional purposes only. By the end of that year the squadron was slightly under strength, having struck off four Parasols between 26 and 29 December, and was equipped with eleven Parasols, one MS type N monoplane single seat scout and one MS type BB biplane two-seat recce escort.

The L had square-section fuselage and wing-warp lateral control; the LA introduced ailerons and some streamlining. The P was a completely new design which lasted until the arrival of Sopwith Camels; by 5 October 1917 three of these had arrived to join fourteen Moranes but within a week the squadron was an all-Camel unit.

The two future CASs: John Salmond and 'Peter' Portal flew Moranes, as did the two VCs: J.T.B. McCudden and F.M.F. West. All this on an aeroplane that was the first to be fitted with a 'stripped' Lewis machine gun, the first successfully to land an allied agent behind enemy lines 18 September 1915 *(flight 17 March 1949)*, and played a leading role in the development of air combat, bombing, contact patrol, aerial photography, wireless telegraphy and Forward Air Control by signal lamp! Performing these duties on the ground at the front Flight Sergeant W. Burns was killed on 28 September 1915; then on the 30th Major E.W. Furse was wounded, both by shrapnel.

On 22 January 1915 Lieutenant A.J. Evans flying 1845 became lost and landed near Schore on the island of Walcheren, in neutral Holland, so both were interned. 'The province of Zeeland soon became the most favoured area for warplane landings as from the air it could very easily be mistaken for a part of Belgium.' Evans' future is not known, but the Dutch paid for all equipment and integrated it in their air arm. Their initial serial allocations were LA-1–50, so 1845 became LA-35, but as more aircraft became available a different scheme was introduced in 1917 with the first 99 numbers allocated to trainers, so 1845/LA-35 became M-23.

McCudden reports:

> A big raid was organised about this time [the end of February 1915] to bomb Brussels. Machines from all the RFC Squadrons took part.
>
> Mr. Birch went from No.3 with six 20-pounder [9 kg] bombs. He didn't come back with his machine, but turned up three weeks later at the Squadron, having landed in Holland with engine trouble, and having got away disguised as a ship's fireman. This, of course, was quite a remarkable effort.

This was our first 'home run', as they were known later.

So most of what could be done had been done by the time the L was replaced by the LA and then the P – the 'BB' and 'N' did the rest until the Camels, when the role, the war and many other things changed.

Painting and markings vary, so here are just a few notes to help date/identify photographs. The Ls were clear doped fabric; struts were black, cowling black or bare metal. Roundels may have been French at first (blue centre, red outer) but were soon repainted; at least one, 1881, had the Union Flag painted under each wing tip, outboard of the roundel. It arrived on 22 March and remained until 25 September 1915 – lasting longer than many aircrew. The intermediate LAs had both the former and latter schemes. The Ps started out clear doped, but by the time they were replaced by Camels they were in the standard scheme of khaki green upper surfaces and sides, with clear doped lower surfaces; this scheme was introduced in 1916 but it took until the year's end before it could be said that all Western Front machines had been so treated.

In his biography of Sir John Salmond, John Laffin describes an incident with Moranes:

> During this battle [Neuve Chapelle, March 1915] there occurred an incident which does much to show up vividly one side of the many faceted Salmond. He found one of his pilots, Captain Reginald Cholmondley, looking worriedly at the tail of his aeroplane, a Morane Parasol, as the aircraft was at rest on the tarmac.
>
> 'What's the matter with you?' S asked lightly. 'Oh, nothing,' C said. 'Out with it,' ordered S. 'Well,' C said, 'have you noticed that the numbers on the rudder add up to thirteen?' 'No, I hadn't noticed,' said S easily. 'But

what of it?' C merely shrugged and did not answer and his CO did not press the point. C was a close friend and they had learned to fly together at Hendon.

The next afternoon C was sitting in his plane as bombs were being loaded on board. Something went wrong. One of the bombs exploded, blowing to pieces C, several members of the squadron and a number of civilians. It was a ghastly scene; the airfield was strewn with broken bodies and fragments of the smashed 'plane.

Dusk was falling and as night came on S ordered everybody well away from the area and passed the word that routine was to continue as usual. He himself took on the depressing, unpleasant and bloody job of clearing the field. With only one NCO, Sgt Angel, to help him, S worked for several hours clearing away all signs of the disaster. He even washed away the blood. Then he and the Sergeant buried the bombs that had not gone off. In the morning when the pilots and mechanics came out to prepare for the dawn patrol there was nothing to disturb or distress them. It was typical of S to want to perform such a task himself.

One of the mechanics was Jimmy McCudden, whose own account reads:

About 5 p.m. on March 12th I had just seen Captain Conran and Mr. Pinney off on a Morane, and on my way back to my flight shed passed Captain Cholmondley and his Morane outside 'A' Flight sheds. The machine was then being loaded with six of the Melinite bombs which have already been mentioned. I had just got to my flight sheds when 'crump-crump' came two explosions in quick succession, and I distinctly felt the displacement of air. I turned round and saw Captain Cholmondley's Morane on fire from wing-tip to wing-tip. Two bombs had exploded during the loading process. I ran over to render assistance and found about a dozen men lying around the Morane, all badly mutilated. Owing to the Morane being on fire and still more bombs being in the machine we got away the wounded quickly.

I well remember the little band of helpers who assisted to get the living away from the burning wreckage at the imminent risk of their own lives. Lieutenants Pretyman, Blackburn, Cleaver and Serjeant Burns were the leaders of the party.

Major Salmond had now arrived and ordered everyone away from the machine, he himself remaining by the wreck – a splendid example of coolness that still further increased our great respect of our Commanding Officer.

This was a very bad day for our Squadron, for in this accident we had eleven killed and two wounded, among whom were some very experienced and valuable members of No.3 Squadron. Captain Cholmondley was one of the best-liked officers in the Squadron, as well as one of our finest pilots, and Flight-Serjeants Costigan and Bowyer, two of our earliest NCOs, were also among the dead. The accident had a generally depressing effect,

63

A 1917 Morane Saulnier type LA showing the external camera mounting, later internal, giving a bulge on the starboard/right fuselage.   (JMB/GSL)

noticeable for days, in the Squadron. I do not think that the cause of the mishap was ever really discovered. It was surmised that during the loading of the bombs a safety wire was accidentally pulled. However, the Squadron settled down to its work again, but those who had seen the accident can never forget it; at least I never can.

Thus are traditions established, to be nurtured by we who followed. Cross-checking this event, I tried to identify the aeroplane in question, and Jack Bruce and I did some head-scratching. The only machine in the squadron at that time with a serial number totalling 13 was a solitary Avro 504, 715, which joined it on 18 November 1914 and was returned to the Aircraft Park on 16 March 1915. The machine struck off charge on the date of the incident was 1871; received on 7 March. Then the penny dropped. British Military Aircraft Serial Numbers were painted on the rear fuselage, but on French machines the manufacturer put his code and number on the rudder! Jack Bruce agreed this was most probable, but even his extensive records cannot provide an M-S number.

According to McCudden:

About this time [18/19 September 1915] *a Morane monocoque* [single-

Morane Saulnier type LA, pilot Lieutenant Roland Taylor. Note camera is now faired in.   *(3 Squadron)*

hull body] *was allotted to No. 3 Squadron from Paris. This was a very small, heavily loaded* [high wing loading] *monoplane, a copy of 'Le Vengeur' which was flown by M. Gilbert. It was one of the first aeroplanes carrying a machine-gun arranged to shoot through the propeller.*

The machine had no interrupter gear to prevent the bullets hitting the propeller, but had a piece of steel fixed on each blade directly in front of the Lewis gun, so that occasional bullets that hit the propeller were turned off by these hard-steel deflectors – as they were called. The deflectors took off almost thirty per cent of the efficiency of the propeller, so that for the smallness of the machine and its ample power [80 hp Le Rhone] *it was not very efficient in climb and speed even for those days.*

Whilst being flown up to Auchel from Paris, this machine had to land near St Pol, owing to the contact-breaker spring in the magneto breaking. I went to St Pol by car to rectify the trouble, and saw the machine off the ground, and then returned. That was my first acquaintance with a gun firing forward in a tractor machine.

This Morane came to No. 3 Squadron about the same time as the single-seat Fokker first appeared . . .

The Monocoque Morane in our Squadron was rarely used in this way, partly because I think our pilots were always busy with their other work, artillery, reconnaissance etc., and partly because the machine was never definitely detailed for the sort of work which at this time the Fokkers were monopolising.

About this time, too, Lieutenant G.L.P. Henderson was wounded whilst fighting two two-seaters over towards Lille, on the Morane 'Bullet'[another name used for the N]. *The observer in the two-seater, who wounded him in the eye, was armed only with a rifle, so our pilot said. Mr Henderson landed on the aerodrome at Auchel and made a good landing despite the fact that he was nearly blinded by blood from his wound.*

On the 14th [December, 1915] *I went out with Sergeant Bayetto* [who later became an N pilot, was detached to No. 24 Squadron then posted to No. 60 and was killed in action as a Captain, RAF in 1918], *a new pilot in No. 3 Squadron, to show him the lines and the principal landmarks. We were out for over half an hour, as there was not much doing on the line that morning.* [Jimmy flew with Bayetto on a number of occasions, probably in L Parasols as he was a junior pilot – the LAs would have been allocated to the more experienced pilots.]

1915 Morane Saulnier type N seen in 1915 with Lieutenant Tone P.H. Bayetto, both went to 60 Squadron. (JMB/GSL)

*Morane Saulnier Parasols at Lechelle in 1917.
Two type Ps are in the centre, flanked on each
side by a pair of type LA. (JMB/GSL)*

'No.5137 was a Morane-Saulnier BB of No.3 Squadron. It was received at No.1 A.D. on 27 January, 1916 and issued to the squadron on 1 February. On 23 February it was shot down at Souain by Leutnant Max Immelman as his 9th combat victory; the pilot, Lt. C.W. Palmer, was wounded and made prisoner; his observer, Lt. H.F. Birdwood, was killed. The aircraft was officially struck off charge on 2 March, 1916.' (JMB/GSL)

What of the N? The squadron's first is that referred to by J. McCudden: 'No. 5067 gave Sergeant T.P.H. Bayetto of No. 3 Squadron a busy

A Morane Saulnier type P, B1604, seen in 1917 with a clear dope finish but shortly to be overpainted with camouflage. The roundels are outlined in white. Note that the engine is fully cowled. (JMB/GSL)

On the 11th [January, 1916] I flew with Lieutenant Lillywhite, one of the former instructors at Hendon Aerodrome, in a Morane biplane, which had just arrived in No. 3 Squadron. This Morane biplane was engined with a 110 hp Le Rhone. The wings, which were of the deeply cambered Morane type, had no dihedral, and the machine was very ugly to look at, but for those days it had a very good turn of speed and climb.

I was up with Mr. Lillywhite [killed in an accident in 1917] for an hour between La Basse and Lens looking for German machines, but we had no luck. The weather was very dull, and I think that the journey was one of the roughest I have ever experienced as pilot or passenger. We landed safely, however.

The next day I was up again in the same machine with Major Hewitt for an hour looking for Germans, but no luck again, although the weather was fine, and the visibility fair.

It is no good looking for Germans during bad visibility, for they do not fly unless they can work efficiently while they are up, but when visibility is good they are up in their hundreds.

Having seen no enemy machines during our hour up, the pilot throttled down, and we glided homewards. In landing an undercarriage V went and we turned upside down, but with no damage to ourselves.

On 24 January McCudden left for England and pilot training.

Jack Bruce, in Aeroplanes of the Royal Flying Corps, says:

The Morane biplane was issued to Squadrons 1 and 3, a policy statement of 29 January, 1916, announcing that 'When Morane Parasols are struck off they will be replaced by biplanes as these become available, until there are four biplanes in each of the two Morane Squadrons . . . These four biplanes will be formed into one flight in each squadron.' Despite slow deliveries of the type this evidently came to pass, for on 1 July 1916, No.1 Squadron had five Morane biplanes and Nos. 3 and 60 had four each.

In service the Morane BB was usually armed with two Lewis guns. One was fixed on the upper wing firing forward; it was fired by the pilot but loaded by the observer, who himself had a second Lewis gun on a rear mounting very similar to that of the Martinsyde Elephant. The Morane biplane performed the same duties as the contemporary Parasols, apparently without attracting praise or blame. More than 80 were delivered to the RFC, and some were issued to No.60 Squadron on its arrival in France.

Lieutenants Edgar Golding, pilot, (KIA 19 September 1917) and observer Freddie M.F. West, who was awarded the Victoria Cross in August 1918. (JMB/GSL)

CHAPTER EIGHT

The Sopwith Camel

CHAZ BOWYER called the Sopwith Camel the King of Combat in the first hard-back book completely devoted to a company aeroplane. He writes:

No. 3 Squadron RFC began re-equipment in that month [September 1917] . . .

By the beginning of March a total of 13 Camel squadrons were available on the Western Front – Nos. 3, 43, 46, 54, 65, 73, 80 and 4 AFC [Australian Flying Corps] *with the RFC, and Nos. 3[N], 8[N], 9[N], 10[N] and 13[N] working alongside their Army counterparts . . .*

On 8 August, 1918, the massive Allied ground offensive swung into action. On that day a total of 19 Camel squadrons were available for operations, located as under: 3 Squadron Major R. St Clair McClintock Valheureux.

Jefford's *RAF Squadrons* gives October 17 Camel (19 February) at Warloy, to Vert Galland 25 March, next day to Valheureux, 15 October to Lechelle. If we Delve into Ken's *The Source Book of the RAF*, in the section on its formation, 1 April 1918, not only do we find No. 3 Squadron missing from Valheureux or the RAF in the field, but from the entire RAF *order of battle*! Jefford's book tells us:

A brand new Sopwith Camel, B6355, seen at Dover in 1917. On 6 November it made a forced landing behind enemy lines and 2nd Lieutenant. A.G. Cribb became a prisoner-of-war. (JMB/GSL)

Lieutenant D. Rogers and his Sopwith Camel of 'A' Flight in 1918. (JMB/GSL)

Sopwith Camel '8' (possibly C8333) of B Flight, with J.L. Butler and Lieutenant J.A. McDonald. (JMB/GSL)

2 Sqn 13 May 12 F @ Farnborough – from No 2 [Aeroplane] Coy, Air Btn. RE

3 Sqn 13 May 12 F @ Larkhill – from det of No 2 [Aeroplane] Coy, Air Btn. RE

We *are* granted the Farman III, but where is the Blériot XI (not until 13 April), and the XXI (not until 12 October)? The Breguet and BE1 are credited only to No. 2 Squadron and no mention of the Blériot XII or Paulhan at all! To say they are pre-RFC would be a 'cop out', as pre-RAF aircraft are described, in spite of the book's title.

Among other squadrons listed for 8 August 1918 are the 17th and 148th Aero of the United States Air Service. Many of their pilots were sent to RAF squadrons to gain operational experience. One American-born Canadian who went indirectly to the RAF was Lieutenant Robert J. 'Brick' MacLeod, who even thirty years ago, said:

I went to France during the latter part of July and went into the pilot pool. I went right back out again, posted to No. 3 Squadron, RAF, during the first week in August . . . just as they were going on a two-week rest period. I was mad as a hornet! I was ready for action. My first Camel bore the numeral '2' on the fuselage, just in front of the cockade.

He was to see plenty of action between 1st and 28th September when he was wounded in the left leg and foot by machine gunners who were defending a balloon. He managed to fly back over the lines to land at Bapaume, from whence he was taken to No. 43 Casualty Clearing Station to have his wounds dressed.

The squadron's first Camel casualty was Lieutenant H. B. New, shot down in B2425, probably by *Leutnant* H. Becker of Jasta 12 on 31 October 1917.

Its worst day was 20 November, when it lost eight Camels, most in a raid by nine aeroplanes on Estormel, home of Jasta 5. Not all were shot down; two crashed in mist on return. Lessons were learned from this, and the prime example of their being put into practice was the raid on Epinoy. 'Shooting Up An Aerodrome' by 'Ham' (3 Squadron), believed to be D. M. Hambly, in *Flying*, describes the event.

'The Low Bombing Raids'

In 1918 in France the German aerodromes were being placed very close to the lines. The result was that the German pilots were saved tiring patrols up and down over the trenches to guard their battle area. Situated as they were, the Fokkers could remain on the ground until they saw a patrol of British machines over their area. They then left the ground, climbing in an easterly direction to get into position for an attack on our machines. As our patrols were invariably carried out several miles on the German side of the lines, the position was still easier for the German pilots.

It was decided by the British 'powers-that-be' that this state of affairs should be altered. The method to be adopted was a series of low bombing raids, each on a large scale with the German aerodromes as objectives. The first was carried out by No. 3 and 56 Squadrons – the former with Le Rhone Camels, the latter with SE5a s.

One day the CO appeared in the mess with a bundle of maps and photographs, and called us all round a table. He then broke the news to us that we were the chosen instrument to move the first aerodrome to be selected. This was at Epinoy, near Cambrai. Aerial photographs of the target had been taken and copies were distributed. There were two aerodromes in the village, one on each side of the road. Squadron 56 was to deal with the one to the north, while we were allotted that to the south, which we divided into three parts, each of which was allocated to a flight.

'Good-Byee'

At that time the majority of us had done no low bombing at all, and the thought of going down low twenty miles over the lines (where a west wind usually blew) was not a cheering thought. As the CO finished his instructions two men crept quietly to the gramophone and played a rapid selection of what they considered appropriate music. The records played were: 'We don't want to lose you, but we think you ought to go', 'Good-byee', 'God send you back to me', and others of the same variety!

The attack was fixed for July 30th and the time of arrival noon, the German lunch-time. The equipment officer gave us all his sympathy and showed it in a very practical form: his stores were ours for the day so far as clothing was concerned! He was quite certain it would be possible to write it all off as 'lost over the lines' in an hour or two's time! Consequently, it was a very well-equipped collection of pilots that left the

Sopwith Camel B6234, 'A' of A Flight, after capture on 5 December 1917. The pilot was 2nd Lieutenant L.G. Nixon: probably shot down by vfw Barth of Jasta 10. (JMB/GSL)

1918. Sopwith Camel 'Z' of C Flight with Lieutenant W.H. Maxted and friend. (JMB/GSL)

ground for the rendezvous over Doullens. Each machine had four 20-lb. Cooper bombs and a certain amount of incendiary ammunition to ignite machines we hoped to find at Epinoy.

The expedition met over Doullens with No. 3 Squadron leading and Wallace, the flight-commander of C flight, in charge of the whole show. With us at 10,000 feet was No. 56 Squadron similarly armed.

At 11,000 feet was No. 60 Squadron on SE5s. A thousand feet above them were No. 87 Squadron with Dolphins. These two squadrons were not to partake in the actual raid, but were to act as an upper escort in case we were attacked. A flight of Bristol Fighters came also at 13,000 feet to take photographs and bring home stragglers.

When we were all in position Wallace fired a Verey light and we set off for the lines. Arrived there, the weather was cloudy and Wallace decided that for all these machines flying so close together it was too dangerous. He accordingly washed out the whole show and we all came home somewhat relieved, but with the horrid feeling that it all remained to be done again!

On August 1st we all met again in perfect weather and crossed the lines at 10,000 feet. From there we flew with our noses down at a steady 120 mph direct for Epinoy, which we reached when we were at 1,000 feet. Squadron No. 56 went to their aerodrome and dropped all their bombs on their first swoop. We went to our own areas and followed each other round, diving, firing our guns and dropping one bomb each time we dived.

'A Hectic Time'

Our arrival was entirely unexpected. There was a number of machines standing on the tarmac, while the officers gathered outside their mess, wondering what it was all about – but not for long, however, as the mess had been earmarked by A flight and their first dive left the Germans no doubt about the reason for our visit.

For the ten minutes or so we were over the aerodrome life was very hectic: Camels all over the place, missing each other by feet, while below new fires of hangars and machines were starting up in every direction. At the end of the hangars was the petrol dump, which was set alight at a very early stage of the proceedings. The smoke from this went up for thousands of feet and was still burning in the evening, as reported by machines sent over then to take photographs.

One or two machine-guns fired at us the whole time and were never spotted. Riley found a staff car on a nearby road and chased it until it stopped in a ditch at the side of the road.

Rudolf Stark, a German pilot, describes this raid in his book *Wings of War*, for he was at Epinoy at the time. He admits that great material damage was done and the units were out of action for several days. He states that no casualties occurred among the personnel – except for one horse. Which, when one comes to think of it, was not an unsatisfactory result.

Captain J.E. Doyle, DFC, also wrote in *Flying*:

'A Planned Affair'

On August 1st, 1918, No. 60 Squadron, of which I was temporarily in command, in conjunction with two other scout squadrons, carried out a crushing attack on two German fighter squadrons on the ground. It was a planned affair, to which much thought had been given by the squadrons concerned. Now the underlying idea was that this attack should be in such strength as would enable us to go right down to the ground without very serious risk of trouble from E.A., so that we could make sure of the job we set out to do. We took with us, in addition to the three scout squadrons, one flight of Bristol Fighters, whose task was to take photographs all the time.

We totalled some fifty machines, not by any means an overwhelming concentration of strength, and certainly a very small force compared to what we could have mustered. However, everything went off according to plan, the only surprise being that we met with no interference at all from the air; even Archie, who sent up a few shells in a half-hearted way as our squadrons crossed the lines, was negligible.

We crossed over, and quickly lost height straight to our objective. Each squadron in turn went down to about two hundred feet [60 metres], while the other two maintained an upper guard at five thousand feet [1,500

On Pass in Abbeville in 1918 J. Sellers, D.M. Hambly (Ham of Raid on Epinoy), G.R. Davis and R.V. Curtis. (JMB/GSL)

D.M.Hamble   R.D.Davis   R.V.Curtis

metres]. *The Fokker biplanes and Albatros of the enemy squadrons were beautifully lined up before their hangars. Then, up they went in flames, one by one.*

What must have been a very big petrol store was set alight, for a column of black smoke rose very quickly ten thousand feet [3,000 metres] *into the sky. The hangars themselves began to blaze, but, of course, our photographs did not reveal what had been inside.*

'A Taste of Lead'

No sooner had we begun than a number of men were seen running across the aerodrome, and we discovered that they were making for a machine-gun post, which, for some reason known only to themselves, was out in the open, remote from all buildings.

Of course, we had something to say about that, and we proceeded to chase those men with our own bullets if they dared to show themelves. This was a sample on a small scale of what air offensive could, and should, mean, and I can tell you we enjoyed ourselves while it lasted. Then we re-formed and went home.

According to our photographs, eleven of the machines that were out in the open were destroyed by fire, and it was reasonable to suppose that some others that had not been caught alight must be badly damaged; and also that some had been in the gutted hangars.

Confirmation of which is now available from the book, Wings of War, *by Rudolf Stark. He was at the time in command of Jagdstaffel* [Chaser Squadron] *No. 35, which, with JG 23, was stationed at this aerodrome* [Epinoy].

Here are some extracts :

> *1.8.18. It is about 1 p.m. We are sitting in the mess, just about to go off for the afternoon patrol. Suddenly we hear a roar and a crash; the next moment bombs come down and machine-guns begin to fire. The English are raiding our aerodrome . . . Several of our machines that stood ready on the tarmac blaze up at once. Other scouts shot up our quarters and dug-outs. Yet others hung over our machine-gun Archies to look after them. It was impossible to fire those guns. If any of us made the slightest move to get near them, down came a shower of bursts all round him . . .*
>
> *One of JG 23's hangars went up in flames, and burnt to the ground with seven machines inside it. The bullets rattled like hail on the roofs . . .*
>
> *We could only look on and take care to show as little of ourselves as possible. Our only hope was that a neighbouring* staffel *to which we had telephoned for help would come in time . . .*
>
> *But the storm vanished as quickly as it came. Up went a Verey light as the signal: off went the machines and vanished in the west.*
>
> *Then it was up to us to salvage what could be salvaged. There were smoking, burning masses all round us, and all our squads were*

1918. Sopwith Camel line up of C Flight at Inchy in 1918, nearest H.
(JMB/GSL)

busy with extinguishers. The burning hangars collapsed; we could do
no more in that direction, but we succeeded in fighting the fire down
and preventing it from spreading to other buildings.

The damage was considerable . . . a tent and two sheds were
burnt down. Eleven machines were total write-offs, and all the others
except 3 were badly damaged.

So two JGs, consisting of 32 aeroplanes, were reduced to 3 serviceable
machines by a raid lasting only an hour from take-off to landing. All our
machines returned safely. Remember, the raid consisted of only three
squadrons, and lasted only an hour, so that by using the whole of our
available strength the entire German Air Force on the Western Front could
have been wiped out on any fine day.

Had this happened, our bombers could have gone over at will and
attacked the enemy's long lines of communication, cutting his roads and
railways and keeping them cut, from a decisive range without fear of being
themselves destroyed.

But it was not to be. Inconceivable as it may seem, such raids, instead of
being instantly organised, were actually forbidden.

Why? Because presumably our army commanders were unable to grasp
so simple a means of bringing the war to an end.

Letter from Captain. T.C. Arnot, RFC & RAF Retd., of Campbletown, Argyll, gives
his version of events.

Sopwith Camel, Lieutenant J. Sellers with his ground crew. (JMB/GSL)

The example given by Capt. J.E. Doyle, DFC, in his article on 'What We Might Have Done' in Flying of July 16th of the attack on Epinoy aerodrome on August 1st, 1918, is particularly interesting to me, as I took part in it. Some of the details are slightly different to Capt. Doyle's account.

The raid was led by Capt. McElroy of No. 3 [Camels], and I was OC 'B' Flight and second leader. No. 56 Squadron was the second low-flying scout squadron involved, and they attacked the Northern 'drome at Epinoy while we raided the southern. No. 60 Squadron I understood to be on escort duty to protect Nos. 56 and 3, but if they were also attacking, then they operated on the Northern drome with 56.

We each had four 20 lb Cooper bombs – full belts of ammunition for our Vickers guns. There was no interference from the enemy worth counting as such; the only danger being that of possible engine failure. 'B' Flight of No. 3 set alight the petrol store and the smoke reached to a height of over 8,000 feet [2,400 metres], higher than the highest machines protecting us. The heat and smoke from this fire prevented 'B' Flight from going close over the remainder of the targets as I should have liked.

A strange thing was noticed regarding the tent mentioned as destroyed by Rudolph Stark in his account of the raid in his book. It so happened that on first going down over our targets, I dropped a bomb upon this tent from about 200 feet [60 metres] and on turning up and round, I heard the *bomb go off but thought I had missed as no apparent damage was visible. It was only on going over it again I saw that the bomb had gone through the roof and blown the contents sideways leaving the roof to settle down upon the debris apparently intact; a tribute to the effective burst of these little bombs.*

One more incident stands out. At the finish of the raid, the Flights were about to re-form when I saw a single machine standing out on the aerodrome. Everyone else seemed to see it at the same moment for every machine of No. 3, and possibly some others as well, converged on this unfortunate bus. It literally appeared to wilt as a hail of lead struck it, and in a moment it settled down upon one wing-tip and the wings on the other side buckled. We returned with the same absence of interference from the enemy.

If those who took part are confused, what hope have the rest of us? Yet another version appears in High in the Empty Blue, by Alex Revell.

In *Royal Air Force 1918*, Christopher Cole gives this account:

A bomb raid was carried out on Epinoy aerodrome by 3 and 56 Squadrons, escorted by 60 and 11 Squadrons. 104 x 25-lb bombs were dropped and a large number of rounds fired into hangars, billets, officers' mess and workshops on the aerodrome, six hangars being observed to go on fire and two to be hit by bombs. Sixteen machines are also believed to have been set on fire, and one machine was blown to pieces. Major Gilchrist, 56 Squadron, dived to within ten feet [3 metres] on one Pfalz scout which was standing on the ground, whereupon it burst into flames. Two very large fires were also started which are believed to be from two workshops, the volumes of smoke – very clearly seen on photographs – ascended to 10,000 feet in one case.

Would that this was the reason the squadron and Camels are remembered, or Captain D.J. Bell for his twenty victories, of which seventeen were scored while with No. 3 Squadron, thereby gaining a bar to his Military Cross. It has even been stated recently that he was shot down by the Red Baron, in confusion with D.G. Lewis? See below:

No. 68 25/3/18 Sopwith Camel C1582 2nd Lt D. Cameron
  Killed
No. 79 20/4/18 Sopwith Camel D6439 Maj R. Raymond-Barker MC
  Killed
No. 80 20/4/18 Sopwith Camel B7393 2nd Lt D.G. Lewis wounded
  PoW

Above are as listed in *Von Richthofen and the Flying Circus* by Bruce Robertson and Heinz J. Nowarra, Harleyford 1958! [but writers and publishers are still wasting paper on proving or disproving Roy Brown shot down Manfred and as for Snoopy and *80 men tried and 80 men died* – which some people believe – the majority were corps reconnaissance two seaters, therefore hardly likely to try, and this writer was corresponding with 'Tommy' Lewis until shortly before his death on 10th August

Lieutenant W. Hubbard DFC, of 'C' Flight in 1918. (JMB/GSL)

1978, or 60 years after No. 80 is supposed to have died]. And Bell? Read on:

25/5/18 Sopwith Camel C6370 Capt D.J. Bell MC MIA/PoW DoW (Missing in Action then Prisoner of War Died of Wounds) in combat with C-type shot down and broke up. Crew of the German 2-seater were *Gefreiter* Rosenau/*Leutnant de Reserve* Heinzelmann (Grub Street references 1990 and 1995).

On Channel 4 TV a Red Baron 'wannabe' told the world the 'facts', so it must be true – his idol was shot down by a 'strine machine-gunner who must have been aiming at 'Wop' May, 'cos if he'd been aiming at the Red Baron he'd have hit Roy Brown, surely?' *1958* reference above refers – and the badge of 209 Sqn RAF is 'A red eagle, falling' or correctly 'An eagle volant recursant descendant in pale, wings overture'. And as John D Rawlings stated in his three volume squadron series books: 'The eagle falling symbolises the destruction of Baron von Richthofen who, in World War I, fell to the guns of 209 Squadron'.

After the Armistice the Camels were retained into the New Year and in February 1919 No. 3 Squadron returned to Britain and was reduced to a cadre until it was reactivated with Snipes in India at Ambala as 'A' Squadron.

A final word on the Camel. In *Tumult in the Clouds*, Captain Graham Donald, RNAS, writes:

The Sopwith Camel was so quick to control. Quick to turn, good performance, wonderful manoeuvrability. For a dogfight the perfect machine: twin machine-guns; Sopwith-Kauper interrupter gear with the guns firing through the propeller; all weights concentrated very close together – engine, guns, pilot, tank – everything close; and very small tail fin and rudder which didn't slow down your movement. She wasn't a machine that you wanted to be ham-handed with but in my opinion she was and still is the finest fighter ever designed by the hand of man!

CHAPTER NINE

Indian Interlude

THIS PART OF THE SQUADRON'S HISTORY is rather sketchy.* Having given up the Camel after the Armistice and been reduced to a cadre it was disbanded at Dover in 1919. A nucleus was formed at Uxbridge the following year and the Air Company then shipped out to re-form at Bangalore on 21 January 1920 as 'A' Squadron, officially becoming No. 3 Squadron again on 1 April 1920. Exactly one year later came a move to Ambala, but after only six months it was again disbanded on 30 September – to appear as if by magic next day! Throughout, the main equipment was the Sopwith Snipe, with two Avro 504Ks for training.

There was a perceived threat from Russia through Afghanistan, but no such threat materialised. The Snipe would have been the best aircraft for air defence in that hot and high environment, but against what were they defending? The best aircraft known to be available to the Russians was the de Havilland 9Ack, but there was doubt about its ability to carry a worthwhile load over the cumulo-granite that protected the subcontinent.

*The author would welcome further information from readers.

An Avro 504K at Ambala in 1921 This photo has frequently been mis-captioned by other units. (P.R. Little)

A Sopwith Snipe at Ambala in 1921. (P.R. Little)

Sunnybank Rest Camp situated up in the cool hills, officers went to Simla. (P.R. Little)

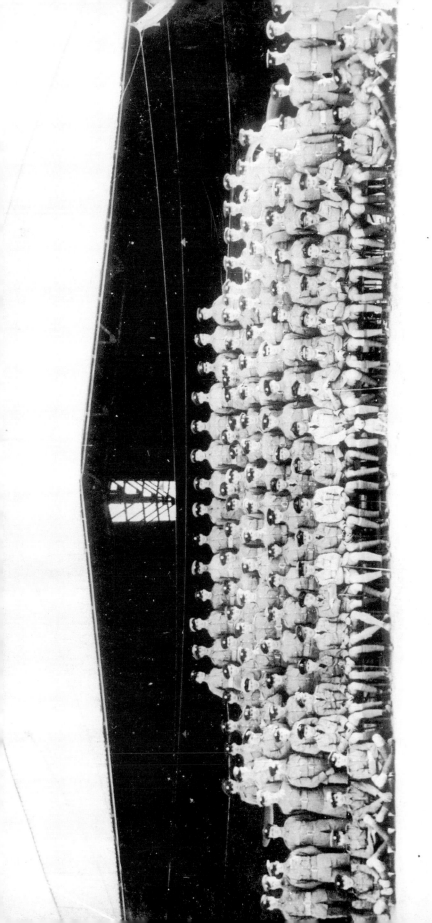

The Squadron at Ambala in 1921. (3 Squadron)

One stalwart of the squadron at this time is known: RFC No. 31 Henry Tom Hamilton Copeland, who tried to keep the Snipes serviceable as Flying Officer (Stores Officer) No. 3 Squadron, No. 2 India Wing. He retired on 3 August 1934, was recalled on 3 September 1939 and retired again in 1960.

'B' Squadron had also formed on 21 January 1920 at Risalpur. It became No.1 Squadron on 1 April, also with Snipes, and was off to Hinaidi, Iraq on 20 April taking most of No. 3 to combine The 'Gas' and 'Air' Companies – a volatile mixture. Michael Shaw writes in *Twice Vertical* and *No. 1 Squadron*:

> No sooner had the first aircraft been assembled from its crate than the squadron was ordered to move down to Bangalore in Madras, where they were to share the airfield at Gaza camp with No 3 Squadron. The squadron arrived at Bangalore 17/5/20 and set to work immediately to assemble the aircraft and settle into their own Mess. The aerodrome was commanded by Wg Cdr George Pretyman [See Flying Moranes in chapter 7.] who had led No. 1 in 1915 and who, ably assisted by his delightful Irish wife, now made sure that his old unit was made welcome in its new surroundings.
>
> Very little flying was accomplished in the early days at Bangalore. The locals in that part of India were fairly law-abiding, and despite the Moplar rebellion in Ceylon [Sri Lanka], the squadrons were not called upon for any operational tasks. There was also the problem of spares. Due to the immense distance from the Air Ministry and the financial stringency of the Government, replacement parts were virtually non-existent. As a result the Snipes spent most of their time firmly on the ground. At one time the situation was so bad that the stores officer, Fg Off. William Bowden, actually had to go down to the bazaar to buy his split pins, nuts and bolts.

This goes some way to explaining how most of No. 3's memories were concerned with leave up in the cool hills at Simla!

In *High Commanders of the Royal Air Force* Probert, in his biography of Salmond states:

> Then in 1922 he went to India to investigate the alleged inefficiency of the RAF and carried out what John Slessor [Then a Flight Lieutenant of No. 20 Squadron, later he became Cheif of Air Staff No. 11] who had been there at the time later discribed as a 'full and searching enquiry'. Not one to mince words, Salmond was highly crictical of the poor material support being provided by the Army, and stated that the RAF in India was to all intents and purposes non-existant as a fighting force. While his recommendations led to much inprovement, he himself was not destined to remain in India. Instead he was to go to the Middle East. [As Air Officer Commanding, Iraq].

While CO he was mentioned in Dispatches twice, awarded a DSO 18 February and then a Bar 24 March 1915. (Which contradicts *Flight 17 march 1949: the Squadron's first DSO was gained by Capt. G.L. Cruikshank 28 September 1915*).

CHAPTER TEN

Novar

O N 1 OCTOBER 1921, SQUADRON LEADER (later Air Marshal Sir) Grahame Donald re-formed the Air Company as No. 3 (Naval Co-operation) Squadron at RAF Leuchars from the Mobile Flight of No. 205 Squadron which was, at the time, the biggest squadron in the service. A year later it went to RAF Gosport where, in January 1923, he handed over to Squadron Leader C.C. Miles. When the Fleet Air Arm was formed in April 1923, No. 3 was split to become 420 and 421 Flights, each with six aircraft.

The equipment taken over was a three-seat version of the DH9a. Thirty years ago this was a 'missing' type, having been omitted from squadron, aircraft and company histories – even former members of No. 3, 420 and 421 denied its existence! With letters as a trigger, this variant was rediscovered. Bruce Robertson provided snaps of the aircraft loaded on lorries; it transpired that detachment from Leuchars to Invergordon for observation of naval manoeuvres was made by road and rail to save flying hours.

A Standard D.H.9a, outside a hangar at Leuchars and used for training. (R.L. Ward)

A three-seat D.H.9a packed aboard motor transport for surface movement from Leuchars to Novar in 1921. It may have been a road and rail journey. (Bruce Robertson)

The Armstrong Whitworth Tadpole was well known as a 'one off' stage on the way to development of the Westland Walrus. But in Westland Aircraft Since 1915 by Derek N. James, we read:

> 'Several DH9a were modified, by the Fleet Aircraft Repair Depot at RAF Donibristle in 1919–20 to carry a third crew member in an enlarged cockpit; they then proved their effectiveness as spotters during the 1920 Fleet Gunnery Exercises'.

So much for the aircraft, what about the people? Here are some quotes by those who were there:

> Two flights of 9a were commanded by Flt Lts Boumphrey and Openshaw [later Gp Capt E. R. Openshaw AFC] . . . There were a number of ex-Naval Warrant Officers who had qualified as observers and were in the RAF as Flying Officers, and their number was gradually supplemented by naval officers trained as observers. So the Squadron was a mixed bag. The main role seemed to be to provide spotting facilities for the Home Fleet when it did its Spring and Autumn gunnery exercises at Invergordon – and then detachments moved up to the provisional airfields near Invergordon. First to Delni [actually Delny, just to the east] and later at Novar [to the west], which was afterwards developed into Evanton.

> Officers' Mess Novar; merely a few large tents – plus a number of bell tents for officers and men. For [some] aircraft [one in each], a few hangars of canvas-over-tubular-metal construction. Rest left in open. They carried

Three-seat D.H.9a, possibly H3536, showing crew positions. Three's Company? (JMB/GSL)

Novar from the air in 1921, it later became Evanton. One lonely aeroplane can be seen outside the canvas hangars. The tented camp is to the right. (R.L.Ward)

Leuchars seen from the air in 1921. (R.L. Ward)

Westland Walrus airborne, a rare sight captured. (R.L. Ward)

Pilot, Observer and Wireless Operator, sitting backwards [the wireless was on a shelf at the rear of the cockpit].

3 Sqn was moved annually to Novar [later called Evanton] *on the Cromarty Firth for spotting duties with the Home Fleet Firings. This move was made by rail, including the aircraft which were stripped down to components and put on long covered wagons. Novar was then just a fair-sized field on the foreshore, a tented camp and a NAAFI hut. You bathed by damming the burn.*

The development of the Walrus is well covered in *Westland 50* by John W.R. Taylor and Maurice F. Allward. This salutary tale is priceless:

When the time came to flight test the first Walrus, [Stuart] *Keep took with him as ballast the foreman of the erecting shop, Harry Dalwood. All went well until Keep tried to throttle back. It immediately became clear that the only way to prevent the aircraft from dropping its nose disastrously was to open up again. Equally clearly, the only way of getting back on the ground was to reduce power. The situation was saved by Dalwood, who hauled himself out of his cockpit, worked his way towards the tail and sat astride the rear fuselage to get the C.G.* [centre of gravity] *right. He was no youngster even then, and the incident may have contributed to the fact that he is remembered as 'a solemn man, with a lined face, whose cap seemed a permanent fixture wherever he went.'*

It is worth recalling that the rear cockpit was designed to contain two people and their equipment, to counterbalance the additonal weight of the Napier Lion engine which replaced the Liberty.

The following extract fom *The Tin-Fish Times*, the newsletter of the RAF Gosport Veterans' Association is interesting:

Dateline: Gosport, 1922. After many vicissitudes and the completion of countless Forms 34, 664B etc. all the officers and airmen of No. 3 Squadron have at last arrived from Leuchars.

As one of the results of the Geddes Commission, we were posted from Leuchars to Gosport six months ago to absorb 'Composite' and 'Observer's Training' Flights, but owing to the summer and autumn exercises of the Atlantic Fleet in the Moray Firth, all but a few officers and other ranks were attached to Leuchars for duty at Invergordon until the completion of the exercises.

During the last three years we have heard a lot of Gosport; some of us have been down on temporary duty, and several of the Composite Flight have been attached to us at Invergordon. But even so we were all in the state of apprehension which one experiences at the thought of joining a new station. But this was soon dispelled. No one could have received a kinder welcome than we have, and our only hope is that Gosport will eventually like us as much as we like Gosport.

The December 1922 issue of *The Amphibian*, the Journal of the Royal Air Force

Base Gosport reciprocated:

> *During the last month the last details of No. 3 Squadron have joined us from Leuchars. We are sure we are voicing the sentiments of the whole station when we say they are more than welcome. Let us hope, however, that the change of atmosphere to the frivolous South will not have too bad an effect on them. Their assistance in all forms of sport will be of inestimable value. The Rugger team in particular will welcome the arrival of S/Ldr Donald.*

On 1 April the Air Company again went into limbo, this time for exactly a year.

Walrus on belly at Novar, after positioning flight from Leuchars. (R.L. Ward)

CHAPTER ELEVEN

The 1920s and 1930s

A FTER A YEAR THE AIR COMPANY re-formed on 1 April 1924 at Manston, but on the 30th they departed for Upavon, remaining there for just over ten years before moving to Kenley for four months. There followed an interruption caused by the Italo-Abyssinian war, and they returned to Kenley eleven months later. They were equipped initially with the Sopwith Snipe, once more, as were so many squadrons in that initial expansion programme. Again, little is known about the period, but a comprehensive record of training for and service on a Snipe squadron of the time can be found in *Sent Flying* by Bill Pegg.

Hawker Woodcocks began to arrive in May 1925 and on 1 March 1926 the Air Ministry selected No. 3 as a night fighter unit, which entailed fitting illuminated instrument panels, landing flares and lights and providing heated flying clothing. During December there were comparison trials between the Armstrong Whitworth Siskin IIIa, the Gloster Gamecock and the Woodcock. During October 1927 Lieutenant Yoshir Kamei of the Imperial Japanese Navy became the first foreign exchange officer, followed by Captain Sersuku Namba from the Japanese Military Air Service, who were to study the organisation, flying operations and daily running of an RAF fighter squadron. On 21 August 1928 all Woodcocks were grounded

Sopwith Snipe two seat seen in 1925 at Upavon. The horizontal stripe is a 'leftover' from another unit and the vertical green band earned the Squadron the title of 'The Margarine Boys' since it resembled the mark of a proprietary brand of the period. (JMB/GSL)

Sopwith Snipes, now overall silver and displaying no squadron markings, probably at Manston in 1924. (Bruce Robertson)

following a series of accidents. The latest of these killed was Flight Lieutenant L.H. Browning when wing failure occurred during air firing over Holbeach Range from the Armament Practice Camp at Sutton Bridge.

The squadron was scheduled to receive the first Bristol Bulldogs, but these were not ready for delivery so Gamecocks were issued in the interim. They were chosen in order to give as much continuity as possible for pilots and fitters, as all three types were powered by the Bristol Jupiter engine. The other types in service, the Siskin and Gloster Grebe, were powered by the Armstrong Siddeley Jaguar. The Gamecocks arrived during late August and September from Kenley and Tangmere, 23 and 43 Squadrons respectively, the majority from the latter which had just re-equipped with Siskins.

Between 3 and 13 September a Bulldog was received for night-flying trials, but

A Hawker Woodcock visiting Northolt from Upavon in 1925. (3 Squadron)

The second prototype of the Gloster Gamecock in 1928. (3 Squadron)

crashed at night before their completion. On 22 May, 1929, Flight Lieutenant H.W. Taylor collected the first to be allotted to the squadron and by 27 September twelve had been collected. But before the full complement had been received, a flight of three was demonstrated at the Hendon Air Display, led by Flight Lieutenant J.L. Airey. This aeroplane is covered in *The Bulldog Fighter* by David Luff.

A Bristol Bulldog II at Hendon in 1929. Assisted taxiing in restricted space was required as no brakes were fitted until the later Mark IIa, which also boasted wheel covers and a concave to convex fin leading edge. (Bruce Robertson)

Bristol Bulldog IIs at Hendon in 1926, overflying a Handley Page Hyderabad; vic led by Flt.Lt. J.L. Airey. (Aeroplane Weekly)

The squadron marking carried on the Snipes was a green band around the fuselage similar to a commercial product, a feature which led to the nickname 'the Margarine Boys'. With the standardisation of unit markings, however, it became a green band running the length of the fuselage and between the upper wing roundels. Flight colours were painted on the wheel discs and the flight commander's fin and tailplane: 'A' was red, 'B' was yellow and 'C' was green. 'B' later changed to blue, probably because it was not thought an appropriate colour to apply to any combat unit.

On receipt of the Mk.IIa, with its convex instead of concave fin leading edge and its wheel brakes, which led to metal instead of doped linen wheel covers, the fuselage band was shortened to the fabric area only, from behind the cockpit to the beginning of the empennage. This was to facilitate the change or removal of markings and transfer between units. A further change occurred, just before the Gladiator arrived, to a 'teardrop' shape.

A move to Kenley, with 17 Squadron, on 10 May 1935 was followed by another trip abroad. No. 3 left for the Sudan with eighteen aircraft (twelve unit equipment plus six immediate reserve), which were flown to Sealand, north of Chester, for packing and shipment on 22 September 1935. Personnel embarked on TSS *Cameronian* at Liverpool on 4 October. Squadrons sent to dissuade Mussolini from further ambition after Abyssinia were 22(B), who disembarked at Malta, 29(F), 33(B) and 142(B) at Alexandria, 3(F) at Port Sudan, and 12(B) and 41(F) at Aden.

Bristol Bulldog IIa, the Boss's kite; Squadron Leader Martyn in white, seen in 1930. (3 Squadron)

No. 3 arrived on 18 October, and after erecting and testing the aircraft, flew to Khartoum.

On 25 January, 1936, there was great excitement when an Italian Caproni Ca 133 colonial bomber/transport landed inside the Sudanese border and was interned by the British. The pilots given the task of recovery and initial evaluation were horrified to find that it outclassed the Bulldog! They were hard pressed to keep up with their leader, Squadron Leader Martyn. Sadly, at the end of March, Martyn became ill with cancer and died soon after the voyage home.

Bristol Bulldog IIAs in Sudan during 1936. Note wheel covers for protection against the sun and sand. The photo is of A Flight on the morning of Air Chief Marshal Sir Robert Brooke-Popham's inspection. (Welch)

Squadron group in Sudan in 1936. It is believed to show two COs, Squadron Leaders Martyn and Lester. (R.C. Ayling)

The tented camp and airfield at Port Sudan 1935/6. (3 Squadron)

Bristol Bulldog IIas of A Flight over Sudan in 1935. (Bruce Robertson)

1935 Royal Review of the RAF at Mildenhall. The King spent some time with the Squadron on the ground and chatted with Group Captain Strugnell MC and Warrant Officer Eley (both on the right}, who were both members of the Squadron in 1912. In command of the review was Brookham (behind HM) and No. 3 led the Fighter Group of eleven squadrons. The King is seen shaking hands with Flying Officer E.M. Donaldson. (Flight Magazine)

Bulldog IIa Pilots 'Warming Up' engines, ground crew ready for 'Chocks away'.

The six pilots and two ground crew for the Sassoon Cup. (Welch)

A Bristol Bulldog IIA at Kenley. Note under-wing rack for four practise bombs and for flares outboard for night flying; navigation lights above upper wing tips. (Welch)

On 3 August 1936, fifteen aircraft started the flight to Aboukir, the rest to Atbara, where they were to remain. The squadron personnel returned to the UK on the *Somersetshire* and assembled at Kenley on 29 August, and after a month's leave commenced flying Bulldogs again on 20 October. The majority of these were ex-17 Squadron, which had re-equipped with Gauntlets in August.

The first Gladiator K6145 was collected by the CO, Squadron Leader H.L.P. 'Pingo' Lester – who

Gloster Gladiators at Kenley in 1937. The multiple refuelling vehicle is probably an Albion chassis and Zwicky apparatus. (Chaz Bowyer)

subsequently used 'P' as his aircraft identification letter – from Brockworth on 2 April 1937. However, on leaving Brockworth 'suffered an engine cut on take-off and, hurriedly switching to his gravity fuel tank, managed to complete a successful cross-wind landing.' *F. K. Mason.* The post-Sudan 'teardrop' marking F.K.M. was soon applied and the upper wing marking was also changed, a parallel band on the centre section but on the outer wings tapering from the join to a point as it reached the roundel. There is photographic evidence to suggest that these were purposely

Gloster Gladiators at Kenley during a VIP Display in 1937. **(Aeroplane Weekly)**

Gloster Gladiator with new spearhead marking applied. (Welch)

assymetric – i.e. either left or right or both – on different aircraft to indicate their position in flight, the standard formation being 1 = leader, 2 = right echelon, 3 = left echelon, possibly therefore 1 = both, 2 = starboard, 3 = port. There is, however, no evidence in writing. Initially the only marking had been the colour flight commanders carried on the upper portion of the fin and rudder, as deep as the aerodynamic balance; all wheel-discs were in the flight colour except that for a period the CO's wheel discs were highly polished metal. Before all aircraft had been 'teardropped' it was decreed that markings were not to be made so conspicuous.

Accordingly No. 3 modified the official spearhead in which fighter squadron badge devices were to be carried, outlining it in a triangle of the flight colour, with

Gloster Gladiator inverted on landing. Note the position of the wheel on the left. (Welch)

The Gloster Gladiator first issue in 1937, Bob Ayling (centre) leads A Flight. (R.C. Ayling)

Hawker Hurricane I first issue in 1938 the early series did not have a ventral fin fore and aft of the tailwheel and were fitted with kidney exhausts, instrument Venturi and a post for the aerial wire. (Welch)

flight commanders filling in the rear upper and lower sections. The device was from the official squadron badge, which was approved on 28 August, 1937, 'On a monolith a cockatrice' – otherwise known as 'bird on a brick' or 'cock on a rock'! The previous badge was the Roman numeral III made up of five monoliths with the RAF eagle and crown superimposed and a scrolled motto below.

On 4 March 1938 the first Hurricane was received and at the end of the month

Hawker Hurricane I L1579, 10 May 1938. The aircraft was wrecked on landing at Kenley, killing the pilot, Hugh Henry May. (Welch)

eight Gladiators were flown to Sealand for shipment to Egypt, the remainder going the following month. Being the second squadron to receive the RAF's latest fighter – the first being 111 at Northolt – it was a proud time, but saddened by the loss of Pilot Officer Hugh Henry May in L1579, who is buried in the airmen's plot at Kenley (Whyteleafe Village) Church Way cemetery. We are indebted to Colin Lee for the eyewitness account of the crash as written on 10 May 1938, by Bryan Prosper.

I was forteen years and seven months of age. Not working during the month in question.

I would often visit Kenley, on this occasion it was a fine sunny afternoon, a Tuesday or Thursday. I arrived about 2.45 p.m., all was rather quiet, Three squadron was airborn.

Standing near the trees on the South-eastern edge of the aerodrome near the end of the married quarters next to Hayes Lane, a few other persons were also there, plus some children about eight of us in all.

At approx. 3.45 p.m. the nine aircraft returned in formation from South to North direction turning left into a down wind leg circuit and landing in loose threes.

The ground staff now were meeting there prospective aircraft on the tarmac and we persons were watching the aircraft taxi in all of us facing North, North-east.

The final three now turning finals over Coulsdon Common I turned to watch them. To my horror one of which perhaps the second from the last

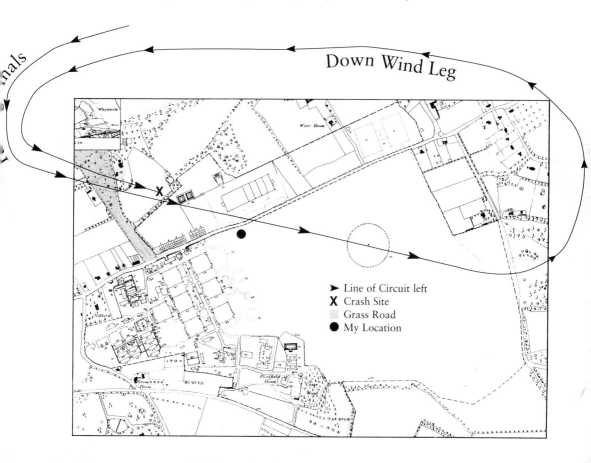

Down Wind Leg

► Line of Circuit left
X Crash Site
▮ Grass Road
● My Location

dropped the port mainplane turned left into a vertical nose down and plunged into the valley out of sight with a muffled crunch.

I stood for a moment frozen to the spot turned to the others watching the aircraft taxi in and said did you see it 'See what?' was the reply.

It would seem I was the only person to see the crash perhaps some small children also but it was not really apparent.

I then called over to the ground staff, they didn't see it, in fact two came over to me requesting directions to the location.

At that moment about six women came rushing out from the back of the married quarters, waving, shouting and some quite distressed, they had seen it.

All this took some five minutes from the time of the crash. The groundstaff about six of them went over to the women then to the site, the RAF Ambulance arrived jumping over the rough field to the wire fence at the top of the bank before the steep slope into the valley.

I waited until the pilot was carried up to the ambulance that made its way back up to Hayes Lane I then proceeded with bike to top of the bank, left bike against fence requested permission from a serviceman and then down the steep bank I went to locate the aircraft. I couldn't find it at first, was walking in the wrong direction. It was very quiet.

I then came out from woodland into a field and only then did I see the aircraft lying flat on a thick hedge the trailing edge was about level with my shoulders, the rear fuse and empenage not a mark on it, as new the prop and complete engine assembly had broken off at the cockpit and thrust forward only the pilots seat remained attached to the fuselage bulkhead.

An airman at the site told me the pilot was bleeding from his ears, nose and mouth and was not expected to survive.

I departed the site some 30 mins later.

About one week later the aircraft had not been moved this I viewed from a different location in the valley known by the locals as the grass Road. part of which is still there to this day.

The inquest reported in the local press, Caterham Weekly Press *stated the aircraft touched the trees. It did not touch any trees.*

On my reflections there are two possible causes. 1. Asymmetrical flaps, if the port side had blown up from fully down position owing to system or linkage failure the aircrafts position was indeed in this type of situation (A well know defect in later years). 2. Before the nose down plunge I noted a slight turn to port, would expect this was to line up for landing because other aircraft were on the aerodrome. If at the line up correction the airspeed had been near to the stalling speed its understandable the aircraft could have developed a stall turn.

This was a very sad outing for me, it was the first time I had seen the Hurricane at close range, also nine aircraft in formation. Also my last visit to this spot which was closed to the public soon after when the new Hayes

Hawker Hurricane I display at Kenley in 1938. Only eight aeroplanes after the demise of Hugh Henry May. (Flight Magazine)

Lane was constructed.

Only five days previously one of the Hurricanes had stalled on take-off and was badly damaged; Kenley was therefore considered too small for these advanced aircraft in its current state and on 4 July they were flown to Digby and exchanged for nine Gladiators of 73 Squadron. These were given a different marking scheme from that in use prior to the Hurricanes (which were always brown and green topsides, with silver undersides on first issue), but not for long. On 30 August the squadron went on block leave, and was then recalled because of the international situation. Orders were issued for the camouflaging of all aircraft, with brown and green on top, and black port and white starboard undersides. At this time Kenley was used as a diversion for Croydon, and on at least one occasion a partly camouflaged Gladiator – the boss's 'P' – is seen surrounded by DH86, 84; DC2s and a Savoia-Marchetti 73. No wonder Kenley was hit so hard later!

In *R.A.F. Kenley*, Peter Flint says: 'No 3 Squadron was having trouble with camouflaging its Gladiators through not having the paint to do it; this was solved by sending someone down to a shop in Whyteleafe for some household distemper.' The camouflage scheme as applied completely obliterated serial numbers, as well as squadron and individual markings; only red/blue roundels were carried. The exception was the aerobatic display team, which had a white chevron on the upper wing to aid station keeping, plus the pilots' names beneath the sliding hood in white on both sides. Later code letters were allocated, but serials were still obliterated – OP-A was K7965, which was flown by the aerobatic flight leader, Flight Lieutenant R.C. Ayling with Flying Officers Fowler and Vickery as his wingmen.

Vickery was 'coming by train' to Kenley on 23 November 1937 in K7896, i.e. following the Ashford – Redhill railway line, flying low due to weather:

> *Suddenly, immediately ahead, the entrance to the tunnel north of Oxted appeared out of the murk with high ground above it* [he had forgotten this]. *Yanking back on the stick, he put the aircraft into a steep climb, but with insufficient speed it stalled and fell on to the sharply rising hill above the tunnel* [near Warlingham]. *The only hurt to Vickery was a sprained ankle and a dent in his pride, but it took a very long time to retrieve the damaged aircraft from its precarious position.*

Vickery was one of the ten Gladiator pilots of 263 Squadron who went down with HMS *Glorious* on 8 June 1940 along with all but two of 46 Squadron's Hurricane pilots, Flight Lieutenant Pat Jameson and 'Bing' Cross.

On 25 March 1939 redeployment to Biggin Hill commenced, partly to allow Kenley to be enlarged and resurfaced. The move was completed by 1 May, with the squadron taking over the South Camp, ready for re-equipping. Then on 2 May the first four Hurricanes arrived. By the 15th, ten Hurricanes and a Battle were on strength, though the Aero Flight retained its four Gladiators, in which they gave displays at various aerodromes. By 24 August, when all flights were ordered to stand by with guns loaded, all the Gladiators had gone, and the day before war was declared the squadron moved to Croydon and took over the two southern-most hangars, previously occupied by SABENA, KLM and Air France.

Gloster Gladiators of the second issue in 1938. This is the Aerobatic Flight at Villacoublay. Four were kept after the second issue of Hurricanes. Note the white chevron to aid station keeping. (R.C. Ayling)

CHAPTER TWELVE

The Outbreak of World War Two

F OR A WHILE AFTER THE OUTBREAK OF THE SECOND WORLD WAR, at least in the west, little happened. Initially the most notable thing happening to No. 3 Squadron was the change of identity letters from OP to QO.

Whenever flying conditions permitted patrols were flown to protect minelayers and convoys in the English Channel, which required frequent moves between Croydon and Manston, with detachments to Hawkinge. Ground crews usually went by road and Ted Burns remembers being issued with a 'Flight greatcoat' for use when servicing in the open; this had been re-dyed from khaki and had long 'skirts' divided up to the waist – probably ex-cavalry – which were most welcome in cold lorries! The first eight months are referred to as 'the phoney war' but it should never be forgotten that the RAF was fighting and dying over old familiar territory throughout this period, and 46 and 263 Squadrons did the same over Norway. First blood for No. 3 came on 10 May 1940 when, soon after arriving at Merville, they were scrambled and claimed six destroyed and three damaged, with one pilot wounded in action and two Hurricanes declared Category 'E'.

Much has been written in recent years about the validity of various claims, but the reports were made in good faith.

Imagine how lonely it must be, in the twilight over the Channel, with no companions and the threat of surprise attack. One of the two Hurricanes written off was N2333 flown by Flying Officer Dickie Ball. Having already flown one mission, in L1901, after flying in from Kenley he was scrambled again. Brian Cull and Bruce Landers explain in *Twelve Days in May*:

> Unable to make R/T contact or find the airfield in the dark, Ball set course for Dover but was similarly unable to find an aerodrome there, so baled out over St Margaret's Bay, near the Dover RDF Station. Unhurt and taken back to RAF Kenley in a Magister, he returned to Merville next day with a replacement Hurricane.

At the end of the twelve days another seven companions had paid the price of other peoples' freedom, two in a collision and one died as a prisoner of war. Eighteen aircraft had been lost in exchange for sixty-two enemy destroyed, five probably destroyed and five damaged. It appears that only five aircraft returned to England.

The following compilation of letters received by Dennis Anstey from Pat O'Connor of No 601 (County of London) Squadron, in Merville Remembered gives a good idea of conditions at the time.

> I had been at Tangmere with No 601 Squadron since January. At the end

The retreat from Merville in May 1940. (3 Squadron)

of a May night shift in the Maintenance Hangar, doing a 60 hr inspection, we pushed our kite out at about 7 a.m. After I had run up the engine, the F700 Serviceability and Work Log was signed and the machine handed over to the Flight. A wash and shave was followed by breakfast, after which I turned in for a well earned kip.

About midday, I was woken by boots clattering on the floor, but I kept my eyes shut, hoping the bods would be a bit quieter and let me sleep. Then I realised that 2 bods were at my bedside. 'You tell him,' said one. 'No, you tell him,' said the other. 'Tell me what?' said I, rolling over, eyes now open. 'Sorry Pat. We've some bad news.' 'Go on, you've busted my bike!,' I prompted. 'No. You're going to France this afternoon. Straight up. Your name's on the list in the Airmen's Mess and you've to be ready by 1430. It's now 1230, so you'd better get weaving.'

A hurried wash, a glance at the list, a quick meal after which I packed my kit, handed my bike and motor-cycle and side-car to a couple of pals who weren't going over, and presented myself and kit on the square at 1425, ready to move off. Inevitably nothing happened till tea time, when we loaded our kit and equipment into Ensigns [Armstrong Whitworth 27

110

4-engine high-wing passenger planes, impressed with most other large transports from Imperial and British Airways which had been merged to form British Overseas Airways Corporation and were usually operated by civilian crews with civil registration letters underlined with red/white/blue stripes on camouflage]. *We spent the night at Manston.*

An early morning take-off found us flying low over the sea with a Hurricane escort. As we cleared the French coast at about 7 a.m., the folks going to early Mass waved to us. I felt a bit guilty – they were going to church and I was going to help kill Germans. We landed at Merville and had another breakfast from the Field Kitchen before putting up tents for our equipment.

Sirens sounded and one aircraft was seen miles up apparently on a recce, taking pictures of our arrival. We mucked in well; there was no demarcation. We got stuck into any work regardless of trade; fitters helped riggers who helped armourers etc. There was a very good relationship with No 3 Sqn. We slept in Nissen huts at the west end of the village – palliasses for bedding – not really first class, but bearable as the weather was great. Field Kitchen messing was not bad considering; we didn't really expect hotel accommodation anyway!

Late one evening they got us all out of the huts because they thought that paratroops were about to land on the airfield? Duff gen! Plenty of that in those days! Also, do you remember that, as there were no NAAFI breaks, they allowed us to go in twos to a Convent just outside the airfield where the nuns sold us coffee and rolls? Rather decent of them! Funny, but I can't remember any guard duties. Somebody must have done them. Strange times, weren't they?

After a strafing sortie a very young pilot climbed out of one of the Hurricanes looking a bit shaken. We asked him how things were going. He said, 'They've got too many tanks, too many guns and too many men – and the Hun column is still coming on.' While checking his aircraft for ack-ack damage I found a bullet hole in the pilot's bucket seat. When he saw it he said, 'God! Where's the bullet?' I suggested that if he hadn't got a sore bum it was probably in his parachute and strongly advised him to change it. This he did and we saw him off on his next sortie. Unfortunately he didn't return.

Flight Lieutenant Churchill (3 Sqn CO, I think?) got me to take a pick-up van to Vitry on the other side of Arras to collect 2 young officers who had baled out. What a journey we had getting through the evacuees. Anyhow, I made it to Vitry a few hours after the Luftwaffe had paid a visit. Eventually I found the 2 pilots in an estaminet and got them back to Merville. One had face burns and the other a damaged arm. Don't remember their names. On arriving back Churchill was like a mother hen to us all. Another time he sent me with a wireless mechanic to get the crystals from a crashed aircraft at Aine-de-lys. This Hurricane was half across the main road and a salvage crew was there first. However, we did

Evacuating Merville Don t forget the bubbly! (3 Squadron)

get the crystals [the number of wireless frequencies were limited in the pre-selector box by the number of crystals that could be carried, capture by the enemy would prejudice communication security] *and once again I was in the CO's good books.*

Late evenings when off duty we used to go to an estaminet cum bicycle shop for our liquid refreshment. Jeannette, the vivacious daughter, was very popular with the lads! Then there was the Hotel Sarafan where I understand you could get a nice bath if you wanted. That was the hotel right next to the level crossing. I was beginning to enjoy Merville – before we had to leave so hurriedly as the result of a visit from the Luftwaffe *when I dived into a ditch and found it full of frogs!*

En route to Boulogne, we were turned on to another road by a despatch rider. We got there in the early evening and found 'A' Rest Camp beside the canal. Not exactly 4 star – the beds were 4 x 2 [inches] battens supporting chicken wire. However, we didn't get much chance to sample them, as the best part of the night was spent in an Air Raid Shelter from which we occasionally popped out to see the fires and the bombing of Boulogne.

Through the early morning mist we could hear machine-gun fire. Not exactly a holiday, was it? We were lined up by an army chap who took our names, next-of-kin, rifle numbers etc. It seemed as if we were to help the 'brown jobs', but after we fell out our Flight Sergeant told us quietly to get in the trucks as his orders were to get us back to Tangmere. We moved off quietly and stayed in the docks till about tea time when we were able to board the Isle of Man ferry Mona's Queen. *As we were going up the gang-plank another army bod was looking for drivers. I'm afraid I felt a bit guilty, saying I couldn't drive, because in my wallet I had authorization to drive all RAF vehicles.*

Before being called up for the Auxiliaries my civvy job was Fitter MT at No 1 MU Kidbrooke. My pangs of conscience were dispelled when our Flight Sergeant said, 'Your duty, O'Connor, is to 601 Squadron, the army can get MT drivers, but we can't get Aero Engine Fitters!'

From Folkstone to Tidworth on Salisbury Plain, arriving after midnight. At Merville I had been issued with a P14 Ross rifle and before we left I had filled my side pack with quite an assortment of cartridges. As we collected our bedding at Tidworth the Corporal said, 'Let's have any ammo you may have.' You should have seen his face when out came clips of ball, tracer, incendiary, AP [armour piercing] etc. 'Christ! You could have put up a siege!' he said. 'Yes mate. I intended to if necessary,' I replied. The next afternoon we travelled to Kenley where there was a big panic by the 'upper crust' who thought that 3 Sqn was going to hang on to us. We really wouldn't have minded as we got on so well. Anyway, back to 601 at Tangmere to prepare for the Battle of Britain. The old Hurricane received more mods, between the fall of France and the B of B than ever in its life. We worked day and night, but it was worth it!

Twenty years later I returned to Merville for a short stay and met some of the people who remembered us. And I took a few photos. In 1960 that road was little different from how it was in 1940.

Other memories of Merville can be found in *Scramble: A Narrative History of the Battle of Britain* by Norman Gelb. The following quote is also worth reproducing.

> *United States Ambassador Joseph Kennedy to the Secretary of State, Washington*
>
> *London, 27 September* [1940]
>
> FOR THE PRESIDENT AND THE SECRETARY
>
> *The night raids are continuing to do, I think, substantial damage and the day raids of the last three days have dealt most serious blows to Bristol, Southampton and Liverpool. Production is definitely falling, regardless of what reports you may be getting, and with Transportation smashed up the way it is, the present production output will continue to fall . . .*
>
> *My own feeling is that they* [the British] *are in a bad way. Bombers have got through in the daytime on the last three days and on four occasions today substantial numbers of German planes have flown over London and have done some day-light bombing . . .*
>
> *I cannot impress upon you strongly enough my complete lack of confidence in the entire* [British] *conduct of this war. I was delighted to see that the President said he was not going to enter the war because to enter*

this war, imagining for a minute that the English have anything to offer in the line of leadership or productive capacity in industry that could be of the slightest value to us, would be a complete misapprehension.

In May the squadron returned to Kenley, which became overcrowded very quickly with fully operational squadrons flying top cover over the evacuation plus No. 3 and others trying to re-equip. There was then a brief respite.

Ten days later, on 30 May, the squadron was retired to Wick to re-form and re-equip. They moved successively to Castletown, north-west of Wick, then to Turnhouse (Edinburgh) with detachments to Dyce (Aberdeen) and Montrose, then to Skebrae in Orkney with a detachment at Sumburgh in Shetland, which was maintained on returning to Castletown. These detachments and movements were dictated by the need to protect the Home Fleet base at Scapa Flow and to maintain the shield as a spoof when this was moved west and south to Inverewe.

After moving to Martlesham on 3 April, re-equipment commenced with the Mk.IIb with twelve .303 inch machine guns and the IIc with four x 20 mm cannon. A month later the squadron moved to Debden and ten days later returning to the Heath kept everyone on their toes and the unit mobile. The tide had turned, and Germany attacked Russia, causing a strategic realignment of priorities. Russia began to insist on the West opening a 'second' front.

To tie down some of the *Luftwaffe*, the 'third front' in the air over Europe was hotted up. Convoy protection became a major task until a shift to night operations began with 'B' Flight. Then in June there was a move to Stapleford Tawney from whence the first intruder sorties over France commenced. The first offensive sweeps in July encountered relatively little oppositon; they then developed into operations involving entire wings, designed to draw up a *Luftwaffe* already suffering large losses in the east and the Mediterranean.

Night operations continued meanwhile, and a move to Hunsdon in August saw co-operation with Turbinlite Havocs for night interception operations. This was a good idea in theory, but in practice quite difficult in spite of formation lights and white stripes on the wings of the converted Bostons/Havocs, which carried radar and an operator and a nose-mounted searchlight! The effect on night vision of all concerned when all this candle power appeared as if by magic was dramatic 'It sure scared the hell out of me, and if it shone on some Krauts they would have surrenderd in mid-air,' was one succinct comment.

There was also an attempt to fit Airborne Interception Radar (AI) into the Hurricane. Not well known is the fact that No. 3 were given the task of early trials, and Pilot Officer Bob Barckley was one who flew such a modified Hurricane. Flying at night and operating these early radars, plus the fact that psychologically it went against the grain for a single-seat fighter pilot to spend more than a few seconds every minute with his head inside the cockpit, meant more trials and practice were needed. A fully operational squadron could not afford men, machines or time, so these trials were continued in the south-west and form no part of this brief history.

Detachments and positioning to rearm and refuel at numerous airfields followed, mainly night intruder operations from Manston and a short period at Shoreham for the Dieppe landing, which took place on 19 August 1942. No. 3's contribution was

114

four squadron-strength sorties; on the 1st Canadian Sergeant S.D. Banks was lost to heavy flak and on the 4th the CO, Squadron Leader Alex Berry, was lost to an FW190 and crashed into a cliff face. Three DFCs were won: Flight Lieutenants H.E. Tappin, Desmond J. Scott and Louis T. Spence.

Tappin recalls:

I joined 3 Squadron at Martlesham Heath on 2 June 1941 after more than two years as a flying instructor and a Hurricane course at 52 OTU at

Hawker Hurricane IIc airborne from Hunsdon in 1941. (RNZAF Museum)

Hawker Hurricane IIc at Hunsdon in 1941; re-loading and calibrating the camera gun. (RNZAF Museum)

Hawker Hurricane IIc BN185 at Hunsdon in 1941 while the pilot prepares for flight and the armourers clean the guns. (RNZAF Museum)

Debden. We moved to Stapleford Tawney on 23 June 1941 and, from my log-book, appeared to operate on a day-to-day basis from Hunsdon, primarily for night work as Stapleford was not suitable for night-flying in the Hurricane. My first flight co-operating with a Havoc of 1451 Flight at Hunsdon was on 2 July. 3 Squadron moved to Hunsdon on 9 August 1941 and so were able to work more closely with 1451 Flight, but although morale was remarkably good, it was difficult to see any real promise in the project, and a final effort was made in September 1942 by forming Turbinlite Squadrons with their own Hurricane flights . . . I was posted away from 3 Squadron in September 1942 to run the Hurricane Flight of 534 Squadron (Turbinlite) at Tangmere, which didn't please me, but I ended up with a Mosquito squadron after a short time, so it had its compensations. . .

Hawker
Hurricane IIc at
Hunsdon. (RNZAF
Museum)

A black night intruder Hawker Hurricane IIc in 1941. The pilot, Squadron Leader Eddie Berry, was killed in action over Dieppe on 19 August 1942. (RNZAF Museum)

1941 Hawker Hurricane IIc Z3068 at Hunsdon in 1941; F Freddy on R & R during refuelling. (IWM CH3510)

1941/42 were fairly quiet times, many convoy patrols, but there were moments, like the *Scharnhorst/Gneisenau* affair and Dieppe, and occasional bomber escorts, plus the night intruders by the Manston Flight.

In 'Appreciation of the MANSTON NIGHT FLIGHT', in June 1943, he wrote:

A wealth of reminiscence remains; the 'all-in' billiards matches between Shaw and Scott which left the spectators convulsed with laughter; mysterious R/T conversations over enemy territory between 'Spike' and 'Joe' which must still be unsolved by German Intelligence; nights in dispersal when the New Zealanders talked for hours of their home country, conversations which were as full of interest to others as they were to the participants; nights when 'Scottie' would leap into the air to shepherd one of his pilots who was in difficulties; these and a hundred other memories help to fill the gap left by the Flight's departure. But to those of us at Manston who knew the Night Flight, there is, and always will be, a gap.

Doug Palmer recalls:

I joined the squadron way back in 1941 as an armourer and stayed until January '46, so I was particularly interested in the Manston Night Flight report [in the Association magazine]. I seem to remember we only had 3 or 4 Hurricanes in the early days . . . and spent many hours waiting for the pilot to return from his very lonely vigil. Where are these gutsy gents now? I shudder to think of the young pilot setting off over France, Belgium and Holland probably worried about finding his way back on a miserable dark wet night and not knowing when an enemy fighter's gun would get him.

Hawker Hurricane IIc BD867 airborne from Hunsdon. (IWM CH3506)

My hero was F/Lt Collins, who I see did two ops in one night! Names like Gilbert, Lumsden, Shaw and others come flooding back. One young Sgt Pilot, whose name I cannot recall, came back with his tailplane partly shot away. I helped him down the slippery wing and after a very quick dash to the tail for obvious reasons [i.e. a pee or to be sick] he told me that those in there ['there' being the crewroom] would now believe that he had been over France.

I cannot think of any other sorties where a lone pilot had to take on such a daunting task. The list of no less than seven awards to the squadron during this period is evidence of their bravery. May I offer this small tribute to them.

The awards were Acting Squadron Leader Scott (NZ) Bar to DFC; DFCs to Flight Lieutenants Collins and Shaw, Pilot Officers Hay (NZ), Inwood and Smith, and a DFM to Sergeant Gawith (NZ). Fifteen and a half enemy aircraft were claimed as destroyed, five probables and seventeen damaged in 208 sorties, totalling 493 hours, during which time six companions paid the price.

CHAPTER THIRTEEN

Wind of Change

ON 1 FEBRUARY 1943 B Flt rejoined the squadron, which ceased to be operational in order to convert to the Hawker Typhoon Ib. Following the conversion, the first action came shortly after the move, on 14 May 1943, to West Malling. Eight aircraft made a low-level strafing and bombing raid on the marshalling yards at Ell, causing much damage. All returned from this raid. A deeper penetration to the airfield at Poix two days later ended in tragedy. Eight aircraft, led by the CO, Squadron Leader L.F. de Soomer, swept in low over the airfield strafing and each releasing their two 500 lb (227 kg) bombs on the first pass. The flak over the target was intense, one of the machines being hit and crashing in flames – Blue 4, Flying Officer D.R. Hall, DFC, RNZAF, in R8979 'N'. The remainder were about to re-form when they were bounced by FW190s, resulting in the loss of a further four aircraft. Red 3, Flying Officer L.G. Gill, R8835 'M'; Blue 3, Pilot Officer R. Inwood, DFC, DN598 'Z'; Red 2, Flight Sergeant F.K.Whitall, DN246 'A'; Red 4, Sergeant V. Bailey, R8879 'D'. All were killed, leaving only three returning to West Malling. These were the leader, Red 1 (Leo de Soomer) plus Blue 1 (Flight Lieutenant Collins DFC, 'S') and Blue 2 (Sergeant Tidy, 'R'), who did not see combat, as recorded in the leader's report of 23 May 1943, which was provided by Doug Palmer and published in Association magazine, 33 5/96, and which triggered the following letters:

> The New Zealander who lost his life was F/O Hall. I did not know his name at the time of meeting him the evening before the raid. We had a few drinks together in the pub called the Startled Saint, just down the road from the airfield. He was on his own and looked very lonely; no doubt thinking about the following morning's Op. Although we had a drink or two I never asked his name, but I always remembered the shoulder flash he wore. I told him I was on 3F also and would look forward to meeting him again, even though I was just an LAC ground crew armourer. But it was not to be. The sadness of his not returning has been with me to this day and now I know who he was. I wonder where he was buried.
>
> PS Have just had a letter from Mike Flannagan and he tells me that prior to the raid Byron Lumsden and F/O Hall had words about whose turn it was to go on ops. that day. The CO stepped in and made the decision. How lucky for Byron.
>
> Lady Luck was not with Ross Hall.

> Leo Canty:
>
> I have vivid memories of the Poix raid. Ross Hall and I were as close as any of us allowed ourselves to become in those days, when one of 3

Hawker Typhoon Ib loaded with 2 x 500lb bombs seen in 1944. (3 Squadron)

Squadron's claims to fame was the casualty rate. We had much in common in that we were both New Zealanders, both Flying Officers, we shared a room and we were friends. Even further, there was an unwritten but very well entrenched understanding that we would fly on alternate missions.

The day before the Poix raid it was my 'turn' to fly, but as we taxied out the show was cancelled. Accordingly, with much 'logic' and a great stand on principle, I reckoned that that didn't count and that when the Poix raid came up it was my turn. With equal logic and great feeling Ross argued that, because the previous day I had started my engine and moved the aircraft, this counted as a 'turn' and therefore it was now his 'turn' to go – in this case to Poix!

I was interested in the story of Ross in the local pub the previous night. I cannot recall its name, but I remember what it looked like! There was certainly an atmosphere about the Poix show. Having been put in line by Leo de Soomer, who settled our argument and ruled that Ross should go to Poix, I recall very vividly standing at dispersal while Ross settled himself in the aircraft and taxied out. One of the groundcrew – a tall Yorkshireman who must have been all of four or five years older than me! – put his hand on my shoulder and said, 'Don't worry, Lum, he'll be OK.' Unfortunately Ross and the other four were not all right.

Having related this, of course I have no problem with you mentioning Leo's PS. In fact it rounds off the tale of Poix and gives an indication of the attitude of the Squadron in those days. You would argue with your best friend about whose turn it was to fly; nobody had to be persuaded to fly!

Byron Lumsden

I know that in the literature of the genre pilots are supposed to get drunk and throw glasses to mark the passing of their comrades. I have to say that

I never personally saw nor took part in such activities. In this I speak as someone who lost 50/60 comrades during my time with the Squadron, including four of the eight COs under whom I served. After Poix the atmosphere was very sombre and contemplative. In my case I had lost my closest friend on the Squadron, namely Bob Inwood, who was our resident 'Ace', having shot down five or six German planes on night intruder operations. He was also a very quiet, modest and most likeable Welshman with a great love of good music. But I remember also my comrades lost before Poix and the very many more lost during the following two years. Could we perhaps pay tribute to them also?
  Bob Barckley

Who would not agree? But in the space available it is not possible to list them all so let Poix stand as an example for all those who died. Meanwhile, let Lefty Whitman's words, written in 1995, stand as a tribute to them all.

'RAID ON POIX AERODROME MAY 18TH 1943

Eight Typhoons all ready, R and Rs complete.
Bathed in misty moonlight With all the world asleep.
We dress with apprehension, Will this show be the last?
And if it comes on this one, Please – make it clean and fast.
Pockets all are emptied, of trinkets, cards or cash.
Sprint to your kite and wait, for the Verey pistol's flash.
Eight Typhoons are airborne, flying just as one.
And then, too soon, our escort leaves with 'bandits' in the sun.
Suddenly, it's all over, and daylight floods the sky.
The world awakes, and five are gone. Three left to wonder why.

In memory of: Vic Bailey, Len Gill, Eppie Hall, Bob Inwood DFC and Ken Whitall.'

In any combat action there is bound to be considerable confusion, but the original brief had been to climb out to 6,000 ft, where a higher-level escort was waiting. For some reason Leo de Soomer had rebriefed to return to base at low level without informing the escort, although 'Scottie' and his 486 Squadron had flown in to West Malling to overnight and were available to rebrief.

On 11 June the squadron returned to Manston where, with its previous experience of the base and night flying, it became one of the few Typhoon squadrons engaged in night-intruder and low-level moonlight bombing missions. On the 16th Sergeant E.K. Ticklepenny was shot down by E-boats while on a dawn roadstead (low-level attack on coastal shipping). He baled out of DN948 'C' off Cap Gris Nez and was rescued. But the fickle finger was not to be cheated, for eleven days later on return from a night roadstead EJ964 'G' hit a balloon on return and went into the sea – his body was found later.

In August 1943 Squadron Leader Thomas, DFC, AFC, took command but within a month was replaced by Squadron Leader P. Hawkins, MC, AFC, who was killed on 5 October leading a raid in JP733 'A' on an oil refinery near Ghent. Squadron Leader A.S. Dredge, DFC, AFC, brought his experience in the Battle of Britain and

Newchurch ground crew at dispersal in June 1944. (3 Squadron)

Malta to bear, and losses were cut considerably following what became an almost standard method of bombing attack by Typhoons: the aircraft was put into a very steep dive at 12,000 ft with the bombs being released at about 7,000 ft.

To give some idea of the intensity of flying, on 19 November Malcolm Edwards flew two sorties in 'R' – first as fighter escort to Hurricanes on a roadstead, then as 'Bombphoon' a Ramrod to Audinghem (Gris Nez); this was repeated twice on the 20th and once on the 22nd to the same target; a note in his log-book states, 'Director of German Works and Bricks killed in these attacks on their HQ at Audinghem. Place completely wiped out.' On the 21st a Ramrod was recalled and two 500 lb bombs jettisoned. They had positioned to Ford from Manston and returned direct.

On the 26th they provided a fighter escort, to 'Marauders plastered military objectives in the Pas de Calais' – a news paper cutting. On the 29th, 'Attacked and set on fire a *Luftwaffe* air base at Moorselle, in Belgium'.

From 10 November many missions were flown to destroy the 'ski sites', which were intended to become V-1 launch ramps, difficult and well defended targets. December saw a move to Swanton Morley, where long-range fuel tanks were fitted, enabling longer sorties escorting Beaufighters on anti-shipping strikes. On Valentine's Day came a return to Manston and at the end of the month came the first 'Typhoon Twos'.

On 29 February 'Lefty' Whitman noted, 'Our first new TEMPEST arrives!' On 2 March in Typhoon 'S', 'Escort to Marauders – St Omer – three shot down by flak over Ostende – one which I was taking home crashed into sea – no survivors.' The same day in Tempest 'C', was his first solo. Bob Cole flew his first, JN742, next day and Malcolm Edwards 'X' on the 14th 'WHAT A PLANE!' On the 15th it was 'X' again, on the 27th 'R' and on the 29th 'Z' – 'MY NEW AIRCRAFT! WIZZO!' Two

124

flights later next day; on the second, 'AEROBATICS – TEDDY DID THEM WITH ME IN FORMATION (NO LINE)'.

In preparation for the forthcoming invasion 3 Squadron and 486 NZ Squadron were equipped with Tempests and, until production caught up, 56 with Spitfire IXs. Together they became 150 Wing of 85 Group and moved to Bradwell Bay in March 1944. After a working-up period, including a week at Ayr to practise shooting it was time to practise for the expected conditions, – so Wing Commander R.P. Beamont led everyone to Newchurch on the Romney Marshes. It comprised a makeshift control tower, Nissen huts, tents and some agricultural buildings.

From here Flying Officer 'Teddy' Zurakowski and Flight Sergeant

His Majesty King George VI presents Buck Feldman with the Distinguished Flying Cross at Blackbushe during a field investiture in July 1944. (Buck Feldman)

"Aw, shucks!" Buck Feldman with DFC ribbon up. (Buck Feldman)

Hawker Tempest V JN862 JF-Z at Newchurch in June 1944 with a pair overhead. The spinner has thin red/yellow/black bands. The aircraft was Belgian Flight Lieutenant Remy van Lierde's mount. (IWM CH16095)

J.L.T. Mannion, were lost on a shipping reconnaissance in the Gris Nez area on the morning of 27 May – Tempest Vs JN736 and JN749. Morris Rose logged them as missing and Lefty Whitman was put up on *Air Sea Search*. Before this he had logged, on 3 May in 'W', 'Fighter Sweep–Belgium–France 1.00 (one hour) First Operational flight of TEMPESTS over enemy occupied territory' and on the 8th, 'To Manston for Intruder .15 then Intruder – Dutch Islands .45 (i.e. 15 & 45 mins) First Night Intruder done in TEMPEST aircraft with Bob Barckley – One E/R Boat Cat.III –

Hawker Tempest V on Diver scramble from Newchurch in June 1944. The background shows Spitfire IXs of 56 Squadron awaiting replacement by Tempest Vs. (IWM CH14096)

Illuminated by searchlights from shore – much light flak'. Numerous sweeps followed, and on 5 June, 'Promoted to Flying Officer – Buck (Feldman) commissioned'.

Next day was D-day. Lefty Whitman in JN743 'P' and Morris Rose in 'J' were two of many flying top-cover to troopships but No. 3 saw no action until 8 June, when three 109s were claimed, one falling to Lefty. Morris Rose also logged this on the 8th when he had over-speeding. He made a forced landing on the beachhead inland of Ouistreham and ran toward Allied troops, to be told: 'You're lucky, you've just run through a minefield!' He came back by launch to Calshot on 9 June'. On the 10th, 'Oxford HM179 F/Lt Wilson Gosport to base .30 (i.e. 30 mins) passenger' – quite a busy forty-eight hours.

In *'Buzz Bomb Diary'*, Bob Barckley remembers:

> *I was stationed at Newchurch ALG with No.3 [F]* Squadron during the V-1 campaign, our squadron having moved there from Bradwell Bay on 28th April 1944, and we remained there until 28th September, when we moved to Matlask in Norfolk preparatory to departing for Grimbergen, Brussels. Whilst at Newchurch, our Tempest Wing *[comprising with ourselves No. 486 NZ Squadron and 56 Squadron]* provided the main fighter defence against the V-1, shooting down 705 of which 3 Squadron accounted for 305, and I am pleased to say I contributed a number to this score. I believe I was the first pilot to attack a V-1 in flight. The event occurred on 8th May 1944, on a night intruder operation, when I intercepted a V-1 in the neighbourhood of Evreaux and eventually attacked it west of Le Havre. It crashed into the sea in the area of Deauville. I would point out this was more than one month before the V-1's were launched against England. At the time I was not aware that it was a V-1, and my log book refers to it as a 'JET-SHIP', which showed a degree of prescience on my part. Our period at Newchurch was particularly interesting as it attracted a considerable number of famous people who felt the need to visit us. These ranged from Sir Archibald Sinclair, the Air Minister, and Sir Trafford Leigh Mallory, the AOC and many other famous senior officers. It also brought many film stars, such as Edward G. Robinson and all the famous war correspondents. One, whose fame extended beyond the war, was Ernest Hemingway, who lived in a tent next to mine, and was the only war correspondent there who got up **at dawn** with us, and shared our meagre repast. I had many interesting talks with him, and whilst with us he certainly was not the bombastic hell-raiser of his popular image.

This book credits No. 3 with 275 V-1s. It should not be forgotten that, although they were pilotless, they were not an easy target. Owing to their small size, close range was required and the fuel alone could cause a violent explosion. Our own anti-aircraft fire and other aircraft were also a danger. Flying Officer George Kosh crashed in JF-K/JN765 on 1 July while in pursuit into cloud and JF-S/JN75 was hit by anti-aircraft fire, which killed Flight Sergeant Stan Domanski two days later. On 6 August Flight Sergeant Mackerras was reported to have spun in with JN759 while in pursuit.

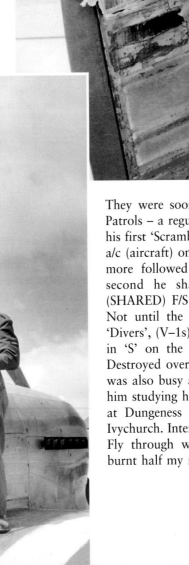

Flight Sergeant R.W. Cole examines the tail of his aircraft that was damaged as he destroyed a V-1 at close range. In the nineties Bob said: 'If you didn't get close you couldn't hit the beggars!' (IWM CH13401)

Pilot Officer G.A. 'Lefty' Whitman leaving JF.X/JN 807. Note ragged edge to hand painted D. Day stripes.   (IWM 14092)

They were soon taken off Beachhead Patrols – a regular duty and Lefty had his first 'Scramble after Hun "Rocket" a/c (aircraft) on the 13th in "P". Two more followed on 16th and on the second he shared 'One Destroyed (SHARED) F/S FOSTER at 410mph'. Not until the 19th does he refer to 'Divers', (V–1s) having shared another in 'S' on the 18th and in 'P' 'One Destroyed over LONDON'. Bob Cole was also busy and there is a photo of him studying his tail captioned 'Patrol at Dungeness shot down a diver at Ivychurch. Intercepted off Dymchurch. Fly through wreckage blazing petrol burnt half my rudder, scorched a/c.' It was necessary to get in very close to hit such a small and fast target, and the resulting explosion often led to the death of the attacker, as recorded by Lefty: 'George Kosh killed after Diver' – 1 July, this was when *JN765 JF-K* 'crashed when chasing a V-1 south-west of Rye'. He also records that Stan Domanski (a Pole) was killed 'shot down by our ack-ack' on 3 July in *JN752 JF-S* on diver patrol. On 14 July in 'S' he was 'forced to break off engagement due to flak'. Having flown over fifty anti-diver missions, on 1 August he was posted by the RCAF Headquarters Public Relations Department, Air Ministry. Attached to Ministry of Aircraft production for factory liaison duties.

He did not log his most interesting 'mission' however. In *Drafted*, by G. A. Lefty Whitman, a Yank in the RCAF, an article published in the Association magazine, he recalled:

> It was May 1944, just after we flew our Tempests to Newchurch ALG, when I received two unexpected visitors. 'Cussy', our Adjutant, informed me that there were two American MPs in the thatched roof cottage that served as our operations HQ. Cycling there across the runway, I found two US Provost Marshals, NCOs all decked out in combat boots, white helmets, holstered .45s and more medals than all our squadron combined. They saluted smartly and presented me with a large brown sealed envelope; they asked me to sign for it and to read its contents in their presence.
>
> On opening it I saw the heading 'Greetings', so I knew I was in trouble. It read, 'This is to advise you that you have been selected for immediate induction into the Armed Forces of the United States of America. Failure to report to the nearest Army Recruiting Office within fifteen days of the receipt of this notice will result in imprisonment . . .' etc. etc. I read on and then said: 'Thank you, Sergeant. What happens if I ignore this notice?' He replied, 'Well, Sir, some one will come to get you, I guess!'
>
> 'Cussy!' I called to the Adj. 'Take these chaps to the Mess tent for lunch; it's about time they had a taste of British Army field rations. It'll be a change from those pork chops and ice cream they're used to!' As they left I spoke to the CO of the RAF Regiment, our 'servicing commandos' who were responsible for aerodrome security, telling him that I'd just been drafted into the US Army. He doubled up with laughter and said it was about time I did some war work, but added that he would get right over to the Mess tent and warn 'those bloody Yanks that if they ever set foot on the base again there would likely be a Court of Inquiry leading to an international incident on their having fired on an operational RAF base.'
>
> I was both amused and insulted. The draft in the US had commenced long after I joined the RCAF and I had begun to receive postcards from my local Draft Board in Pennsylvania. They informed me that my number was S.1511, but that under section 3[C] I had been classified as 'engaged in war work', I would tear off a section of the card and return it to the Board. With moving around there was always about a six month delay, but they were always the same; 3[C]. Now someone back there thought that I should be upgraded to 1[A] and serve my country! By this time I had

already turned down two offers from the US Army Air Corps to transfer, first on an equal rank basis and next to join a squadron in the USAAF 4th Fighter Wing. Firstly, I didn't like the kites they were flying and also I didn't like joining up with newcomers.

My squadron, No 3[F] RAF, was formed in 1912 and had fought with distinction ever since. There was no way I would leave such an elite outfit voluntarily and, when I discussed this with the WingCo and the CO, they both agreed that the matter should be resolved as quickly as possible.

The flight from Romney Marsh up to Croydon took about ten minutes and upon arrival I took a cab to London. It soon pulled up in Grosvenor Square where a US Recruiting Office had recently been set up to collect merchant seamen for induction. It was a tiny ground floor office that had once housed a dress shop. Benches lined each front wall and sitting at a table under an 'Uncle Sam Wants You' poster was a Sergeant frowning at a pile of forms. Two civilians, obviously merchant seamen, were reading newspapers; one had on his lap a brown envelope similar to mine, which was tucked inside my battle dress jacket.

The Sergeant never looked up as I went to his desk. I waited a moment

CO, Squadron Leader Alan S. Dredge, with the squadron mascot Squirt, a kitten born on the day the first V-1 appeared over England. (IWM CH13431)

1945 An alert Alsatian awaits its master – Flight Lieutenant Collins. (3 Squadron)

and then said, 'Sergeant, I have some business of an urgent nature to discuss with your Commanding Officer.' He raised his eyes just far enough to see the colour of my faded blue pants and snarled, 'Sit down and wait to be called!' Well, I had never pulled rank on anyone; not that a Flying Officer had much rank to pull! But now I thought it was called for, considering the circumstances. I placed my fingers under the edge of the table and after slowly raising it two or three inches I let it drop with a bang. It immediately got his attention! He leaped to his feet but before he could speak I barked at him, 'Sergeant, do you recognise this uniform?' Before he could reply I fired the second barrel, 'Either you parade me to see your Commanding Officer, now, or I'll drag you in behind me. Move!' He saluted like a wind-up toy and marched me into the Lieutenant's office. Obviously fresh out of Fort Dix and resplendent in Army 'pinks', on his tunic was a good conduct ribbon [for not getting VD!] and merit badges for various accomplishments. He had the kind of haircut you'd see in a delousing camp, fully half an inch brush cut. He seemed startled at being disturbed at his work for he slid a copy of Life magazine under some papers with such force that it skidded out the other side and landed on the floor.

'This officer, Sir, says he has urgent business,' the Sergeant said standing stiffly to attention. 'Very well, Sergeant. You may leave,' the officer replied. Without waiting further I produced the document. A malevolent smile spread triumphantly across his face as he drawled, 'Swearing in every day at 1400, train same night to Liverpool and in two weeks you'll be Stateside in boot camp. We get all you draft dodgers sooner or later.'

Now it was my turn to burn, but with great difficulty I restrained myself. Tearing the document in half I dropped it on his desk and said, 'Come and get me! Don't send anyone else; just come yourself!' Picking up his Life magazine, I threw it at him adding, 'Be sure you finish this first!' Once out in the street I cooled off a bit. Boy, you really blew that one, I said to myself and headed across the square to the Ambassador's office, [John G.

Winant] *where I suppose I should have gone in the first place!*

He received me at once and when I told him my story and of my intention to return to my squadron he apologized for the reception I'd had at the Recruiting Office saying, 'That Lieutenant will remember you for a long time, I'm sure. I'll send a cable to your Draft Board and have your classification reinstated.' Thanking him I returned to Newchurch.

The entire operation had taken less than three hours and a few days later a signal came through, 'Congratulations on your success with the RAF. Deferment granted for the duration.' Signed, Wm. Ditters, Congressman.' So an international incident was avoided, peace was preserved between the US Forces and her Allies and the Lieutenant at the Recruiting Office probably finished the war in his little back room.

As for me, I had been duly reclassified by the Draft Board who apparently had been convinced that employment as a fighter pilot in the RAF was in fact 'war work'.

Ordinary life continued – and a brief quote from Wing Commander Ted Sparrow shows the difficulties faced on the Home Front, for which the ladies seldom get any credit. From 56 Squadron Ted went to Millfield for the Day Fighter Leader's Course and took over 'B' Flight as a flight lieutenant on 25 August 1944.

Having moved to RAF Manston the weather remained closed-in for several days and the wing was stuck there. It was not until the evening of

RAF personnel examine a V-1 brought down by No. 3 Squadron in 1944. One of the first reasonably intact for examination. (IWM CH13400)

22 September 1944 that I gained Wing Commander Beamont's approval to depart from Manston on pre-planned leave. The reason for my having to absent myself from the Squadron while it was grounded at Manston was because I was scheduled to be married on 23rd September 1944.

I completed a very hazardous journey from Manston to my brother's home in Blackheath, South East London, travelling partly by train, partly by thumbed lifts in privately owned cars and for considerable distances on foot. My family and bride-to-be had more or less decided that I would not turn-up and that there would be no wedding when I finally appeared on the scene, very foot-sore and weary at about 3.00 a.m. on the 23rd September 1944.

The wedding took place as planned, followed by an excellent Reception, which was attended by members of both families at my brother's home in Blackheath. My bride and I then managed to travel to Cambridge the next day to start our honeymoon. In the early hours of the next day, however, i.e. Monday, 25th September 1944, we were awakened by the Hotel Proprietor who handed me a telegram. The message in the telegram directed me to return immediately to the squadron and to report for duty ASAP at RAF Matlaske, Norfolk.

By the end of that day I had managed to take my wife back to Blackheath, where I left her in the company of my family. I then travelled by train to Norwich in Norfolk and by Military transport from the railway station to RAF Matlaske to rejoin the Squadron there.

The weather was still very poor with low cloud covering the whole of the East coast of the UK and Western Europe. I learned that most of the Wing had managed to fly from Manston to Matlaske in small Sections and in pairs of aircraft during the preceding days. Unfortunately, several of the aircraft and their pilots had become dispersed at Aerodromes and Airfields en route to Matlaske because of the bad weather conditions or aircraft unserviceabilities.

I seem to recall that most of our time at Matlaske was spent in reassembling and servicing our aircraft in readiness for our next move, which we were informed was to be to Europe. I believe that No 56[F] Squadron, led by its CO, Squadron Leader [Digger] Cotes-Preedy, did complete the odd operational mission from Matlaske. The Wing Commander also paid a speedy solo visit to Belgium to review the facilities at the next Aerodrome that the Wing had been allocated to use.

Then, on 28th September 1944, Wing Commander Beamont led the three Squadrons, which comprised about 30 servicable Tempest aircraft to our next location at Grimbergen Aerodrome [B.60], Brussels in Belgium. On reaching our destination the Wing Commander decided that he wanted the Wing to arrive in style. He then formed up the Squadrons in close formation to give a low FLY-PAST of both the town and the aerodrome before breaking to complete the swankiest of fighter aircraft style 'stream landings'.

Flight Sergeant Morris Rose sketches a V-1 for his colleagues during 1944. To his right are Flying Officer Bob Barckley, Pilot.Officers Rodney Dryland (upper) and Kenneth Slade-Betts. This photograph appeared in Life *magazine June/July 1944. (IWM CH1348)*

It would appear that the local inhabitants were delighted to see so many Allied fighter aircraft arrive in such style and so soon after their Liberation from the Germans.

The Wing was renumbered immediately on arrival at Grimbergen and it became No. 122 Wing under the Command of the 2nd Tactical Air Force [2nd TAF], with Air Vice Marshal Harry Broadhurst as its new Air Officer Commanding [AOC].

We recommenced operational activities immediately on arrival at Grimbergen to aid in the mopping-up of residual pockets of German resistance in the surrounding countryside and to assist the advance of Allied Ground Forces in the Nijmegen Bridge area, Holland. Our stay at Grimbergen was very short lived, however, and having arrived there on 28th September 1944, flown operational missions from that base for a couple of days, we moved on again on 1st October 1944. This time the move was to Volkel Aerodrome [B.80] in Holland, where the Aerodrome was in such a mess with bomb craters over the whole of it that we had to land and take-off for the next few days using the taxi ways. The Germans were also so closely installed to the Aerodrome that they shot down and *killed one of our pilots, Warrant Officer Reid, while he was in the circuit preparing to land* [Warrant Officer F. McG Reid AFM JN812 'M' 1 October 44. Buried in Venray War Cemetery] *and they damaged several other aircraft in the same manner. If my memory serves me correctly, the Wing Commander's aircraft was one of those damaged in this way.*

I never did get my honeymoon and the next time my wife saw me after our wedding was in Hospital in December 1944.

His engine failed and he force-landed south-east of Nijmegen on 29 November 1944.

The move from Newchurch to Manston was flown by Bob Cole in JN738 on 20 September 1944 and on to Matlaske three days later; he then managed two days flying in the 'hack' Tiger Moth T7791 with 5 and 3 flights on 25th and 26th, before taking JN868 to Grimbergen.

On 13 September the CO, Squadron Leader K. A. Wigglesworth, in JN818 was believed to be hit by debris and crashed near den Haag. Buried in The Hague General Cemetery. Bob Barckley, records:

Eight aircraft of No. 3 Squadron led by Ken Wigglesworth were carrying out a 'Ranger' operation east of the Hague the objective being to locate and attack V-2 weapons at their mobile launching sites. A weapon was

Hawker Tempest V JN796 JF-A. Following propeller overspeed and engine failure Morris Rose force landed on the Normandy beach-head. After running to the Allied lines a British Tommy said, 'You've just run through a minefield!' (IWMCH13109)

Hawker Tempest V on return to Volkel 26 February 1945. Pop's comment: 'Very tall trees in Germany'. (Pop Ewens)

located and Wigglesworth instructed 'B' flight to provide top cover whilst he led 4 aircraft of 'A' flight in an attack on the V-2.

Harvey Sweetman of 486 Squadron, in SA-I logged: 'Strafing, V.II site outskirts Hague. 1.30 target strafed. C.O. 3 Squadron killed.' And on the 16th in JF-Y: 'armed recco–North Hague. 1.40 Promoted to S/ldr C.O. of No 3 Squadron.'

On 25 September Flying Officer W. Davies was killed when escorting Liberators; EJ652 crashed into the sea 35 miles west of the Hague because of an engine fire. On 13 October Bob Cole was in EJ758 on 'patrol Grave. see Me 262 make a head on attack. no result. chase him and overhaul 20m N. of Arnhem. open fire at 600 ft. fire again at 150 and it blew up. pilot baled out.' On the 23rd he was awarded the

DFC. On 26 November, in JN822, he 'shared a 109 with F/O Dryland' then was 'hit by flak whilst attacking MT on Rheine/Hopstein – baled out.' He became a prisoner of war.

Bay Adams had joined 'B' Flight on 15 August. He went by Harrow to Brussels then to England by Dakota as a patient. Upon returning to duty on 23 January, he logged 'Lost W/C Beamont, Ted Sparrow, Ken Slade-Betts, F/L Edwards, Bob Cole, Pottinger.'

On 29 December, Flight Lieutenant M. F. Edwards in EJ803 was shot down by a 109 of JG27 north of Rheine. He had just returned to the squadron after suffering injury during harvest time at Newchurch. He was sent to Halton RAF Hospital with a septic foot, then to the West Country flying target tugs. He returned to No. 3 on

Airfield B.80/Volkel in 1945, damaged by Allied bombing and retreating Germans. Dutch workers repaired the runways and taxiways. (IWM CL1418)

A low-level attack on an ammunition train 1945. Credited to Squadron Leader Bruce Cole DFC, 24 February 1945. (Flight Magazine)

8 December, and on the 25th 'had a squirt at an Me 262'. He was killed on his ninth flight after return.

A Kiwi who had joined No. 3 in December, Harold W. Longley logged on 29th, 'Eddie and Slade-Betts missing on morning sortie'. Flying Officer Slade-Betts was in JN803, also shot down by JG27 north of Rheine.

This sortie was led by Squadron Leader J. F. Thiele, DSO, DFC**, RNZAF, who had been posted from 486 on 14 December as 'A' Flight Commander and who then took over as CO from Harvey Sweetman on 6 January. He was shot down on 10 February in NV644 'H' and taken prisoner. His notes for 29 December read 'A/R (air raid) Rheine Munster .55' 109 destroyed – Ken Slade-Betts & Eddie missing'.

CHAPTER FOURTEEN

Victory to Cold War

CELEBRATIONS WERE, OF COURSE, THE ORDER OF THE DAY when Germany capitulated, followed soon – too soon, some said – by numerous formation flights to 'show the flag' over recently freed (and occupied) territory, frequently positioning to operate from other than the base airfield. A letter in the Association magazine described one effect of this practice.

> *The picture of Pierre Clostermann's Tempest . . . brought back quite a few memories. When I was posted to 3[F] [in August 1945] I took over JF-E, which had about 20 Swastikas painted on the side. After I took it over these remained on the aircraft until it went in for major overhaul. As you can imagine, it was most embarrassing when we landed at different aerodromes.*
> *Leon Pitt*

During one celebratory 'wing ding' over nearby German towns, 3(F) were at the back, with Bay Adams as 'tail end Charlie'. At briefing the wing leader emphasised 250 ft minimum height – and then proceeded to fly at 250 ft himself! So Bay ended up down in the trees and commented in his broad Australian accent: 'If this is 250 ft, my cock's a kipper!' At the debrief the wing leader looked straight at Bay and

Tempest Vs at Wunsdorf after WWII. (3 Squadron)

criticised his radio discipline. To which Bay responded, again in pure 'strine': 'Jeez, Boss, how d'ya know 'twas me?'

Les Dowey recalled a short detachment to Berlin Gatow:

The flying area allocated to the squadron at Gatow [surrounded by the Russian Zone] was so small that it was impossible to fly straight and level for more than 30 secs. So occasionally aircraft strayed across the border resulting in an immediate phone call of complaint from the Ruskies. This was most annoying as every morning around 10 a.m. an old Rusky bi-plane stooged across the airfield at about 500 ft obviously checking on activity and most likely taking photos.

Lats Latham [Flt Cdr], never one to sit around and wait for instructions, decided to take action. With me as his No. 2 we took off at about 9.30 a.m. and hung around at 5000 ft waiting. As the biplane crossed the airfield we dived underneath him and pulled up sharply in front of his nose, causing him to wallow like a canoe in the rapids. Needless to say, as soon as we landed we were whisked off to the CO's office for a dressing down, but nothing more was seen of the old bi-plane. [Probably a Polikarpov Po2].

Ron 'Tak' Wright wrote of Lats Latham:

All who were at Fassberg will remember his 'experiments' with rocketry. The pellets from Coffman [engine] starter cartridges being the means of propulsion. The only time it could be considered safe was when he was flying or on leave! Fassberg was an 'Aladdin's Cave'; the Luftwaffe had buried so much of their equipment – tools, radios, personal kits, uniforms and of course aeroplanes. These were in various states of demolition. In one hangar we found two Bücker biplanes, both extensively damaged, but from two we managed to make one good 'un. Now we needed a test pilot; Lats couldn't refuse the challenge.

I had several flights with him around the German countryside looking for parts of gliders which were stashed away in the pine trees. These were retrieved, made serviceable and flown using either the Bücker as a tug, or the CO's jeep. His comment when flying the gliders: 'I keep running out of sky!' Then there were his 'Thoughts for the Day' which he would write up on the Notice Board. One I recall: Confucius, he say, "Woman who cooks cabbages and peas in same pot unsanitary"!

I think it was at Lubeck where S/L Bruce Cole asked me if I would like to fly up to Copenhagen. He and Lats would be going in the Auster. We would have to take our own fuel and stop about half way on some island to refuel. Duly loaded with jerry cans, with S/L Cole in the LH seat, Lats in the RH seat and me behind with the fuel. Take off was a lengthy business; it took some time to unstick. However, once airborne Lats lit a cigarette and offered me one – with all that fuel beside me! Only Lats could have done that with Bruce.

Of course it was not all fun; the primary purpose was to delay the Soviet 'steam roller' which was expected on the Channel and/or North Sea coast in forty-eight hours. Therefore weapon delivery accuracy was paramount and there were regular detachments to the Sylt Armament Practice ranges, which were made interesting by the nude bathing which took place in the area. Squadrons were expected to be able to demonstrate their proficiency. Alan 'Lefty' Wright recalls:

> *For some years, 3[F] had been the preferred BAFO squadron to enhance big airshows, including the Royal Air Force Display at Farnborough in 1950, with dive-bombing or live rocketing demo – albeit with concrete heads, since a 'twirler' could rather spoil the runway. One of the last such displays was on 10 October 1952 for VIPs at Gutersloh, which was attacked by 8 Vampires from Wildenrath.*

Colin Allsop recalls:

> *In the early 1950s aircrew training was being expanded rapidly to cope with the threatened spread of the Korean War. In addition to flying schools in the UK, aircrew were being trained in Southern Rhodesia [now Zimbabwe], USA and Canada. With the rapid build up of the RAF, Flying Training Command was struggling to keep pace with demand. My instructors on Tiger Moths and Chipmunks were civilians, and on Harvards and Meteors were mostly reservists who had been recalled. The first major hold up which I encountered was at gunnery school; there simply were no places available, so at least nine of us were posted directly on to Vampire squadrons in Germany for our final training.*

In 1948 the Vampire F.1 replaced the Tempest V. This squadron group shows the pilots and ground-crew at that time. In the foreground: Flying Officer P. Pennifer, P.IIs W. Hart and E.C. Wheatley, Squadron Leader C.H. Macfie DFC (CO), P.IIIs M. Milton and L. Zappe, P.II J. Collinson and Flying Officer E.C. Rigg. (Flight Magazine)

This photo, taken in 1948, shows Vampire F.1 VF/267 J5H. The ground crew are draining the engine after a wet start [failure to ignite], failure to do this would lead to a blow torch next time. (3 Squadron)

Vampire F.1 TG/385 J5M in the late WW2 high-altitude colour scheme with topside light grey and the underside PR blue. (3 Squadron)

Frank Brittain and I had the good fortune to be posted to 'Three', which had just moved from Gutersloh to the newly built airfield at Wildenrath. This must have imposed quite a burden on the seventeen or so pilots already on the squadron, and the temporary attachment of two French Air Force pilots from the Vampire wing at Dijon complicated matters even further. The other two Wildenrath squadrons, 67 and 71, either sarcastically or perhaps enviously referred to us as the Troisieme de Chasse. *The spirit on the squadron was quite incredible; a six aircraft formation aerobatic team* [shared with 71 Sqn] *and a solo aerobatic pilot* [Des Blake] *took part in many displays around Europe. With some of the more experienced pilots being posted to Korea there was a definite pilot shortage. For the last six months of compulsory military service our pay became the same as the more permanent pilots, which just about doubled my income of £17.10s.0d per month.*

1948 Vampire F.1 VF/279 J5T in overall silver. (3 Squadron)

Regarding aerobatics, the following query was raised in the Association magazine by him:

Around the autumn of 1952 or perhaps very early in 1953, while the Squadron still had a few Vampires pending the delivery of the Sabres, the squadron aerobatic team were asked to provide a display near the Hague to celebrate the Dutch Queen's birthday. I flew the spare aircraft alongside the other four until reaching the start of the show, when I was dispatched back to Wildenrath. Apparently, at some stage the formation pulled up into a loop, whereupon the formation leader's fuel control barostat failed and his engine dropped back to idle. The resulting avoiding action by the other three was very symmetrical, resembling the Prince of Wales' feathers manoeuvre developed by later – and lesser! – formation teams. All four landed safely – I think at Soesterburg? – and the Queen of the Netherlands was sufficiently impressed to award a medal. For some reason I got one. Can anyone remember what this medal was? I am almost certain that the leader was Des Blake and I think that George Cole and Pat Stride were also there. Can anyone remember?

Alan Wright replied:

About April/May 1952 an aerobatic team competition was staged at Gutersloh. No. 3 Sqn did not have an aeros team at that time, but usually provided the Command RP [rocket projectile] attack demonstration when required. I recall that, on a 4 x single-RP 'precision' attack sortie, Arthur Vine had achieved an average error of 27 inches [69 cm] firing 3" [7.5 cm] 'drains'.

Nearly all the half dozen or so squadrons competing entered a team of four Vampire FB5s. But I believe the competition was won by our base-mates, No 71 [Eagle] Sqn with their firmly established team of 3 Vampires. Their Boss/Leader, Sqn Ldr 'Andy' Hardy, recognised better than most that the gutless Goblin engine and its calendar-measured response severely restricted the number and variety of tidy formation changes that a 4 could employ. A team of more than three really had to choose between being boring or being scruffy! After the competition we understood that the C-

1948 Vampire F.1 formation in 1948. The Boss leading Collinson and Wheatley. (Flight Magazine)

1949 Vampire FB.5 formation. Having just replaced the F.1, the newly arrived
aircraft had no identity markings. (Alan East)

A Vampire FB.5 at Wildenrath in 1952. It is silver overall with green acorn
fairings. (John D.R. Rawlings)

in-C BAFO had decreed that every DF/GA [day fighter/ground attack] squadron was to form an aeros team so that each base could lay on an ad hoc display for any visiting Government Ministers, embryonic German generals etc.

Prior to joining 3[F] from 26 Sqn in November 1951, Des Blake had gained considerable experience of individual aeros, albeit in the much more powerful Meteor T7; so our Boss appointed him Team Leader and, in effect, told him to get on with it. Several times a day, the new team of Des, Don Arnott [2] and Archie Lamb [3] would take off in vic, disappear for about 40 minutes, reappear in echelon, break and land. The Boss – and the rest of us! – wanted to see 'our' team do its stuff overhead the airfield, but Des steadfastly refused to let it be seen until he felt it was ready. Came the day, they arrived overhead at about 1745 hrs inducing a rush from various Messes at tea-time. Everyone was genuinely impressed, not least OC 71 Sqn, who could identify a threat when he saw one! Very soon he suggested to our Boss that the teams from 3 and 71 should separately practise near-identical routines and subsequently work together on a co-ordinated display. This proved very effective because one team would be performing a manoeuvre while the other was positioning between manoeuvres, thus leaving little scope for spectator boredom.

The whole routine began with the arrival of a six – Andy Hardy leading his vic with Des Blake's vic in close line astern on them – pulling up into a loop. When they were over the top the two vics separated into their co-ordinated display, including many formation changes. This must sound very puny 40 years after the Black Arrows' 22-a/c loop, but you can thank the RR Avon and high-speed flaps for that!

The first show of note for the six was a NATO Air Day at Maelsbrook, near Brussels. During the entry into the routine-opening loop, Des Blake's engine suffered, as Colin said, barostat failure. This not-too-common fault resulted in rather more than idle power, but restricted max. obtainable RPM to 7,000 – spot-on for a QGH [ATC and D/F assisted let-down], but useless for anything more ambitious! After their prompt unscheduled landings Des, Don and Archie walked their 3 separate ways, roughly 120 degrees apart, to ponder over 3 separate cigarettes.

Approximately a year after the above, 12 Sabres of 3[F] Squadron were among the 620-odd aircraft flypast as part of the Queen's Review of the RAF at Odiham on 15 July, 1953. We returned to Germany the following day, then on 18 July, participated in another big fly-past celebrating 40 years of Dutch Military Aviation. Was that at Soesterberg, Colin? Commemorative medals were distributed later – can't remember exactly where mine is now! – and I expect that is the one to which Colin refers.

Additional information was provided by John Daly.

It was not given for the aeros show they put on, nor for any Vampire show; but for the flypast of the Queen of the Netherlands on 18th July,

1953, on the occasion of the 40th birthday of the Royal Netherlands Air Force. I got one too. We had just returned after the Coronation Review flypast at Odiham – On 16th July from Duxford to Wildenrath. So [having had them for only a couple of months] about the only experience we had all had on Sabres was close formation flying! Anyway, we flew a box of boxes, i.e. 16 Sabres, and all participating pilots got one, even the squadron sprog – me! More than we got for the Odiham do!

Mark you, the time we all really deserved a medal about then was two days later when we flew the 20 miles [32 km] or so in close formation from Wildenrath to [newly constructed] Geilenkirchen. Again a box of boxes, tucked in nice and close to impress our new base, when John Sutherland led us into the blackest cu-nimb I have ever seen! And then called, 'Air brakes, Go!' I was number 4 of the last box – still Squadron sprog, lucky me – so I just closed the throttle fully, popped the boards and went downwards quite safely. Sixteen individual aircraft emerged from the cloud to make ignominious separate landings, amazingly with no collisions or accidents.

Because we had more aircraft than pilots there were three visiting pilots helping with this ferry; I remember one of them saying, 'AFCs for the lot of you!'

The difficulties of British aviation in the post-war years are well covered, so I will just mention the cancellation of the Miles M.52 and the 'sale' of the Rolls Royce Derwent and Nene to the USSR, which helped in no small part to trigger the Korean

The CO's Canadair Sabre F.4 stands behind the Squadron personnel in 1953. (Alan East)

Canadair Sabre F.4 undergoes line servicing and maintenance, obviously not a Quick Turn Round. (Alan East)

War. As a stop-gap it was intended to use the Canadair Sabre with Orenda engine, but time was of the essence and the Sabre Mk4 retained the J-47 engine. In *The Canadair Sabre*, Larry Milberry describes the Sabre:

> *The aircraft handles beautifully and has normal take-off and landing characteristics. Its climb to height compares to the Meteor F.8 but of course at higher forward speed. Two snags: [a] Instrumentation presentation is bad and would make all-weather flying unduly difficult. Possibly overcome by fitting the standard RAF [blind-Flying] panel. [b] More importantly, starting procedure is highly complicated and a single mistake may necessitate engine change.*

148

Air Marshal Sir Basil Embry, then Air Officer Commanding-in-Chief, Fighter Command, was emphatic that the F-86A was not acceptable as an interceptor until the latter difficulty was overcome.

Needs must when the devil drives, so Canadair built the F-86E as the Sabre 4. Under the Mutual Defence Assistance Programme (MDAP) this could only be authorised for the supply of tactical fighters, which influenced the RAF's decision to deploy most of its Sabres in Germany as part of the 2nd Allied Tactical Air Force. Transatlantic ferrying was done by Operation Bechers Brook, a story in itself.

RAF Wildenrath, a newly constructed NATO airfield in Germany close to the Dutch border, became the main conversion training centre for 2 TAF squadrons with the formation of the Sabre Conversion Flight (SCF), tasked with giving tuition on the new fighter. Initially the 'pupils' comprised the flight commanders and more experienced pilots of the squadrons earmarked to re-equip with Sabres, usually from Vampires.

No. 67 had the distinction of being the first operational RAF squadron to take delivery of Sabres and also the last to retain one. No. 3 Squadron had been the first in Germany to be equipped with Vampire F.1s in 1948, later exchanging these for

Canadair Sabre F.4 echelon formation. (Alan East)

the Mk 5 fighter-bomber variant. In 1952 the squadron had been notified that it would be the first to receive the new de Havilland Venom, and there was great disappointment when this failed to materialise, so there was great joy at the news that No.3 had been chosen as the first squadron in the RAF to fly the Sabre and change roles from ground attack to interceptor.

The first Sabres to be received at Wildenrath were delivered direct from Canada on 13 March, 1953. Although they were for the SCF, No.3 Squadron 'borrowed' these for the purpose of beginning their own conversion from Vampires – with only a few sets of RCAF pilots' notes for reference, since the SCF was itself just in the process of formulating a Sabre training programme. George Cole was among the youngest pilots on 3 Squadron at that time:

> I flew my first Sabre, XB616, on 7 April for an initial 30-minute familiarisation flight, and thereafter had very little Sabre flying until after 11 May, when the first of 3 Squadron's own Sabres were delivered. I adopted XB590 as my personal aircraft whenever it was available, and flew it for the first time on 19 May, 1953, the day after its delivery, in the 'box' slot of the first four-ship squadron formation, hastily organised to pre-empt our rivals on 67 Squadron!

Together with 67, No.3 Squadron deployed to Duxford for almost a month to prepare for the Royal Review flypast, in which the two squadrons put up a crisp combined formation of twenty-four Sabres, even though pilots averaged less than twenty-five hours on the type. Immediately after their return from Duxford No.3 Squadron moved to its new base at Geilenkirchen on 20 July, and was soon given its first taste of 'combat' in the NATO air defence exercise, Coronet, held from 23 to 30 July.

George Cole was chosen to demonstrate the Sabre at the annual Battle of Britain 'At Home' at RAF Biggin Hill on Saturday, 19 September 1953, and flew XB667 via Manston and Duxford, where he stopped the night before. The aircraft was the star of the show, representing the RAF's first operational swept-wing fighter, and George gave flying displays with sonic booms at both Biggin and Hornchurch. At that time there were no restrictions on such activities, though towards the end of his tour on 3 Squadron, George recalls that pilots were advised to avoid banging the larger German towns! He has more recently been piloting RAF Hercules to the Falkland Islands yet his impressions of flying Sabres remain as fresh as ever:

> The aircraft was grossly underpowered, taking over 20 minutes to get to 35,000 ft, but once there it coped well. Handling was good at low level, but performance fell off at altitude. Occasionally one slat would come out and stick out, producing some interesting manoeuvres! In mock combat the Sabre was good against the opposition at the time – Meteors, Vampires and Venoms. Venoms could go higher but nobody could perform like the F-86 at high Mach numbers. Hunters could out-accelerate the Sabre every time, but the confidence given to the pilot knowing that at the high-speed end of the performance envelope the Sabre simply reached terminal velocity with no awkward handling problems and no fear of spinning gave

The CO's Canadair Sabre F.4 in 1953. (Alan East)

one an edge over aircraft with a theoretically superior performance. *Handling in the circuit and during landing was excellent and viceless; you could do an approach without ASI by riding the slats at about 185 knots – it happened once to me, and several other people.*

I sometimes used to fly No.2 to G/C Johnny Johnson, the station commander at Wildenrath, and later at Geilenkirchen, whose Sabre [XB686], like his Vampire before it, had a red fin and carried his initials 'JEJ' in large letters. He was quite keen on leading 'wing dings', seldom less than 24 Sabres, and we would often whistle low over other fighter airfields to encourage them to come up for sport, or get into furious dogfights with anyone foolish enough to be airborne at the same time. More usually we flew in 'finger fours' and the majority of the flying was either air/air combat [cine] or firing on the flag, or ground attack for which the Sabre was not really suited with its 0.5 inch guns.

George Cole completed his tour with 3 Squadron in October 1954 but continued to fly Sabres in the UK with 92 Squadron. No. 3 Squadron began to phase out its Sabres in favour of Hunter 4s in the spring of 1956, and there was a special ceremony at Geilenkirchen on 22 June of that year with the departure of XB670/S, billed as the last RAF Sabre in Germany, although this was actually not true; it was XB693/C of 67 which left Bruggen on 21 August 1956.

The unit markings on the Sabre were bright (apple) green rectangles, thinly outlined in yellow on each side of the fuselage roundels. Nose cones were also green, edged in yellow. Code letters were in flight colours (red for 'A' Flight; blue for 'B' Flight) outlined in white, on the fin, and repeated in black on the nose-wheel door of some aircraft. Most aircraft had the squadron badge in a white disc below the cockpit. XB984/K differed in having a broad green band across the fin, edged in white, within which the code letter was painted in red, thinly outlined in white.

It is interesting to note that in a recent TV programme General Chuck Yeager, USAF, was seen and heard to say: 'It took the Europeans and the Russians a while to catch on to that little trick.' And in the book *Yeager* the impression is given that Larry Bell invented the adjustable tailplane for the XS-1/X-1, at first only on the ground and then in flight, which appears to be 'that little trick' curing control problems and enabling 'Glamorous Glennis' to bust through the 'barrier'. Years later the F-86D and 100 had 'slab' tailplanes without elevators. It is most unfortunate that the 'not invented here' psychosis of the Yanks so often ruins a good yarn.

Earlier I referred to the Miles M.52 cancellation, which from the start was designed with a 'slab' tailplane. So the first part of this *crie de coeur* expands on this fabulous 'might have been'. And remember, it was designed to take off under its own power, climb to height, go supersonic, RTB (Return To Base) and land, all without external aid – the Bell XS-1/X-1 was carried to height in a B-29 or 50, the pilot having climbed down from the bomb-bay to enter it and then be *locked in*, followed by a dead-stick landing occasionally requiring to jettison highly volatile fuel on the way down.

According to Don L. Brown in *Miles Aircraft since 1925*:

> *Thus, in February 1946, over two years of concentrated and dedicated work on the part of the two teams was thrown away, together with over £100,000 of the tax-payers money: and, by this cancellation, Great Britain threw away the honour of being the first nation to achieve supersonic flight. The following year on 14 October, 1947, this was achieved by Major Charles E. Yeager in the rocket-powered X.1 built by the American Bell company whose engineers and designers had, on the insistence of the Government, had access to all the drawings, calculations and design data relating to the M.52. Furthermore, the Bell X.1 did not have sweptback wings.* [One of the many reasons given by that Government experts for cancellation!]

In his book, *Yeager* with Leo Janos, Chuck is apparently unaware of our contribution, in particular the 'moving tail' seemingly invented by Bell, and he writes off the film *The Sound Barrier* as hokum, instead of an attempt to simplify for the average person the onset of the exponential drag rise approaching M 1.0. And to quote: 'They used a World War II Spitfire to break the barrier, which was amusing because that airplane wouldn't go faster than .75 Mach in a power dive'. Earlier in the book he describes having control difficulties in a P-51 Mustang in a power dive, and was unaware that in 1943 Squadron Leader J.R. Tobin reached an indicated M 0.92 diving Spitfire XI EN409; then in 1946 Squadron Leader A.F. Martindale achieved a definite M 0.9 in another XI.

He also talks down the second D.H. 108 TG306, a Vampire fuselage with 45 degree swept, slatted – but lockable by the pilot – wing and swept fin, plus power controls like the Comet's, in which Geoffrey de Havilland was killed. No mention is made of the third and improved VW120 in which John Derry exceeded M 1.0 on 9 September 1948, the first British aircraft to do so, and in which taxpayers were 'banged' at the Farnborough SBAC show – less than a year after Chuck, and in an aeroplane which, like the M.52, was able to take off, climb to height and go supersonic (albeit in a dive to 30,000 ft) [9,000 metres] descend and land under normal power.

It is not my intention to put down or deny the achievements of Chuck and his buddies or their mounts. To do so would be to deny their so very spectacular achievements; this particularly in Korea, and specifically with the F-86, which was made available to us when we needed it.

In *F-86 Sabre, The Operational Record*, Robert Jackson says:

> *It is interesting, at this point, to make a comparison between supersonic fighter development in the United States and on the other side of the Atlantic. In November 1951 – the very month in which North American was awarded the F-100 contract – Hawker Aircraft of Great Britain began detailed design work on a project designated P.1083; this was in effect a supersonic version of the Hawker Hunter, the prototype of which had flown in the previous July. The P.1083 was a straight-forward development of the Hawker Hunter, featuring a lengthened fuselage to accommodate an afterburning Rolls-Royce Avon RA.19 turbojet and married to a new thin wing, swept 52 degrees at the leading edge and with a thickness/chord ratio of only 7.5.*
>
> *Performance estimates for the P.1083, at a loaded weight of 17,700 lb with half fuel, included a maximum speed of 820 mph [1.248M] at sea level, 790 mph [1.2M] at 36,000 ft, and 690 mph [1.05M] at 55,000 ft. Estimated initial rate of climb was 50,000 ft /min at sea sevel, 28,700 ft /min at 20,000 ft, and 5,400 ft/min at 50,000 ft. Estimated service ceiling was 59,500 ft, while time to 30,000 ft at an all-up weight of 20,000 lb was estimated to be one minute fifty-seven seconds and to 55,000 ft five minutes twelve seconds from the start of the take-off roll.*
>
> *There is no reason at all to doubt the accuracy of these estimates. Neither is there any doubt that the performance of the lighter, more manoeuvrable P.1083, the so-called 'Super Hunter', would have been superior in many respects to that of the F-100, particularly in time-to-altitude. But in July*

1953, with the prototype 80 % complete, the RAF Air Staff turned aside from the use of afterburning engines like the RA.19 and the P.1083 was cancelled. The RAF would not have a supersonic fighter until 1960, when the English Electric Lightning entered service.

The decision to cancel the P.1083 had a considerable impact on Britain's future military export market. Apart from Britain, no fewer than sixteen other countries went on to use the Hawker Hunter; and when some of them, particularly those in NATO, came to look for a supersonic successor in the late 1950s, they chose the F-100 because Britain had nothing to offer them.

Sabre F4

Reproduced from Squadron Prints coloured bookmark

CHAPTER FIFTEEN

The Hawker Hunter

AS HAWKER HUNTERS BECAME AVAILABLE through the Super Priority
Production Programme they released Sabres for other NATO nations under
America's MDAP rules. In Germany the routine continued as before, with
manning 'battle flight' and practice interceptions. The Chairman of our Association
was involved in one.

GREEN ENDORSEMENT
Flying Officer A.C. East
No. 3 [F] Squadron
1. On the 16th November, 1956 Flying Officer A.C. East of No. 3 [F]
Squadron, Royal Air Force Geilenkirchen was the pilot of a Hunter Mk. 4
[XF948/J], flying in the No. 4 position during a Battle formation sortie.
2. On the completion of a snake climb [single or pairs, at timed intervals,
leader calling turns which were supposed to be made at the same interval]
through cloud and at a height of 20000 ft [6,000 metres] he reduced
engine power on joining the rest of his section, the engine continued to lose
power and eventually flamed out, three attempts were made to relight but
without success.

In 1956 the Hawker Hunter F.4 replaced the Sabre. (Alan East)

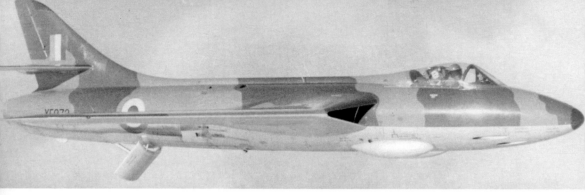

A Hunter F.4 with airbrake extended. This could not be done on the ground as it risked ground contact with gear down a test switch was therefore fitted. (Alan East)

> *3. Flying Officer East carried out a modified flame out QGH and in spite of marginal weather conditions successfully made a safe landing at his home base, without damaging his aircraft; throughout this emergency Flying Officer East displayed airmanship and judgement of the highest order, thereby, undoubtedly saving a valuable aircraft.*
>
> > *H.A.V. Hogan Air Vice-Marshal, Air Officer Commanding, No. 83 Group.*

In his telex signal the AOC also paid tribute to Pilot Officer Williams, the duty Air Traffic Controller. A.C. East added, 'The Green Endorsement incident was my ninety-sixth Hunter sortie and added just ten minutes to my 63.10 hours on type!'

He contributed three pages to the Association magazine on the Sabre to Hunter change including the following:

> *We feigned to miss the comfort of the Sabre's 'armchair' seat – ignoring the superior performance of the Martin Baker one, and the fact that we no longer had to carry our personal back pack parachute to and from the aircraft each sortie! . . .*
>
> *Something we did frequently was to fly a high-level sweep to the south looking for Canadian Sabre 5s and later 6s [both with more powerful Orenda engines] or American F.86Ds or F.86Fs to play with. Their performance had often proved too much for our Sabre 4s with only 5,200 lbs, of static thrust – 2,000 lbs less than the Sabre 6. We soon learned to appreciate the Hunter's better climb and dog-fighting performance. It was on one such sortie that XF976/B diverted into an RCAF base [Marville] with a problem. When Chas Boyer ['A' Flight Commander] went to collect it a few days later he found that No. 441 Sqn had 'Canadianised' it with their squadron's black and white chequers and by changing the red centre of the roundel into a maple leaf! [and while waiting for the engineers to finish their checks, had time to find a Sabre 6 for a quick comparison sortie].*
>
> *My tour on No 3[F] Sqn finished in April, 1957, just a few weeks after all personnel had assembled in The Astra, the Station Cinema, to be addressed by the Station Commander. Duncan Sandys' 1957 Defence White Paper had proposed that the manned fighter was virtually obsolete; its role could be filled by missiles! The Second World War had finished only 12 years earlier. Just half a generation! As the Group Captain read out a long list of squadrons to be disbanded, including our own No 3[F] Sqn –*

Hunter F.4 'The Clean Mean Machine'.

Hawker Hunter F.4 XF990 K at Le Bourget in 1956.   *(Aeroplane Weekly)*

the first in the world ever to be fully equipped with heavier-than-air machines! – most of those wearing medal ribbons were near to tears. The squadron was disbanded on 15 Jun 57. Eventually the folly of not keeping alive the identity of the senior low-number squadrons was acknowledged. In Jan 59, No 96 Sqn, a long-standing night-fighter squadron with a noble history of its own and then operating Javelin FAW 4 a/c, was renumbered No 3 Squadron.

Gordon Browne has his own memories of the Hunter, as recounted in an article entitled 'Lucky 13'.

Virtually all my flying has been on single-engined jets or pistons. Although this makes life relatively simple [only one go-faster lever], it does mean that if Messrs Rolls Royce, Armstrong Siddeley or any other maker's product cannot stand the strain, then things tend to go very quiet. This is a tale of one such incident, one of many suffered by that classic aircraft, the Hunter.

The early days of the Hunter were not trouble-free. It was rumoured that to be declared operational on the Mk 2 equipped squadron at Wattisham, you had to have done at least one real forced landing! The problem of engine surge and/or flame out at high level was solved by introducing an automatic fuel dipping system which meant that, at the critical moment in a dog fight, you suddenly lost 1000 pounds [450 kg] of push. Also, if you pulled a little too hard in the thin air at high altitude, the leading set of static blades of the compressor could flutter, touch the first row of rotating blades and – blatt! – you have stripped the compressor down to the blade roots.

13 May 1957 was a typical spring day at RAF Geilenkirchen, the southernmost airfield in the soon-to-be demolished Second Tactical Air Force [2ATAF]. Just one month before, Duncan Sandys had produced his infamous Defence White Paper and nine of the thirteen Hunter squadrons and all the Venom units in Germany had gone or were awaiting disbandment. As a very wet behind the ears first tourist I had only joined 3 [F] Squadron [the first RFC squadron to fly heavier-than-air machines] in the previous November. Our Boss, Squadron Leader Tim Hutchinson, decreed that, until the Benson Ferry Wing pilot's arrival, we would get every last hour we could, and attempt to drain the Officers' Mess stocks of Carlsberg. After a weekend heavily involved in the latter noble cause, we assembled to continue the former.

My first trip was a singleton general-handling sortie finishing off with three practice forced-landings, this was continuing a trial of a new way of bringing home your broken jet. Developed, I believe, by the Fleet Air Arm, the new pattern required only a good overhead to be given and then, making use of the excellent glide of a clean Hunter, punching down at high speed to below the cloud. If you got it right, you could come down to a 1000 feet cloud base and still leave room to either eject safely or land. As I signed in after the sortie, I noticed that it was my 12th trip of the month so far and the 12th successful test of the new forced landing pattern.

The next trip was to be a routine four-ship-battle formation fighter sweep into 4ATAF airspace; I was flying No.2 to the flight leader, Peter Vangucci. Our standard ploy was to climb to about 20,000 feet to the north of Geilenkirchen then turn south so that we would be at 40,000+ feet before entering 'hostile' airspace. For months we had been hassling with the USAF F-100s and the RCAF Sabre 6s based in southern Germany and north-eastern France. The Sabre 6 was the most dangerous – the Canadian pilots were far more experienced and the '6/3' wing of the Sabre

1956 Hawker Hunter F.4 XF976 B freshly painted in dispersal. (3 Squadron)

Hunter F.4 XF976 B after additional attention from No.441 Squadron RCAF at Marville after its forced landing. (3 Squadron)

gave it the edge at high altitude.

Sure enough, somewhere over the cloud-covered Eifel hills came the call – '8 at 6 o'clock climbing'. We turn hard into the threat – watch the power setting – gun sight up – 36 feet on the wing span setting [ever hopeful of catching the Sabre on cine!] *– tighten up to hold position on Peter – bang! – RPM falling, jet pipe temperature* [JPT] *rising – must be a surge. Throttle back, and dive below 30,000 feet – 'Nailcream Black Two engine surge – descending to 30 thou to sort it.' 'Nailcream Black Two – Roger, I'm behind you.' 30,000 feet, speed below 300 knots, um, max RPM available only 6,200* [should be 7,800], *JPT a bit high, no sign of any push. The penny drops. To prevent stator and first stage compressor blades touching at high revs and angle of attack, Rolls Royce had introduced 'Mod 441', increasing the gap between the rows of blades by a quarter of an inch. Earlier this month Bob 'Leadfoot' Hillman had had a similar failure. I wonder – yup dear ol' B Bravo was unmodified.*

So here we are at about 29,000 feet somewhere over a cloud-covered Eifel, rpm 6200, no thrust, speed to glide 230 knots – about 1600 feet a minute rate of descent. No idea where the nearest airfield is and Pete can't help as he doesn't know either. Oh well: 'Mayday Mayday Mayday.'

A rather bored, heavily accented American voice answers: 'Nailcream Black Two, this is Yellowjack [the 4ATAF emergency fixer service]. *We hear your Mayday but are unable to assist you at this time'. To pre-date Victor Meldrew by many years: 'I don't believe it.' 25,000 feet and still nothing but cloud and the odd glimpse of German pine trees. Then, faintly, a Canadian voice. 'Nailcream Black this is Marville we have a slow moving target 075 40 miles steer 255 for ident' – hope at last. 2 miles per 1000 feet is the rule of thumb so should just make it.*

The ruined engine is still running, giving hydraulics and electrics. Marville's voice gets louder as I glide down now in and out of the stratocumulous cover. 'Cloud base 6/8 at 1500 you are advised to eject.' Stuff that. Finally, joy of joys, a runway, well the upwind half anyway. Hydraulics still OK but remember Bob lost his engine in the last few seconds on finals, so prepare to blow down the wheels and flaps and revert to manual. Three Greens – keep the speed up round finals – aiming high because full flap really dumps you, like now! Full flap, over the threshold at 140 – and the engine finally dies.

Let it roll – sign of fire wagons – touch of brake and turn off at the 2000 yard mark. Made it. Pins in the seat, climb out to be met by a grinning fireman – 'Sir, you have one very silvery jet pipe.' He's right, all that lovely metal melted and sprayed down the full length. A more senior Canadian, the Wing Commander Flying, demanded to know why I had done a dead stick in a cloud base of only 1500 feet. Their SOP [Standard Operational Procedure] *was 5000 feet minimum or eject. They still had the very inefficient US-designed seat not that greatest life-saver the Martin Baker.*

So that was it – almost. After a suitably alcoholic spree with the

Canadians of No 441 Squadron and others, Les Elgey picked me up in a Vampire T11 and we returned to find the other '13s'. My sortie in the authorisation sheet was the 13th as the duty authoriser had forgotten to write 12A. It was also the 13th pre-mod 441 failure in the Command. I should have stayed in bed.

Afterwards, Les Elgey went back to collect 'B' with its new engine. 441 Squadron had got at it and resprayed it in their well known black and white checks with mapleleafs in the roundels. We kept the checks but quickly removed the mapleleafs because, as Tim Hutchinson said, we are combatting nations.

In 1964 when flying Gnats at RAF Valley we were searching for a name for the first Gnat aerobatic team. Flight Lieutenant Lee Jones, the leader, and I were swopping stories over a beer. 'Why not Yellowjack,' I suggested. Lee had had a similar experience with that organisation a few weeks before my episode. So 'Yellowjack' they became – I still prefer it to the 'Red Arrows'.

And the moral? Black cats, walking under ladders or one 13 – take it in your stride. Two or three 13s – take care. But four 13s is too much even for a Rolls Royce!

CHAPTER SIXTEEN

The Javelin

I N BEWARE THE JABBERWOCK, or Some Tales of No. 3(F) Squadron Javelin Days, Bob Burgess.

As I joined the squadron on 21 September 1959 I cannot comment on the events prior to this date except to say that one of the crews suffered a fatal flying accident while returning from an air show during this time [96 Squadron became 3 Squadron on 21 January 1959].

I travelled to Geilenkirchen via the ferry from Harwich to the Hook of Holland, the 'Blue Train' [troop carrier] to Heinsberg and thence by car to the squadron at Geilenkirchen, courtesy of Mike Morgans, another No. 3 Squadron pilot. On arrival the four of us [two new crews], met our CO Wing Commander Don Farrar, and I have never served under a better Boss before or since. Don was a real expert on all aspects of fighter operations.

After settling in and completing sector recce flights and familiarizing myself with the Mk 4 Javelin, my Nav/Rad operator Bob Bonas and I plunged into cine weave practice before the forthcoming Armament Practice Camp at Sylt. Our first operational flight of night PIs [Practice Interceptions] on 1 October allowed Bob to put into effect his professional expertise, taking control of the interception from the Ground Controlled Intercept Officer and guiding us into a killing position approximately 150 yards behind and slightly below the target [another Javelin, with which we were paired.]

The next two weeks were employed preparing for APC by day and flying practice interceptions by night. One of the pre-APC requirements was to fire in the guns following reharmonisation for air-to-air shoots on the towed drogues at Sylt. This involved flying in pairs over the North Sea ranges in battle formation descending to low level before firing the cannons into the sea. I recall one day when my leader called 'fire' as I spotted a small cluster of fishing boats in my gunsight and called abort. I didn't think the fishermen would appreciate being sprayed with 30 mm shells, albeit ball ammunition. We subsequently found a clear area and got the job done.

APC took place at Sylt between 19 October and 19 November, and due to consistent poor weather alternating between fog, drizzle and low cloud, it was not a great success with only a small number of shoots achieved. As a result much time was spent grounded, awaiting weather clearances. It was on one of these days that my Nav/Rad. became involved in a nasty accident while ground checking one of the Javelin AI [Airborne

Interception radar] *sets. To achieve this it was necessary to taxy the aircraft up to a pre-determined white mark on the tarmac and lock the radar onto a reflector 1,000 yards away to check the range shown on the set. On this occasion, as it was a non-flying day and we were all playing bridge, Bob volunteered to carry out the task with another pilot also free at the time. On arrival at the ranging site Bob stood up in the rear cockpit to locate the reflector and inadvertently disconnected his intercom. About then the rain began to come down heavily and having warned Bob on the intercom, his pilot tried to close the hood, without success as Bob's shoulder was trapped by the mechanism at the time and, with no intercom he had not heard the warning. The outcome was that Bob was unable to fly for about a couple of months as a result of his injury and I completed my live firing with Al Carter as my Nav/Rad. before returning to Geilenkirchen.*

Back at base the Squadron returned to normal routine i.e. one flight on day operations and the other on nights interchanging weekly. In additon to normal ops. the Squadron maintained a Battle Flight of two aircraft at night, a duty shared with No. 11[F] Squadron at Geilenkirchen. When scrambled and ordered to steer east and make maximum angels, one never knew if it was a practice or for real! We could have given a good account of ourselves being armed with 1,000 rounds of 30 mm shells per aircraft but invariably, we were turned round approaching the ADIZ [Air Defence Interception Zone] between West and East Germany. I often wondered if the GCIs got a bit bored at night particularly at weekends or if they could see a real threat approaching from the east.

During this period a few interesting incidents spring to mind. A. Flight Commander was flying along one fine day when one of his fuselage tanks became detached and tumbled earthwards. Fortunately it did no damage to anything on the ground but the impact didn't do the tank much good.

Another time Bob and I were turning finals at Geilenkirchen when a voice over the air using my callsign said 'You are on fire, get out.' I ignored this transmission which referred to a Canberra on the ground and the speaker had used the wrong callsign.

Later during my tour Trevor Betterton had an unusual experience. On return to Geilenkirchen, after an otherwise normal sortie, he found that one of the main wheel undercarriage legs would not extend. After discussion with Don Farrar, via the Air Traffic Control Tower, having tried various G force applications Trevor elected to land with fuselage tanks attached. He pulled off an immaculate forced landing, holding up the wing of the affected side until the last moment, resulting in only minor damage compared with what might have been. What upset Trevor most was that when he later kicked the offending undercarriage leg, it came down of its own accord! Rumour has it Trevor swore for some 10 minutes thereafter without repeating himself.

My final personal tale of woe occurred when on the downwind check I saw that my port brake was not functioning. Being short of fuel I decided

Javelin dispersal. *(John Wilson)*

to land at Geilenkirchen using maximum aerodynamic braking and as slow as possible. [The Javelin's delta wing makes a good airbrake.] We went into the overrun area and stopped without damage. The aircraft was soon recovered but the following fire engines were stuck in the mud and took somewhat longer. An ensuing report in Flight Comment *[RAFG Safety Magazine] suggested that standard braking technique on Javelins was to lower the nose on touchdown and apply full braking. In this case the result would have been to leave the side of the runway at about 90 kts, taking some runway lights with me, and possibly leaving the undercarriage in exchange! Don Farrar subsequently wrote a rebuttal to* Flight Comment *suggesting that any pilot following their advice would be considered very much at fault.*

On the humorous side, the Squadron flew up to Gardemoen, Norway, on an exchange visit to a Norwegian fighter base. We set off in loose Battle Formation and approaching our destination the Boss called for echelon starboard. About this time a Norwegian F86 [-K probably] took up the No. 2 position on the Boss's starboard wing. The pilot was somewhat surprised on looking to his right to find five more Javelins in echelon starboard on his own right wing.

In May 1960 Don Farrar was succeeded by Arthur Peers who continued

'Boss' Farrar with the Air Officer Commanding, during thhe Annual Inspection.   (John Wilson)

as CO until the Squadron disbanded as a fighter squadron on 31 December 1960, later reforming as a Canberra B18 Squadron. Of the Javelin crews about 50% including myself were posted to No. 11 Squadron Geilenkirchen remaining with our new squadron, flying Javelin Mk 5s, until November 1962. I have not included the 1960 A.P.C. which was much the same as 1959 except the weather was better, the scores higher and Bob didn't hurt himself.

Al Carter remembers the 'Crash of Javelin XA640 at RAF Geilenkirchen on 8 April 1960:

I was a young navigator on 3 Squadron at that time. It was my first squadron and you can always remember details from your early days. As night fighters we usually flew in pairs with one aircraft acting as target. I was in the other aircraft of this particular pair and can recall the incident quite clearly. We took off together at 2305 on 7 April 1960 and the crash

Pre-flight inspection by ground crew – not strapped in, no 'bone-domes'. (John Wilson)

occurred at the end of the mission after one and a half hours, so at about 0030 on 8 April 1960.

The aircraft which crashed was the leader of the pair, flown by my Flight Commander, Squadron Leader Peter Stark, and his navigator was Flight Lieutenant John Lomas. The pilot was originally South African and a powerful man. At the end of our trip doing night interceptions we returned overhead GK [Geilenkirchen] at FL40 and at the 'dive circle' started a steep let down to the east for a GCA pick-up at around 1500 ft range 15 miles. The second aircraft would complete one full rate-one turn at the 'dive circle' and follow the leader down with 2 minutes' separation. This gave the GCA controllers more practice than just handling the pair together.

During the steep descent 'Boss' Stark experienced double hydraulic pump failure leaving him with only half his flying control and no auxiliary services at all, no airbrakes or wheel brakes, no undercarriage or flaps. He would only have enough spare fuel in reserve for safety reasons but his priority would be to get the aircraft on the ground in case he lost his third hydraulic pump necessitating immediate ejection.

He was busy and called 'Pan, Pan, Pan' as he turned in for the GCA, then said he had double hydraulic failure and very sluggish controls. On his final straight in approach he blew his undercarriage down with emergency air but this also means he could not raise it again even on the ground. Without flaps and airbrakes he was 'hot' and found it very difficult to get rid of his speed.

As wingman we joined him on his final approach to help if we could and saw him land centrally on the runway but very fast indeed. Without

Gloster Javelin Lima, after transfer - with John Wilson - to No. 11 Squardon.
(John Wilson)

wheelbrakes he tried to reduce speed by holding his nose high and then he managed to operate an awkward lever to put the last of his 3 pump pressure into the wheelbrake system but there was a leak on a common union which is why the aircraft suffered double hydraulic failure in the first place.

So there he was going like the hammers of hell and there was nothing he could do, not even raise the undercarriage to stay on the airfield. I watched him go over the end of the 3000 metre runway with flying speed, at least 180 knots.

So he roared through the perimeter wire and into farmers' fields going on for at least 2 km and finally crossing a lane which is the border, so he reached Holland.

As the aircraft slowed gently neither crewman was injured but the aircraft was very severely damaged and written off.

CHAPTER SEVENTEEN

The Canberra

THE FOLLOWING MEMORY OF FLYING THE CANBERRA by George Payne was published in the *Association* magazine in 1997:

In 1961, when I joined the Squadron, we had a close brush with World War Three. There was a crisis regarding Allied access to Berlin. My introduction to the Squadron Commander, David Ross, was grim. He had only one thing missing from his office – a sandwich board carrying the device 'The end is nigh!' He greeted me with the comment that he was glad that I didn't have my family with me as it seemed that WW3 was just about to blow, with buckets of instant sunshine being tossed about the place. I crossed my fingers that the powers-that-be would come to a more amicable arrangement because I had a 'cross posting' in which the lucky recipient went to the head of the married quarter waiting list, thus eliminating a 9-month separation from the nearest and dearest. 'What a nuisance!,' I thought.

Besides lobbing nuclear weapons, one of our potential tasks was to fit the gunpack and shoot down enemy aircraft. In that sense we were, say, 3[B] in the morning and 3[F] Sqn in the afternoon. Hell, let 'em all come! We could meet 'em with anything! But a little notice would be appreciated. Strictly, we were not terribly serious about the interceptor role. It was only

1960 Canberra B(I)8. One careful previous owner. No.59 Squadron's unofficial fin badge which was replaced by our Cock on a Rock in 1961; green band added late 1963 author was responsible. (Les Bywaters)

1962 Canberra B(I)8 with 'Cock on a Rock' in white circle on fin. Note the practice bomb carriers underwing, no gunpack betrays nuclear role. (Author)

supposed to be in regard to helicopter gunships. And we never practised the role, possibly owing to the large shortage of British helicopter gunships, i.e. zero! Well, officially never . . .

A chance opportunity arose during a detachment to the LABS [Low-Altitude Bombing System] range near Castel Benito in Libya. We [Bob Latchem and I] were on the range when we noticed a small civilian helicopter apparently observing our results. I notified Control and tried to make it go away by practising interceptions on it. It was rather like trying to fix a crazy flying bluebottle to the wall with a 6-inch masonry nail. It sat in the centre of our left- and right-hand pursuit circles and refused to budge. If only we had been flying a Boulton Paul Defiant – or a Harrier! The next tactic was to climb well above the little blighter and turn back on to it. By the time our two Avons had got us sufficiently high into the sun to turn back, there was no sign of it. It had probably run out of fuel!

Canberra B2s were definitely bombers. But the B[I]8s of No 3 Sqn, with their fighter type cockpits and gunpacks were a different delight. Jacking the pilot's seat up fully into the glasshouse gave one a splendid all round view. It was the original MRCA [Must Refurbish Canberra Again]. The on-board navigation system was deadly accurate. My own was labelled Bob Latchem. This was a version that could get you on target, on time, anywhere, day or night, low level. There was another one on the Squadron labelled Bill Drake with a contour visual interpretation capability in Norwegian valleys that would have made a Tomahawk cruise missile seem half blind. They made a pilot's life easy, but there was yet another one who gave all instructions in Esperanto. That was a cold shock on a dark night. We flew all over Europe, but never did find his homeland!

We mainly practised normal LABS runs, pulling up to toss the bomb well ahead because we were advised that the real bombs went off with a bit of a WOOMF, which could be uncomfortable if one dallied after release. Planning the run-in was based upon this normal tactic. But one day Bob said, 'There's the IP' [initial – or initiate – point] 'Where's the IP?' 'S#@ the IP!' So we selected the alternate fry-up manoeuvre to release the bomb after pulling up through 110 degrees. The triangular target appeared directly below us and up we went, expecting a direct hit. But the Range Officer gave us 800 yds off. That was like aiming for the runway intersection and hitting Station Headquarters, a complete waste of time. In our haste and lack of planning we had forgotten to apply the wind factor which, of course, is much greater anyway for the longer bomb flight-time of the alternate manoeuvre. Red faces all round!

We called the Squadron Commander 'Sir', to avoid rhyming his name in an undignified way with 'Boss'. He was quite old, being 39; and he told me he had learned to do two things very well. He could fly and he could write. He showed me the paper he wrote on and it was true. Having been on a joined-up-writing course myself, I had only learnt to write obscure American words like 'mission' [to redeem loose women?]; but David showed me how to write words like 'what?', 'where?', 'when?' and half a dozen others of that ilk which, when you applied your needs to them, could transform a vague idea into a concrete operational plan. It was beautiful and it worked!

There were other craftsmen in language on the Squadron. I was shocked when I first heard 'my own' Bob's nickname. Fortunately, I am not mean enough to repeat it – and too cowardly to do so anyway! Cruel nicknames were in vogue. The best one was 'Twittering Fred Drawers'. I wonder who that was? It could have applied to any of us when the hooter went for WW3. [All right, lads. Only a practice!].

John Corby on Our American Allies

Serving at Geilers [Geilenkirchen] as a young navigator with 3 Sqn, I quickly learned that our friends in the USAF were well trained, cool and, of course, generous.

QRA [Quick Reaction Alert] 1
Bells clanging, hooters hooting, Murphy swearing. I am first out to the aircraft, down on the ground rolling under the bomb bay to get at THE WEAPON when a huge weight on my right arm prevents all further movement and all thoughts of anything except 'Help!' Despite the excruciating pain I eventually manage to open an eye to find the sharp end of an American carbine three inches [7.5 cm] from my nostrils and a size 12 American issue field boot the cause of my immobility. Boot and carbine belong to a young black USAF enlisted man who, from where I am lying is definitely 10 feet [3 metres] tall – at least! He says, 'Suh, Ah bin practising with ma weapon lately an' Ah guess Ah could hit you from this

range, now you just git out from under there nice and quiet so's we can first give you permission to git under there, then you can do it see?' I saw. I did. I learned.

QRA 2

Boring old QRA again! Thank goodness for this poker game and the chance to win the large, nay, very large, pile of chips in the pot! Suddenly the radio music courtesy BFN [British Forces Network] stops and a very agitated and emotional voice booms out: 'President Kennedy has just been assassinated . . .' The rest was lost on us as we dropped our cards, jumped up to run about like headless chickens, convinced we were about to be told to go to war! Another voice booms out 'SIT DOWN', we stop, look, and see the American Defence Officer [ADO] has us all covered with his handgun, we knew it was loaded too! John Wayne this was not. We could see, however, that he was deadly serious. Confused, we sat. 'Pick up your cards and I'll see you,' he said throwing another chip into the pot. We turned over our cards and he triumphantly laid out his four Jacks, scooped the pot into his hat, holstered his gun, real cool! He then ran off down the corridor to his personal panic phone shouting, 'Jeez! Jeez! Waddowedonow?'

TO A FAULT

A weekend of child-minding for the senior ADO's family whilst he went off with wife for a special couple of days. Having to get used to being called 'Sir' and 'Ma'am' by tinies was compensated for my wife and myself, by unlimited use of the family freezer which seemed only to be stocked with T-bone steaks the size of skateboards. We ate very well! A few weeks later we were invited as guests of the said ADO and wife to dine at 'Au Coin Des Bons Enfants' in Maastricht. Fab foods, fine wines, great hosts. A really special event way outside the experience of a young Fg Off and wife (who just happened to be in the early stages of first pregnancy). We emerged from the very warm restaurant into the cold night air and, as we stood on the pavement and I struggled for an idea of how we might return his generosity for the wonderful food – my wife threw up her entire meal at his feet!

38 years later and we have still never returned to Maastricht!

The stories of my own time flying 3 Squadron's heaviest fighter, appeared under the title Cranberry Daze:

I was supposed to arrive at Geilers for New Year's Eve 1962/3. So the day before I drove away from our OMQ at RAF Marham, via my folks in London, to pick up Mick Collins, who was to join 14 Sqn at Wildenrath. We awoke to a blanket of snow, unable to get to Lydd, so back to Mick's folks for the night. Next day we reached Lydd, but the only aircraft flying was a SABENA Superfreighter taking off in conditions one step up from zero/zero. Ticket swopped for boat and off to Dover, but the boat was

1963. Canberra B(I)8 Dave Jackson comes alongside to allow Bill Scragg to indicate to Spud Murphy and John Corby "Two minutes to go!" (John Corby)

Canberra B(I)8 closer, now only "Two seconds to go!" (John Corby)

docked until the wind died down, so in harbour we celebrated French New Year, then ours, then Iceland, Greenland etc. Somewhere about Kamchatka I had to rush to the lee side – we were just passing the mole! My first continental drive was not too well remembered, except for one long zizz in a lay-by. Hairs of the dog at Wilders, then off to Geilers – to find a survivors' party in full swing. The Dunwoodies were administering Brandy Alexanders the next day, then 'Hey ho, hey ho! it's off to Flights we go!' Lots of time for induction as it was 'Harry Clampers' until 15 January, when a 'lunch time sucker hole' appeared, and so did Ted Sadler, the Squadron Trainer, beckoning from the door of the bar!

On the climb Ted asked, 'What's that buffet!' Airbrakes? No. Bomb doors? No. Wheels? No. Whoops! Forgot the transition from IAS to Mach number at which point the returning blizzard prompted ATC [Air Traffic Control] to issue an urgent recall. So, power off – but not to idle in the T.4 in icing conditions; brain almost in gear again! – roll over inverted, pull through, airbrakes out then bomb doors open and RTB pdq.

Conversion to the B[I]8 included a detachment to Idris – south of Tripoli, in Libya, where the Italians built all their airfields far enough inland to outrange naval bombardment – with Catch 22: 'You can't land at Idris until you've experienced landing a Canberra there before.' My many landings there as a Valiant co-pilot did not count. So I lay in the nose while Nick Allen [I think it was] did it. Scary stuff! How did the navigators do it? Or did they know no better? Particularly in view of someone else's tale of an undercarriage problem. They landed on the grass, stopped rather suddenly and the navigator, who should, of course, have been strapped into his seat – not ejectable – below and to the right of the pilot, shot through the transparent nose cone and came to rest dazed but uninjured – until the ambulance ran over his legs! Will the owner of this tale please stand up? He should have recovered by now.

At Idris we used to practice LABS with 4 x 25 lb practice bombs, two on each underwing pylon. Off to Tarhuna range, accelerate to 400+ kts at 250 ft, trigger the 'pickle' switch, follow the needles – similar to an ILS dial but, to help confuse us poor pilots, the pitch operated in the opposite sense by pulling it to the centre – completing a half loop with a roll off the top. The on board elastic would unwind to release the 'weapon' either at 45 degrees up for maximum range, 60 for maximum time or 100+ if you had missed the pre-IP and or IP and had to pass directly over the target. Due to the reduced escape time this was known as the 'Kamikaze' as there was a likelihood of your being passed by your own 'Divine Wind'! On one of these detachments the Buccaneer S. 2 was there on tropical trials. On one run in a black shadow appeared off our starboard wing-tip, rock steady while our bucket of bolts was bouncing about. As I fought to fly smoothly and precisely through the manoeuvre he accelerated away – with the usual cheery wave indicating two minutes to the bar.

After dropping the first four bombs it was back to Idris for an engines

1964 John Corby escorts hatless Ron Winfield at Akrotiri, Cyprus, Holiday Camp. (John Corby)

running – therefore the pilot could not leave the cockpit – quick turn round [QTR] to load four more. Having dropped those, return to shut down, refuel, drain and refresh the pilot before repeating the process. The canopy was fixed so QTRs were hell and copious quantities of orange juice consumed; I was a lot slimmer then. That Buccaneer had a sunshade over the open cockpits and an air conditoning unit plugged in. But we were not jealous; we knew we were getting TSR2 and Bea had just written to me – for the unit history – and described how he left a Lightning standing using only one afterburner. So HMG cancelled that, ordered the F111K and then cancelled that, thereby spending a fortune abroad that would have been better spent at home – where the workforce would have paid taxes instead of being Paid Off! Our 'best informed Defence Minister' stood up in the House to state: 'I am not aware the French are developing a variable geometry aircraft' when the Mirage G was being described in Flight. So we went to AFVG [Anglo-French Variable Geometry] and then MRCA 75 [Multi-Role Combat Aircraft [for service in] 1975]. Now look up the entry into service date of the Tornado, which is what became of all this, and which I described to a TV personality at Farnborough as 'the ugliest Javelin I've ever seen' – hence no career in TV or politics.

Once we became reasonably competent we were sent off to do this at night at Nordhorn, back in Germany. On one occasion we had a hang-up, so did a low, slow fly-by the tower. Despite my request to train the light on the left wing-tip in line with the tail, it was aimed straight into the cockpit and nose. Who says you cannot fly by the seat of your pants? – whatever state they are in! Years later a Senior Management and Training Pilot in Manx Airlines gave me a mini-lecture on instrument flying, 'particularly at night'. When I told him of our night operations, particularly LABS, I was told, 'Never! No Squadron or Flight Commander would authorise such a flight' – but then, he was a 'Pickfords' Nigel [Transport Command Co-pilot/First Officer in 'civvy street'].

The 'serious' business was NATO nuclear deterrent. In a compound to the east [i.e. wrong] end of the runway, ready to go at a moment's notice, 24 hours a day. Initially fully clad the whole time, I mentioned that when I was a V-force co-jo we went into pyjamas at night. Naturally, I was on the first night this was allowed and, equally naturally, HQ 2ATAF rang the bell in the early hours. It added less than 30 seconds. Knowing the effects of cold-soaking, I also suggested a trial scramble after an aircraft and weapon change. I got that one too! The first two port cartridges failed to fire, but the third one 'bit'. Then so did the first on the other engine and away we went – leaving behind a worried looking ADO [American Duty Officer]. No one thought to warn anyone else and the Jabberwock crews of 5 and 11 Sqns had just completed their daily inspections on Battle Flight. Keith McRobb was halfway down the ladder when he heard us start up in the QRA dispersal – and the gates were open! He nearly got a double hernia reversing up the ladder, to reach into the cockpit for the tele-scramble and ask, 'What time did World War Three start?'

Previously Nick Allen and I had been on Valiants at Marham. There we developed a 'scare tactic' for the weekend goofers on the Downham Market to Swaffham road. At Geilers we had a 'duty spy' on a knoll to the east of QRA. As we strolled around the compound with our 'significant other' [navigators 'Benny' Goodman and Paul Nagle for me and Nick] we were talking of this and noticed our 'spy' with telephoto lens. 'Shall we?' 'Yes, let's!', so ran at the chain-link fence to jump and cling as high as we

1963 Canberra B(I)8 under tow, interdictor fit with gunpack. (John Corby)

could shaking back and forth going 'Ook! Ook!' Very quickly we heard: 'What seems to be the trouble, Sirs?' A USAF sergeant with .45 and two airmen with Armalites escorted us back to our hut, ostentatiously staying between us and our aircraft as we went. I often wondered what would have happened if the bell went, also if our 'monkey-business' pictures were on our reserved room at the 'Lubyanka Hilton'. We had to phone the Boss and John Field came down with the Colonel to explain away our antics as British humour, not stir-crazy!

The reason for the USAF? The weapons were Uncle Sam's and his representatives had to 'enable' them. I once asked, 'Enable them to what?', but their humour doll's eye went white again. Several wheezes were aimed at our transatlantic cousins, the best was achieved one Easter. The weapons were stored on the opposite side of the airfield and once loaded on a trolley were draped in a tarpaulin and conveyed to QRA. One of our smallest airmen ducked under the tarpaulin and during the journey tied a speed/duct tape bow around the bomb, adding the message 'Happy Easter, The Bunny'. Amusement was not the word when it was uncovered at QRA. Why shots were not heard above our laughter we'll never know, but the score was one-nil to our lads and remained so, at least until the end of my tour. But you had to laugh in a situation where we had just four minutes to get airborne and yet the evacuation plan for our families was to coach them to the Eifel mountains – in four minutes?

Another wizard wheeze. For added security no one was allowed to cross lines painted across the front and rear of the hangar to get to the armed aircraft unless and until the ADO and an aircrew member went across together. Naturally on some practices we would both halt at the line to let the ADO go across on his own – none was ever shot. With a new ADO, on daily checks the pilot would sit or squat at the front of the bomb bay *as he went up one side of the weapon and the nav. up the other. With a fat tin of their 'Instant Sunshine' in our narrow bay they were quite restricted, so when the nav. lowered a thumbs up the pilot would use both hands to clap on the hollow nose cone of the bomb – you could always tell a new ADO by the bump on his head, often with a deep crease if the positioning was exact.*

One of our regular mission profiles was a hi-lo-hi to go low level over Devon and Cornwall. Frequently as we came out over the sea down an inlet Benny would yell 'Britannia!', especially effective if the ship had buff funnel and/or black hull. 'Ha ruddy ha ha!' Then we started going the other way round – just to get a forward oblique shot of the Cerne Abbas giant. Left at Dungeness and go round the Isle of Wight southside. Once again 'Britannia!' But this time 'Ha ruddy . . . etc' became 'Oh bother', or words to that effect, as the camera button was pressed. Result: a superb shot of Betty Windsor's Boat. A few months later the Queen came to Germany and we were to provide a B[I]8 for static display at Gutersloh. Everyone was hoping to be in the fly-past of course. I suggested to the Boss that we frame my photo of 'the boat people' for the static crew to present. Wisely, he decided against this, overflights of the Royal Yacht being verboten. Thus he again preserved what little career I might have had.

All squadrons provided aircraft for the fly-past, 3 Sqn having two flights of three in vic. plus a spare. Ron Winfield and I took it in turns, one flying as No 6, the other as spare. As the four 'clutch' wings assembled [bases at Bruggen, Laarbruch, Wildenrath and Geilenkirchen] and flew through a cloud layer somebody 'lost it' and I volunteered our services. It was the No. 3 of another unit and 5 moved up to take his place while 4 and 6 went line astern on the leader to make an arrow. When I arrived they resumed their original positions so I had to join like a mating porcupine – very carefully. As we approached Gutersloh ground control told us we were early. Whirlwind helicopters led and had no problem, nor the Pembrokes; the Hunter leader called 'Airbrakes, Go', the Javelins nearly stopped and from the Canberras a voice cried 'God save the Queen'! Laughter took away the tension and witnesses claimed it was the tightest formation seen for a long time, but I never saw the film. The original plan was for the spare to land at Gutersloh, pick up cans of film and depart for Heathrow. Meant to go by BEA actually it did not; John Field and Peter Broadhurst took it.

Earlier I mentioned Ted Sadler. One night, again in the T4 on a recurrent check, he asked if I minded his doing the last landing. Now, in the event of engine failure the drill was the mnemonic C WATER, standing for Control the aircraft, Warn the crew, Adjust the power, Trim, Examine for cause and Rectify. On my asymmetric overshoot – nowadays called go-round - Ted took control and turned down wind over Married Quarters. As he was easing the 'failed' engine up and the other one back, the 'failed' engine actually failed! I think what he said was 'What the heck's happened here?'

At the subsequent debrief next day, in front of others, he said: 'While I was doing a ten fingered ballet I had to admire the way Jack just sat there with his arms folded calmly saying, 'What happened to C WATER?' I had to own up that my 'folded' arms were poised to reach either the face-blind or seat-pan handle in the event of a Martin Baker let down – to join our Flight Commanders at the Bridge table.

One of these was carrying out a night check on another occasion. On the approach to Wildenrath, with the first 200 yards of the runway sterile, he commented, 'That was a bit low.' Truthfully I replied, 'I always land low, Sir,' to which Benny was banging on his chart table in applause. 'Hydraulic hammering!' yelled Sir, and nearly cut short the sortie in the overshoot area.

And so to my most embarrassing moment. Squadron scramble, start up, thumbs up, taxy out, check controls – oh! oh! rudder lock still in! Luckily the caravan controller could reach it, so I was still leading – albeit by having blocked the runway . More haste means less safety. Everyone in aviation is trying to kill you, including you!

My happiest moment, apart from family, was the Düsseldorf British Week – and the beginning of battles with Germany. On the Sunday start we were on static display with a Javelin and a Hunter. Talking with Ted Heath we all persuaded him to get us permission to display. This was given. The Hunter first, who took photos of an Il-12 'Cub' by flying between it and the terminal. We were next, and having seen the film of Bea's demo to the USAF in which he was done, down and dusted in the time it took the Martin XB-51 to do a circuit, we kept within the airfield boundary and, although by doing so could not achieve 400 knots, finished with a dummy LABS manoeuvre. The 'Flat Iron' was of course limited to tight turns and banging the afterburners in and out. It was mostly this noise which caused the main Saturday fly-past to be curtailed and the aerobatic team to be cancelled. A good note to end on? No way! Towards the end of our tour the Javelins were given a low level interception task. Returning from a low level mission through Area 2, Benny called in a Javelin at 1 o'clock just as I spotted it. I formated on his left, no reaction. Telling Benny to keep an eye on him, I crossed over the top – and this giant black shape/shadow caused him to break left. In the Mess later that evening, as the pilot entered I was able to say 'Splash! One Javelin in Area 2.' My proudest moment on No. 3's heaviest fighter.

John Field recalls a detachment to Malaysia in an article entitled Canberra + Confrontation = Kuantan.

In the mid 1960s I was lucky enough to be in command of 3 Squadron, RAF, based at Geilenkirchen, Germany, and equipped with Canberra B[I]8s in the nuclear strike and conventional ground attack roles. On 24th October 1964 my wife Marylou and I had just arrived in Shropshire for some leave when the Station Commander telephoned to recall me to

Geilenkirchen from where, within 48 hrs, I was to take a B[I]8 detachment to Malaysia. At that time Malaysia, with UK support, was 'confronting' an expansion-minded Indonesia. FEAF [Far East Air Force] had little if anything in the way of offensive capability and, though not known to us beforehand, there was a contingency plan for RAFG to fill the gap. Our task was to practise this reinforcement.

Marylou and I drove to Valley where Eric Denson and Peter Broadhurst were waiting to fly me back to base. They had brought Norman Roberson with them, tasked with driving Marylou back to Germany in our Fiat 500 [We were waiting for the BMW at the time – and still are]. Those of you who know the dimensions of Norman and of the 500 may wonder how he managed to get in, let alone drive the thing. I never asked.

At Geilers Dave Collins and Peter Little [Flight Commanders] had crew and aircraft selection in hand and the change from nuclear fit to gun packs and wing pylons was underway and fresh tyres etc. were being fitted. The groundcrew had already left for a VC10 ride to Singapore. I was concerned to find that the detachment was to be mixed – four aircraft and crews from 3 Sqn, four from 14 Sqn [Wildenrath]. This arrangement may have facilitated the maintenance of both the Geilers and Wilders QRAs but it had many disadvantages, particularly when we had less than 48 hours to liaise and to prepare for departure.

So, on 26th October, we were off: self and Martin Fortune, Peter Little and Mike Richards [Navigation Leader], Greg Marsh and Paul Nagle, Eric Denson and Peter Broadhurst, for an uneventful transit to our first night stop at Akrotiri, where we met Peter Rogers and his 14 Sqn crews. Akrotiri's Canberra wing had been tasked with providing an HF-equipped lead aircraft to take us round the Turkey-Iran route to Bahrein so we briefed at some length with OC Operations [Peter Latham] both on the ground rules for 3/14 integration and on transit formation flying. The B[I]8 squadrons had little opportunity to practise formation flying so we all had to be quite clear about how best to move 9 aircraft in safe company.

I commanded 13 Sqn [Meteor PR10, Canberra PR7] from Akrotiri's bare base opening in early 1956 through the Suez operation to late 1958 so I was interested to see how the place had developed since 13 Sqn's dispersal was in dilapidated ex-Canal Zone caravans parked on the eastern 300 yards of the runway, protected [we hoped] by a 5 ft earth barrier – 'Boyce's Barrier' [the then SASO] – from over-runs from the 09 direction but not protected at all from any undershoot problem on 27. We had moved to safer ground before the French F84Fs arrived for Suez, which was just as well – loaded they needed 3000 yds before they even thought of getting airborne. But I digress.

Day 2 saw us following the Akrotiri leader northwards in a more or less orderly gaggle. The long haul to the Gulf gave us time to get used to keeping station and by the time we descended into Muharraq we were able to close up and make a reasonably tidy arrival. Leaving our Akrotiri guide behind we refuelled and pressed on to Masirah, on the Arabian Sea coast of Oman, for an overnight stay. By this time there were a couple of stragglers. One of the 14 Sqn aircraft had arrived at Akrotiri with enough mainwheel [tyre] canvas showing to worry even an Aeroflot engineer, and Peter Little had dropped behind to act as whipper-in. Although Masirah's facilities were very basic – salt-water showers and rationed drinking water from their desalination plant – they were adequate for a night stop.

We planned a crack of dawn take off for Gan, the RAF's base in the Maldives. I remember sitting aboard, door open in the cool, still pre-dawn, waiting for the huge orb of the desert sun to climb over the eastern horizon. Shades of Lawrence of Arabia for those who remember the film. But it wasn't Omar Sharif who galloped out of the sun – only an Arab boy on a donkey, complete with mood-shattering ghetto blaster at full pop tune volume. The ocean legs were quite sporty for crews that had only DR [deduced reckoning] plus doppler radar to keep them on track and, where possible, we planned to fly in loose company with one of the H/F equipped PR7s that were frequently travelling to and from FEAF. Not on that particular day though. We found that the doppler worked quite well on the ocean swell and there was comfort in the company of others but I think we were all relieved to hear the Gan approach controller.

Gan was one of those 6 month postings where, we were told, people arrived wondering how they would survive the boredom of life on an isolated, tarmac-covered coral islet and left grumbling about the hobbies, studies etc. that they hadn't had time to complete. The Maldives are now a popular holiday destination of course and the RAF is long gone. We only had time for an hour or so's snorkelling on the reef before an overnight rest and another dawn departure for RAAF Butterworth on the north west coast of Malaysia. The headwinds at our cruising level turned out to be much stronger than forecast and it was a long 5 hour grind, only enlivened, if that is the right word, by Greg having to descend to relight a flame-out, accompanied by Eric Denson for moral support. Diversions were in short supply and we were glad to hear Greg's relight call. About half an hour later Greg and Eric's climbing contrails appeared several miles ahead. We really should have picked a lower cruising height.

Butterworth was a well developed, comfortable base not far from the holiday island of Penang. The RAAF made us very welcome – air conditioned rooms, plenty of cold beer. I thought of pressing on to Kuantan but we were all tired and it seemed prudent to take advantage of Butterworth's hospitality overnight. So we made another early start for Kuantan, where a descent through lowish strato-cu [cloud] brought us into the gin clear visibility that was to make low level flight such a pleasant change from north Germany's clag/winter gloom. Our ground crews, who had arrived ahead of us, gave us a well organised reception and turn round. Peter Little brought in the stragglers a day later and by 1 November we had 8 aircraft and crews ready for whatever FEAF had in mind.

The 1960s facilities at Kuantan airfield, a few miles inland from the town, which is in turn about 200 miles up the east coast from Singapore, were basic; a 2000 yd runway with a drainage ditch alongside and lots of tall trees off each end, a taxy loop to 8 pans, a tented camp, bowsers for fuel storage and supply, and not much else. The short runway would have limited our offensive radius of action unless we staged through Butterworth or Tengah. Masses of rusty barbed wire lay around in heaps, and there were several zigzag trenches, plus one gun pit. I didn't see any AA guns but Martin Fortune remembers receiving some AA training. He also remembers being briefed at Geilers to avoid the temptations of the local girls. I didn't receive this briefing: perhaps Wing Commanders were considered to be temptation proof – or beyond hope?

Contact with FEAF, apart from an early half hour visit by the Senior Air Staff Officer [Air Vice-Marshal Hawkins], *and one or two trips that I made to Tengah to liaise with the Ops staff, was by signal. Otherwise we were left to our own devices.* [FEAFs B15s had been moved back from Kuantan to Tengah just before we arrived and were on a 'high state of readiness' so FEAF were probably pre-occupied with possible ops in the Borneo theatre at the time]. *We had an FEAF Int. officer and a certain amount of rudimentary target information so we spent our working days studying possible targets and flying low level training sorties. We expended quite a lot of 20 mm shells and many practice bombs on China Rock range off*

1964 English Electric Canberra B(I)8 in dispersals at Kuantan, Malaysia in 1964. Note the lack of fixed base buildings. (John Field)

the south-east coast. This was enjoyable but did little for our accuracy as the rock was quite large, wasn't instrumented and hits didn't stir up much guano dust. On most afternoons we sent Landrover loads to Kuantan beach, deserted and unspoilt then, and we had a makeshift screen for the occasional film show in the evenings. One or two brave souls spent a day learning what a formidable barrier to movement is presented by primary jungle and I think that every crew managed to make one landing at Changi or Tengah for urgent operational reasons – Noritake china, fast-tailored clothes etc. On one trip to Tengah I found a RNZAF Canberra on a Lone Ranger [single aircraft training trip abroad]. It would have been nice to have entertained the crew at Kuantan but like everyone else at FEAF the idea of visiting our primitive home did not appeal.

Orders to return to Germany arrived in mid-November, again with 48 hours' warning. We left one of our aircraft behind and sent one crew back by VC-10 as a 14 Sqn crew suffered a collapsed port leg and a bent wing tip during their after landing checks in mid-detachment. At first the finger pointed to the pilot but when I climbed in to check I found the flap lever to be up, the u/c selected down and three greens lit [indicator lights].

The return trip was quicker and easier because we were gaining on the clock and had more daylight to play with. We couldn't fly directly to Gan, Kuantan's 2000 yds being too short for full tanks and tips plus the weight of all those essential purchases stowed in the gun pack ammo trays, so we made a quick fuel top up at Butterworth before crossing the Bay of Bengal, in company with a PR7, for a night stop at Gan. I lost a generator on take-off the next day so Martin and I inspected the Maldive lagoons at low level for an hour or so whilst burning off enough fuel to land back at Gan. By the time our snag was fixed our return flight whipper-in – Peter Rogers – had arrived and gone to bed. We persuaded him that the place to sleep was Masirah, where we arrived that evening. The next day the pair of us

1965 Canberra B(I)8. Intasun holiday flight in the Mediterranean on the way to Idris in Libya, bombing Tarhuna range on the way. (John Corby)

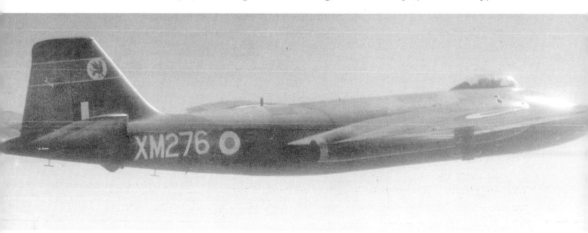

flew through refuelling stops at Muharraq and Akrotiri, catching up with the rest of the detachment at Luqa that evening. The following morning we said farewell to the 14 Sqn crews and headed home for a GCA through the usual November gloom to Geilers [where Jack Long was waiting to be relieved from seemingly endless confinement, deterring the might of the Warsaw Pact, in the Quick Reaction Alert cage].

There followed the usual report writing [remember stencils and pink correcton fluid?]. RAFG agreed that there would be no more mixed squadron detachments and although Akrotiri sent a squadron there once or twice I think that there was only one further RAFG visit to Kuantan – by 16 Sqn who brought back our abandoned aircraft. As a reinforcement exercise it was reasonably successful in that we all arrived in good shape, ready for work. We could have cut at least a day off the outbound journey but I didn't know enough about the 14 Sqn crews and aircraft to push them. Whether we could have operated against targets in Indonesia to best effect in our rarely practised role, for a Command not acquainted with B[I]8 capabilities and limitations and hampered by primitive C + C [Command and Control] facilities, will never be known. Shortly after 16 Sqn returned Indonesia changed Presidents and the 'Confrontation' chapter closed. Malaysia and Indonesia are now members of South East Asian Nations and Kuantan is now the base for, amongst other aircraft, the Royal Malaysian Air Force's Mig 29Ns.

Another memory of Canberras comes from Dave Mackenzie. In the Association magazine of June 1998, entitled *Canberra Capers*, he wrote:

Ron [Ledwidge] and I had been on QRA overnight [on 9 May 1967] and were just signing off. The morning Flying Programme detailed me to have the first slot and Ron the second. Ron needed to get away early as soon as the sortie was over, so we swopped slots and aircraft. Ron flew with Jack [Stewart] and Andy [Leddy] came with me.

A couple of hours later, just leaving Nordhorn Range, Andy and I saw a tall plume of black smoke a few miles off track. Smoke and flames were coming from a pit in the middle of a field. It did not look like an aircraft because there was no debris scattered about. We climbed up and advised the Radar Unit. They had heard a brief Mayday call, but nothing further.

When we got back to Geilers Ron and Andy had still not returned. We waited to hear the inevitable news. About an hour later Ron phoned Ops. It was quite a long time later before Jack called in.

The ailerons had jammed and the aircraft had rolled – at 250 feet! Ron had successfully barrel rolled it up to 10,000 feet when Jack finally got his chest parachute on and departed. Ron then used the Martin Baker assistor. The aircraft hit the ground vertically.

I had been on the Squadron for only a few months, but Ron was just Tour-ex[pired]. The results of the incident could have been very different if the programme had not been changed! I believe that this was the first time

Canberra B(I)8 escorted by two No.11 Sqn Gloster Javelin FAW9s in 1965. (3 Squadron)

both crew had successfully abandoned a Canberra B(I)8. Ron got an AFC for his achievement.

Alan East, the magazine editor, added:

Knowing that Ron feigns surprise that anyone should be the least interested in this story, I offered him the Right of Reply! Claiming that memories will be unreliable after 31 years, he sent me copies of official reports from Air Clues, Flight Comment etc. But he did add the comment, 'I notice that my ejection report stops short of the actual perfect parachute landing in a big heap in a field. This was shortly followed by a gaggle of German farmworkers excitedly asking, 'Starfighter?', before I could explain that I was an Englander.' [At this time the 'new' Luftwaffe, having been persuaded that the Lockheed F-104G was the ideal aircraft and/or weapons delivery system, were losing quite a number – the German joke was, 'If anyone wants a Starfighter, buy a field and wait.']

Modesty also prevents Ron adding that he was subsequently selected as one of twelve 'Men of the Year', who also included Francis Chichester, Jack Hawkins, Topol and Chapman Pincher. The London Gazette 25 July 1967 *explains how he got the aircraft to [in fact] 8,000 feet. It is quoted here with Jack Stewart's approval.*

> *. . . the major part of a low-level navigation and bombing training mission had been successfully completed and the aircraft was returning to base. . . when, at 500 feet [150 metres] above ground level the aileron control suddenly jammed at about half deflection. The aircraft immediately started rolling on to its back. Realising that his aircraft was in imminent danger, Flt Lt Ledwidge could at this point have used his ejector seat to escape; however, he was aware that his navigator, who was not equipped with an ejector seat, would have no chance of escaping before the aircraft crashed. With complete disregard for his own safety, Flt Lt Ledwidge attempted to regain*

Canberra B(I)8 in 1965 led by an F-104 Starfighter and flanked by F-100 Super Sabres with F-84F Thunderstreaks outboard and another in the box. (3 Squadron)

Paul Nagle is forced to substitute Coke for Amstel. (3 Squadron)

188

*partial control of the aircraft and, although he could not prevent it
from continuing to roll, he was able, by a superb display of
airmanship and piloting skill, to use differential engine power, rudder
and elevator to prevent the aircraft striking the ground. He then
continued to climb the aircraft through a series of full power climbing
rolls, using rudder to influence the rate of roll at different stages and
thus gain as much height as possible during each manoeuvre.*

*He had warned his navigator of the emergency immediately, but the
harsh use of the contols and the reversals of 'g' during the early stages
of the recovery had caused him to be disconnected from the intercom.
and thrown around the aircraft cabin. Not until the aircraft was
climbing was the navigator able to re-establish contact . . . Flt Lt
Ledwidge then waited until the navigator had fitted his parachute
pack and the aircraft was approaching a wings level attitude during
one of those climbing rolls before giving the order to abandon the*

Taking the "Cock" back to its "Rock", taken by his No.2

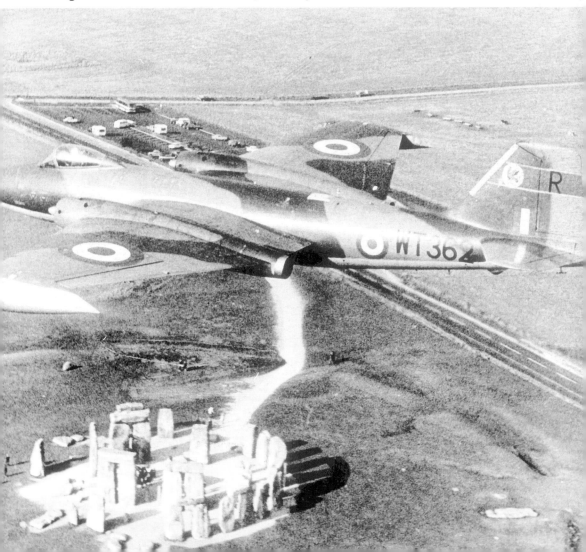

aircraft. *Only when he had seen his navigator leave through the escape exit did he operate his ejector seat . . . Both made a successful descent by parachute and were quickly picked up by rescue services alerted by the distress call which the pilot made before abandoning the aircraft.*

Throughout the whole of the emergency, Flt Lt Ledwidge displayed exceptional presence of mind. His handling of his aircraft in a dire emergency showed superlative judgement and outstanding skill, determination and sense of duty. These qualities, allied to a courage which is an example to all and in the very best traditions of a fighting service, undoubtedly saved his navigator's life.

What a superb note on which to end what was the longest aircraft chapter in 3's story – until the Harrier's arrival.

1972 Canberra B(I)8s. Gone but not forgotten. Redundant aircraft awaiting disposal at Warton in 1972. (Les Bywaters)

CHAPTER EIGHTEEN

Hawker's Bird of Prey – The Harrier!

DEVELOPED FROM THE HAWKER P1127 through the Kestrel to the Harrier GR1 and 3 with 'tin wings', then to the GR5 and 7 with 'plastic wings' and a proper fighter cockpit – which is why I count them as two separate types – it should have been the P1154 supersonic Vertical take-off and landing (VTOL) fighter. But politicians knew better and encouraged inter-service rivalry so that it, and the TSR2 plus the Vertical Short take-off and landing (V/Stol) HS 681 tactical transport, could be cancelled – but at least the latter became the 146, whereas TSR2 vanished completely, replaced by the F-111K also cancelled, to be replaced by the AFVG also cancelled to be replaced by the Navy's Buccaneer. Thank all the gods that while all that was going on the Third World War was put on hold.

By 1982 successive upgrades of airframe and engine resulted in the GR3, via the GR1 and 1A, during which time the original Bristol Pegasus 2 engine cleared for flight at 11,000 lb thrust had been developed by Rolls Royce (Bristol) to the Pegasus 102 with 20,000lb in the 1A and the 103 with 21,500 lb in the GR3 & AV-8A by McDonnell/Douglas. The latter was operated by the US Marine Corps who, with MD, opted for a total redesign with 'super-critical wing, improved lift devices and carbon-fibre epoxy-based construction'. 'The American AV-8B will provide the basis for the proposed Harrier GR mark 5' – echoes of Anglo-American co-operation with P-51/Merlin and the Canberra/B-57.

My first extract in this section is a series of articles in the Association magazines of July and December 1994 and December 1995 by Clive Handy, entitled '1975, Life in the Field':

> Since the start of this Association, apart from the occasional CO's Report, I don't think we've had many stories more recent than 1960. To redress the balance I offer these scribblings from my Harrier era, just to keep the more senior members in the picture as to how the Squadron has changed – or not!
>
> I joined No. 3[F] Sqn in February 1975. At that time there was an 85% change-over of personnel because so many of those who had been involved with the re-forming of the squadron with Harriers two years previously were now tour-ex. My boss was Stu Morgan. Our Junior Engineering Officer [JEngO] at that time was Les Walsh and our senior one [SEngO] was Ned Billings. We were a happy bunch; ignorant, but happy!
>
> Like many others, I had completed my Harrier GR1 course at Wittering the previous year, but working on the actual aircraft was a different kettle

1982 Hawker Siddeley Harrier GR3 in 1982. Gutersloh is in the distance above. (Alan East)

of fish altogether! We were all inexperienced about the workings of the 'Bona-Jet' and there were few experienced colleagues left to whom we could refer. Nonetheless, we somehow muddled through. As an Electrician, I found the wiring system completely unlike any I had come across before. Engine changes were delightful! For the first two or three months things were very hectic because we were due out on our first deployment in April. For the uninitiated I shall explain a deployment in Harrier parlance.

Deployment is the doctrine behind Harrier operations. Initially the Harrier was devised as a VTOL aircraft. This means it doesn't require conventional runways from which to operate; virtually any flat surface will do. In practice, of course, the Pegasus engine was not powerful enough for a fully fuelled and armed Harrier to take off vertically. So field operations involve STOVL, in which a fully armed Harrier can take off in less than 800 yards, carry out the mission and land vertically. This became the SOP [standard operating procedure] *and, since the Warsaw Pact were likely to* destroy airfields, our deployment involved setting up a mini airfield in a remote location, usually on the Sennelager or Paderborn ranges.

The logistics of these operations was enormous. Fleets of lorries loaded to the gunwales with tents, tools, machines, water, test equipment, spares, fuel, oil – you name it! – would deploy to two sites, Primary and Sub. Other sites involved station personnel, including Logs [Logistics], FWOC [Forward Wing Operational Control] and, of course, the other squadrons then at Wildenrath, 20 and IV. But we'll draw a veil over them and concentrate on the important people – 3[F] Sqn! The lorries were driven by Squadron personnel and we usually set off in convoy early on Monday morning to arrive by midday. It was at my first site near Paderborn that I was introduced to the pleasures [or otherwise!] of 'camping'. The standard issue 12' x 12' tent was used to house up to 8 chaps, with an NCO i/c each tent. You couldn't make yourself too comfortable or spread out too much, because at any time a 'crash out' might be called. This involved rapidly packing up and moving to another site because the original one had been compromised. So kit was kept packed and everything made easy to strike camp. The Royal Engineers [RE] had already been to each site and laid PSP [pierced-steel planking] and a 'Maxipad', a vertical landing pad. In addition, the REs also erected camouflage netting hides in which to park the jets between sorties. Each site was prepared like this, so a pre-planned 'crash-out' meant moving to a site similar to the one just left.

In order to break up their outline and make things 'invisible' to the enemy, general camouflage had to be applied to all static objects, of course. This became quite an art form and some ingenious methods were used to disguise the lorry, machine, Ops. Caravan or whatever. Each Harrier was housed in its own hide, each with its team of engineers led by the 'hide boss', who was usually a Corporal. Later, the use of higher ranks in certain jobs meant that this role was sometimes filled by a Sergeant, but in my time it was a very good grounding for a Cpl. to be i/c a team of 5–6 blokes and to be responsible for the operation of 'his' aircraft. In charge of each pair of aircraft was a Chief Tech., usually assisted by a Sgt armourer. The 'chief' coordinated everything, did the paperwork and was the direct link via Storno radio and land-line to the Ops tent/van.

After setting up camp on Monday the most important part of this first day was the evening meal! Without doubt, the catering on site was superb. The cooks erected and camouflaged their own tents and then produced some splendid meals. Not only for us but for everyone, because a Harrier deployment site was in effect a miniature RAF station with Air Traffic Controllers, RAF Police, clerks, RAF Regiment, grocers [Supply Sqn], Ground Equipment fitters, Safety Equipment, Ops. personnel, medics. and even stewards.

I also remember that first site I was on because of a visit from the then SACEUR [Supreme Allied Commander Europe], General Alexander Haig. He came to my hide to listen to the conversation over telebrief between the pilots and Ops. He then spoke to me but, being surrounded by more brass than I could shake a stick at, I was terrified and stuttered the usual incoherent replies to not-very-taxing questions. Gen. Haig went on to become the US Secretary of State for Defense and later a Presidential candidate. I'm still in the RAF and a Chief Tech.! I wonder who has the most satisfying career?

This particular occasion was meant to be a show-case for Harrier operations. But the whole place was a quagmire with everyone in Welly boots. It rained practically non-stop for a week, but we operated through it. The first week was the work-up, with moderate sortie rate and no OTRs [operational turn-rounds]. Normally an OTR involved refuelling and rearming an aircraft on turn-round with the pilot remaining strapped in, although sometimes a crew change would take place at the same time.

As well as maintaining the aircraft, we were also expected to dig trenches and determine arcs of fire from these trenches to repel potential attack. Digging the trenches was sometimes no more arduous than asking the REs to dig one with a JCB! At other times it involved more strenuous work. The work-up lasted until Saturday when all the 'Bona-Jet' pilots would have a dog-fight practice, which they called air-combat. It seemed to be their favourite activity. It also involved the ground crew in furious activity because the sortie pattern was usually short take-off, vertical landing, refuel and off again. But on Saturday afternoon the whole camp relaxed. Aircraft were repaired, people caught up with their dhobi [washing], others preferred something less strenuous such as Egyptian PT.

Then came Saturday night – and cabaret. If I say so myself, the fame of our cabaret spread far and wide, particularly to IV Sqn. But then we were/are better than IV Sqn at anything! The talk of the whole deployment, to those members of the Squadron who had never been in such a thing it was all rather bewildering. It was something akin to a school play, but with a certain indefinable ingredient. Of course it was definable – it was drink! It was strange, but with its help people lost their inhibitions and became stars of the stage for one night. The stage was the good old 5-ton Tasker trailer, with the sides dropped and draped in canvas or cam. nets. A 4-tonner with the tilt rolled up on one side became the MC's perch, complete with fire bell for keeping 'Best of order! Best of order!', a la Wheeltappers and Shunters Club, a popular TV programme of the time. These two MT pieces formed two sides of an amphitheatre and the clientele stood in the middle and jeered, sorry cheered! The bell-ringing role of MC was usually played by Ian Hudson, a Cpl Nav Inst fitter who, with his large moustache and even larger glasses, certainly looked the part!

The acts were members of hide crews or from one of the other support sections – like aircrew! All week they had been practising and making costumes out of whatever could be begged, borrowed or stolen. Many of the skits took the Michael out of various execs. such as the Site Boss and the Eng O. Some were just a group of drunken chaps singing rugby songs;

but some were absolutely brilliant singers or joke tellers. For instance, Dick Chadwick could usually leave us in stitches with his jokes, especially the 'not that twat, ya twat, this twat!' joke, which I'm sure many will remember [or imagine, but probably best left out!]. Coming from Wales, Merv Cook naturally had a fine tenor voice and was one of the few acts which could actually silence the crowd. He was – and I hope still is – a marvellous singer. Other acts included three chaps dressed as women in grass skirts and singing 'Happy Talk' from South Pacific. I don't know who they were, but maybe their 'last three' were Ward, Currie and the author! Another member, a certain Maj. John Hickie, the GLO, did a marvellous skit about the correct way to wear a tin helmet. The culmination of the whole thing was 'The Dance of the Cockatrice', usually performed by one A. Grant complete with feathers, head-dress and lots of dr . . . er, Dutch courage. To see this 17-stone electrician jumping and leaping about like a demented chicken on heat was a sight to behold! The audience had plenty of refreshing liquid to help them cheer along the participants and the party usually lasted well into the night. For now we'll brush over the wild pig chases and the midnight skinny dips in the river, and go on to Sunday.

Sunday, of course, was a day of rest and worship. Well, for the local German population it was. For a squadron on exercise it was just another working day in which aircraft were serviced, hangovers tended, sleep caught up with and NBC [Nuclear, Biological and Chemical attack] drills practised. On one memorable day in 1976 we were at a site through which a public road ran. The great German public love relaxing on a Sunday and could not resist the opportunity to see a Harrier at close hand. Soon the road through the site was chock-a-block with traffic and people. They particularly liked the home-made shower, which was an engine compressor wash-pump and a shower-head rigged up to a tree with a canvas or cam. net modesty cover. Our hide was nearest the road and contained a T4 [two seat training and periodic check trainer variant]. So this particular Sunday, our hide chief Mick Harding decided to relieve the boredom by allowing the Germans to have a look round a Harrier. We rigged up some lashing tape as a makeshift barrier, built a bit of hi-way staging to allow easier access to the cockpit and invited the locals to look around. They seemed to think the whole show had been put on especially for them and it occurred to us that if we charged an entrance fee, of say 1DM, we could make a fortune! Somebody thought that collecting money like this would reflect badly on the Royal Air Force, so the idea was dropped . . .

One other thing happened on that Sunday I think I can now tell without fear of retribution. For most of northern Europe 1976 was the driest and hottest this century. In Germany the average daytime temperatures were in the 90s [Fahrenheit – 30s Celcius] and that Sunday was no exception. I realise that there is some effect on engine performance, but the main trouble with being in the field in these high temperatures is – the beer is warm! Without access to a fridge, the best way to keep it cool is to immerse it in ice. But where to get ice when we were 15 km from the nearest town? Well, luckily the Harrier is fitted with a liquid oxygen [LOX] system in which the LOX is stored in removable bags. The bags had to be replenished out of the aircraft from a LOX trolley which held 50 litres of the stuff at -250 F. An ideal source of ice! Would you like the recipe? Put a couple of gallons of water in a plastic bag. Insert the LOX trolley hose in the water and turn on the LOX. The water becomes lumps of ice in seconds. Introduce warm cans into the bags of ice and you very soon get severely cold beer.

While doing this Mick Harding looked a picture. With the temperature in the 90s he was wearing his LOX protective apron, mask and gloves – and little else. Just a pair of shorts. The Health and Safety Inspectors of today would have a fit! Next day when the Logs. Park [Field Stores Depot] checked on the LOX remaining in stock, they wondered why our site had used 5 x 50 litres containers of LOX in one day. The explanation was easy; the LOX packs in the aircraft had got particularly hot and were venting off excessively. The aircraft systems had to be kept topped up, otherwise the whole system would need re-purging, which would cause unacceptable delays – and an even higher consumption of LOX. It was amazing what bulls**t the suppliers took in, especially when they didn't ask why the other sites hadn't experienced the same problem! Other stunts and pastimes took place on Sundays, but we were there to fly.

After the weekend festivities it was down to the nitty-gritty for the rest of the week. For those taking part this was the raison d'etre for their existence, especially the bung-ho bona-jet pilots! The format for the week's exercise was pretty standard: work-up phase, attacks, being attacked, gas attacks, sometimes ground attacks, then denouement and finally a few wind-down wets. [Beers, Bloggs!]

The three days of the 'Exercise' were hard work. Not only did the aircraft have to be maintained, rearmed, refuelled and fixed; but the site had to be guarded from air and ground attack. At any time this could involve donning gas masks and working in these hideous objects. NBC clothing was haute couture for the period of the exercise and was removed only to go to bed. If the exercise was in October even this didn't happen because usually it was so bloody cold! On the Monday morning the first thing that happened was a gas attack, followed by launching the aircraft. They usually took off conventionally on the 600 ft [180 metres] maxi-strip and landed vertically on the maxi-pad. Between the flights we often had to carry out an OTR. This involved all trades helping the armourers to load the aircraft with weapons while one airframe man did the kick-the-tyres-and-wiggle-the-flaps routine, as well as doing the refuelling. The other ancillary trades did the humping and grunting with the armourers. Needless to say, it was a well practised routine so each man knew what he was [supposed to be] doing!. Trying to load rocket pods and 1,000 lb *bombs while wearing gas gear was interesting, to say the least. Sometimes the OTR took the form of a 'show' to demonstrate to the Taceval DIStaff that we were able to do it. Often the OTRs were live, i.e. waiting for an aircraft to come back from a sortie and then carry out the OTR for real. Obviously that gave us more of a buzz than doing it in front of a load of Taceval people!*

This is not to say social life didn't get a look in. We were effectively 'confined to barracks' for the duration of the exercise. But there were ways of getting to the local pub – resplendent in gas gear and with 'gatts' [SLR rifles, Bloggs!]. The locals treated us with respect and more often than not we could end up getting rather sozzled! The journey back sometimes involved subterfuge in getting back within the boundaries of the site without being spotted. I hope anyone who is reading this who was in charge at the time didn't think we were tucked up in our beds with a cocoa by 9 o'clock! The resourcefulness of trying to get a drink sometimes outweighed all other considerations! But since we are now 20 years down the road I don't suppose it matters much. But it wasn't me. Honest! At the end of the day's flying, after the aircraft had been A/F'd [After Flight Inspection] and refuelled and we were waiting around for the night attacks, people could be seen walking around with cans of coke. Well, they were coke cans, but sometimes the contents were not pure coke! Obviously beer was a no-no during an exercise; yet every site had a beer lorry. I remember ours was run by an armourer named Dougie Harmer; I wonder what happened to him. Also, there were methods of concealing liquid in one's water bottle. If this makes us sound like a bunch of drunks – well, it was one way to get through the exercise!

The week continued in much the same vein. The aircraft usually flew their sorties 'dry', i.e. with no weapons attached. Occasionally they would go 'live' in order to practise OTRs, but not very often. In the main we were doing turn-rounds and refuels throughout the day without many breaks. The site was split between three teams. Each team had two hides and each hide accommodated two aircraft. So one aircraft from each hide was in the air while the other was being worked on. The routine for team 3 was different because they usually had one aircraft and the T-bird [the 2-seater] plus the main rectification experts.

At the end of the day's flying, after the aircraft had been put to bed, any outstanding rectification had to be carried out. Sometimes this could stretch well into the night and would require assistance from the 'Logs Park' who would provide back-up such as engine change teams. There were particular problems associated with changing the engine of a Harrier in the field because the aircraft had to be jacked up into the flying attitude. The whole mainplane was then lifted off before the engine could be removed. Back at base this was fairly easy because power cranes and hangar lifting devices were available on concrete floors. But in the field other problems presented themselves, such as soft ground and lack of hangar cranes. Usually an HIAB on the back of a 4-tonner could be used. HIAB are the initials of the Swedish company making this crane, which is truck mounted and hydraulically operated, the hydraulics driven by the truck's engine. Apart from major component changes such as this, everything else was very easy to change. Of course, a lot of things could be deferred until we got back to base, in order to keep the aircraft flying.

On Thursday of the second week the exercise was terminated – to many cheers from everyone! The aircraft were prepared for transit and the camp partially dismantled. Camouflage netting was removed, fox-holes and trenches filled in [again courtesy of the Royal Engineers] and unwanted tents were struck. Then we wound down by finishing what was left on the beer wagon. The next day was the mass exodus with the remainder of the tents struck, the remaining equipment packed into trucks and trailers and the convoys formed up for the arduous journey home. All this was started early so that the three hour journey back to base could be completed before it got dark.

The convoys home were usually uneventful, although there was the occasional break-down or getting lost. Then we would swing into the camp gates at Wildenrath, with all the women and children standing and waving Union Jacks. No, just kidding! There was a lot to do before we saw them. The lorries were unloaded, piling the equipment ready to be sorted out on Monday. An advance party would already have met the aircraft. Depending upon the flying programme, some would be made ready for next week's flying while the rest were left in the hangar or readied for rectification. Then there was personal kit to be sorted and the vehicles to be cleaned. Finally, when all that was done – home!

Things didn't always go like clockwork there, either! When I arrived home I was directed to the cellar to strip off. No, nothing kinky, it was just that the smell after two weeks in the field was something less than subtle, so I'm told. Then it was bath, a whisky and bed – to sleep on a MATTRESS. What bliss!

So that was it for another few months; then the whole process would be repeated. Looking back it was an enjoyable time in many ways. I made firm friends, most of whom have remained so since. That has not always been the case of friends made subsequently. You could say that the bond of working 'in the field' with a bunch of disparates is one of life's worthwhile experiences. It taught me lessons which I practise to this day, particularly resourcefulness and adaptability – two traits which are the hallmark of the Royal Air Force.

And, with apologies to Maggie May. . .
It's lovely to see you, you've been gone so long;
And you're looking suspiciously brown!
Why can't you write when you're out 'in the field'?
And what's in that bag you've put down?
It's full of your washing? That's all I need!

> *I suppose there's a lot to unpack?*
> *What do you mean, there's a beer call and you've got to go?*
> *Well, thanks a lot! Welcome back!'*

In 1999 came the following article entitled *Sea, Sun and Lots of Sand* by Dave Perry:

In the mid 1970s British Honduras was coming up for independence. But there was a slight altercation with its neighbour Guatemala over a strip of land on the south British Honduras border. As British Honduras, or as it was later known Belize, was a British protectorate No 1 [F] Harrier Squadron from RAF Wittering was detached to form a close air-support flight for the British ground forces. As the situation progressed into an ongoing commitment the task was spread over the whole Harrier force and by 1978 RAF Germany had taken over the commitment with No's 3 [F] and 4 [AC] Squadrons rotating every three months.

The Belize detachment contained enough ground crew to support four GR3 Harriers in field operations. It was split into three areas. Two of these being the operating hides named Charlie/Delta and Foxy/Golf after the phonetic alphabet. These were situated outside the main perimeter of Belize International Airport, Charlie/Delta being situated alongside the Belican Brewery, and Foxy/Golf alongside the Fire Station and the Puma detachment. Each hide setup had a two aircraft allotment with nine engineers and a cook. The aircraft were parked outside under camouflage netting which resembled the hides used in Northern Europe Deployments, hence the name. Each hide complex was self supportive with enough fuel and weapons to maintain two days operations without resupply from the main camp, where engineering support and operations control were situated. The standard operation was a Dawn and Dusk patrol along the border with additional flights during the day to keep the Aircrew and Groundcrew current for Northern Europe Operations.

It was the 3 [F] Sqdn Christmas detachment and I was on my second tour in Belize. There we were on a clear November day in 1978, 34 degrees [C] or 90F in the shade, the sun over the yard arm. The last flight of the day due back shortly, followed by a warm shower and a cold beer. Do all such dreams come to such an end? The small intercom box in the corner indicated that it was going to emit words of wisdom and out they came. 'Is Dave there? Trev's on his way over, Tango's bogged down on Key Chapel [XV796, 3 (F) Squadron used the tail letter rather than the serial number to identify aircraft]. Grab a turn round kit and meet him at the Puma line.' This was followed by *'See what's wrong and sort it.'* As Trevor Browning and myself boarded the Puma clutching a shovel, a turn round kit [enough tools to make the Harrier ready for flight] and one toothbrush apiece we were fully expecting to be returning late evening.

Key Chapel is one of a string of coral islands from the isthmus of San Pedro running parallel to the barrier reef about 10 km off shore. At that time it was owned by a Kentuckian coal magnate who used it for his holiday home. About 1.5 km long by 800 m wide its main building, the holiday hotel, sat on the seaward side with an airstrip running down north to south almost the length of the Key.

As we approached the hotel looked majestic in the setting sun, not so Tango sitting in the middle of the airstrip looking all forlorn and lonely. On deplaning we approached the pilot or should I say he approached at a trot. 'Got stuck so I dropped the nozzles and gave it some oomph.' Was the greeting an understatement? On close appraisal it became evident that a shovel and a toothbrush were not going to be enough kit to solve this problem. The GR3A Harrier stood on four mounds of coral where it was found out later that lowered nozzles had caused the depressions by moving fifteen JCB bucket loads of sand, most of which I think had disappeared down the engine and auxiliary air intakes. The Harrier was now resplendent in Caribbean livery of grey, green and light brown due to the clinging sand. After passing through the hot and cold nozzles the sand had attached itself in a solid crust to the intakes, laser pod, puffer ducts [flight reaction nozzles used in the hover to change direction] and the rear fuselage.

Standing there wondering what the powers-that-be would make of this Trev and I pondered on the approach to the problem. 'Best see how far it's been ingested,' was Trev's best offering as I headed off to check the engine air filters.

The Puma crew who had by this time finished the in-flight rations joined the party. All stood with bated breath as I made two sand castles; one the size of the Air Motor Servo Unit filter. This is the main filter for the motor that moves the Nozzles, and one matching the air inlet filter to the Fuel Control Unit which controls the engine fuel management system. 'Well that's that!' was muttered and it was decided to phone home to report in. Hold on! It's not quite that easy, the Belize telephone service did not run to Key Chapel so the aircraft radio was used to transmit the news. After a short conversation with a lot of head shaking from the cockpit it was decided that Trev and I would stay to guard the aircraft. Seeing meanwhile if we could come up with a solution, the pilot returning to base as they were in short supply.

After waving good-bye to the departing Puma we headed off to check the accommodation our host had kindly offered us. Not bad, air-conditioned with a sea view, so to the second problem; guarding the aircraft. The dictionary definition states: 'To guard. To prevent unauthorized personnel approaching the guarded object.' As the Harrier was in full view of the hotel bar we invited the other six occupants of the island to a 3 [F] Sqdn welcome party, which kept them nicely away from the aircraft they had been around all day.

As the meal and the night progressed, Anglo-American relations were well into the second phase with the main topic of conversation being how to retrieve Tango back to Charlie/Delta. On our own little island enclave isolated from the real world we were at this time unaware just what was going on and how far the recovery procedure had escalated. After a typical American breakfast we attempted to phone Belize International switchboard using the local telephone net, it was approaching lunch time when we eventually got through and by mid afternoon a Puma was in circuit with two 12´ x 12´ tents to use as a radio shack and rectification office.

This was accompanied by two Royal Corps of Signals Engineers and a full radio communication setup, so at least we were not devoid of outside contact. Whilst the radio shack was being set up Trev and I checked over the engine to ascertain just how many ancillary systems were down or affected by the enforced sand ingestion. Our main worry was that as most of the systems are operated with air taken from the main engine compressor they would be contaminated beyond recoverable repair. It was discovered that most of the air systems had been dusted but not those protected by filters. So although both Compressors and Turbine oil pressurization systems had sand ingestion it had not progressed into the fuel control system, nozzle control system or the fuel tank air pressurization and transfer system.

Our final worry was how far the sand ingress had contaminated the cooling system for the rear nozzle bearings and what was the state of the blades that made up the rotating components of the Pegasus engine. A quick inter-service radio message and 45 minutes later a Royal Navy Scout helicopter that had just happened to be on base from a visiting frigate, was in circuit carrying an intrascope and – doom and gloom – an Engine Change kit. The intrascope is a piece of equipment that is used to look inside the engine through removable ports to check the rotating assemblies. Whilst I had my eyeball to the intrascope Trev was pondering the engine change kit and wondering how all the other ancillary equipment was going to arrive at a small coral island 3,000 miles from home. After I had found no damage, apart from a good sand blast to the Compressors and Turbines it was time to disappear into the cool radio shack to pinch a cup of tea and ring home. 'Hello Belize, this is Key Chapel.' 'Send Chapel.' The speed of reply should have indicated what the state of play was, but at the time it did not register. 'Compressors clean, turbines good, no serious damage to Engine.' 'Wait one Chapel.' 'Engineering Officer plus full Engine change and Wing off team on their way over, please confirm accommodation for an extra six persons.'

To remove the Harrier engine the wing must be removed first. This normally requires a team of two Airframe fitters, three Engine fitters, an Instrument fitter and an Electrical fitter. Due to the manpower restrictions imposed by the need to fly normal sorties from Belize our team consisted of Trev Browning, Ron Brown the Airframe Technician, Paul Horth the Instrument fitter and myself. An electrician to be flown out when required. What Paul did not know was that he was there to turn the handle on the crane as it was manual.

Whilst we had been in our own seclusion the channels of communication must have been red hot as that night over a debrief we got the message: We have three options:

1. Fly the fuselage, engine and wings out under a stream of Pumas.
2. Fly the fuselage, engine and wings out in three Lockheed C130 Hercules [What!].
3. Engine change, systems flush and fly it out.

Right! So whichever way we go we have to remove the wing and engine and make sure that the fuel tanks don't dry out in the process as this was the number one problem with engine changes in Belize.

The morning was greeted by the first helicopter flight of the day, I won't say Puma flight as every helicopter available was seconded into use. The kit required started to arrive, personnel came courtesy of the Royal Navy, heavy equipment under-slung from Pumas. The Wing stand was the first to arrive followed by the 'A' frame Crane and engine egg box; this doubled as an engine stand and transport box. It was split into two, the top becoming the bottom for the removed engine and the bottom becoming the top; it was empty at this time as we did not have a spare Pegasus ECU. Then came the lifting slings, jacks, power units and tool kits, finally the field fuel-canister that looked like a rubberized version of Barnes Wallace's famous bomb. Amid all this activity one of the Loadmasters came over with a spares container. 'Jeff Castleton says the last one you sent was no good can he have a new one.' On opening I found the contents to be a coconut I had sent for the hide flower-garden, so unbenown to the next RN flight they transported a highly relevant serviceable component for the operation. The team was now fast expanding and closing on a dozen personnel so in came the Compo rations and the evening meal was an introduction to our hosts of Sundowners and Compo stew. All that was required now was the final shipment of Royal Engineers and the Harrier maxipad so the work could start in earnest.

The following morning was greeted by a not so bright and bushy tailed crew who started to set about arranging all the equipment into some logical order to split the Harrier down; in amongst all this the REs had arrived and the pad was completed, resplendent in all its glory with the Harrier up on jacks. When the Harrier was first designed all the clamps and connections that had to be disconnected to remove the wing and engine were painted yellow for ease of identification so non Harrier-trained technical personnel could be used in the removal. After a quick briefing to all available manpower on how all you needed to pull a Harrier engine was a pair of wire snips and a 7/16″ ratchet socket-spanner. A combined work force headed off to remove all the yellow-painted engine pipe-clamps. With the wing removal almost complete a report came in from base: 'Hold on. The Pumas can't fly it out as they have tried it and the wing starts to fly above 15 knots.'

What next? was the burning question as we had a Harrier almost in kit form and nowhere to go. We decided to go as far as engine disconnect and wing off, either way the engine needed to come out. The wing was removed without any undue problems and the author was in the inverted position disconnecting the rear nozzle drives that are situated under the water tank between the rear nozzles, when Trev's face appeared at the nozzle opening. 'Fat Albert in circuit', this being the nickname for a Lockheed C130. As I disentangled myself from the workings I was greeted with the picture of Fat Albert approaching the Key at treetop height, Dunlops dangling and all flying surfaces flopping and dropping. At this point there were personnel stood on ground equipment to obtain a better view, but the C130 descended even lower, so the ground crew tended to remove themselves to a safer vantage point. The C130 carried out a low level pass along the strip just above ground level and left in a cloud of burnt aviation fuel and coral dust. When the cloud had cleared the ground crew looked like bakers and the engineering officer was following the aircraft paperwork across the Key. 'Don't think that will work,' 'Could have warned us,' and a few more unprintable statements followed in the C130's wake. By the time the site was recovered it was closing dusk on Friday night and we all adjourned for a well needed shower.

Saturday morning saw the sun rise over a calm sea and a leisurely breakfast, when the duty radio operator reported 'Comm from UK 1000 local, all technicians to stand by.' That started a discussion of what the plan was and 1000 came with everybody in the radio shack. It was OC Eng Wg Cdr John Manning. John, who was like myself an ex Halton Apprentice, had considerable experience in aircraft recovery – both the wrecked variety and unservicable ones stuck in strange parts of the world. 'How bad is the engine?' was his first question, 'So-So', 'Will it run?' 'Don't know.' 'Are the auxiliary systems contaminated?' 'No.' About twenty minutes of this ensued. 'Will call you back in two hours.' Two hours later and the radio sprang to life. 'Put it back together we are going to try and fly it out.' It had transpired that the situation was getting a bit political and no spare engine could be delivered for a week, so plan 'B' was in operation.

The rest of Saturday and Sunday morning saw the reassembly and by mid afternoon it was discovered that the undercarriage would not fully retract as the bottom of the engine bay, where the main undercarriage leg pivot normally housed itself, was full of sand and would require an engine pull to clear it. The decision was taken to run the engine anyway to see what would happen.

Monday morning saw the whole population of the island stood at a safe distance as Trev climbed into the cockpit. 'Here goes' and the canopy slid shut. At clear start the Auxiliary Power Unit/Gas Turbine Starter sprang into life, faltered, coughed once, and ran up to standby mode accompanied by a large exhalation of breath. Now for the big one, the APU/GTS ran up *to start mode and the engine started to rotate. At which point the rest of the missing sand disappeared aft in a cloud. Dry run r.p.m. was reached which is when the engine is rotated but no fuel is injected so the combustion chambers do not ignite. After 30 seconds dry run Trev shut down the engine and allowed the APU/GTS to cool down. 'OK Dave, let's check the rest.' The engine was restarted and when all systems were on line and checked Trev stirred the stick to puffs of sand from all the extremities as the reaction nozzles opened. 'No problems there. Acceleration checks next.' As the engine and aircraft ground checks continued it became more and more obvious that the Harrier was not unduly upset about eating a large portion of a Caribbean island. When the engine finally wound down and the Key was once again peaceful, all systems were working normally.*

We still had the problem with the undercarriage and without tie-down equipment we could not check top end acceleration times or max. r.p.m. Tie-down equipment was needed for two reasons, the first being that the brakes gave in at 55% r.p.m. and you could not check the nozzles below 10%. This information was relayed to Belize and the reply was 'Put the ground locks in, we will fly it back legs down, the pilot can check top end pre-take-off.' With this we all wondered who the 'WE' was.

The following morning produced the answer as Flt Lt Paul Hopkins climbed out of a Scout to greet us: 'I lost the draw.' 'It's all yours, sign here.' 'Thanks a lot,' and carried out his walk-round and slid into the cockpit. The engine started and with a quick radio transmission [I am not sure whether it was terrestrial or heavenly], Paul taxied out onto the strip. The engine wound up to full power and Tango moved about 100 ft [30 metres] down the runway and stopped; a voice cut the stillness of the moment: 'It's OK he's checking out the max. r.p.m.' The engine wound up to full power again and Paul started his take-off run, nozzles down and our last view was Tango heading home with legs down as fast as safety permitted.

About 20 minutes after take-off came the message to confirm a safe landing, but what this failed to admit was that the Harrier stopped mid-runway and was towed the final few hundred yards to the Puma hangar. It seemed that providence was not to be tested too much. 'Well that's that, let's pack up and go home.' We now had to dismantle all the equipment and await the helicopters, which would take another two days, leaving Trev and myself till the end. Whilst all this was in progress the Harrier was recovered with a good vacuum and an engine change.

It was a credit to all responsible for design and maintenance of a unique aircraft that was designed for the European theatre, that it took to Caribbean cuisine so well. Or was it just an indication of things to come a few years later.

In September 1994 Alan East reported on a visit to Bentwaters by Association members:

'Be at the guardroom by 0945,' said Fred. But the main gate had apparently been locked since the Americans vacated the place over a year ago. However, we found the appropriate side gate and awaited our escort. 'We' being: Bill Brindley, Alan East, Fred Dolman, his brother Arthur and friends Charlie Hale, Dave Keeble and Adrian Cotton. Before we could be led across the runway to the 3 Sqn site we had to wait while a 4-ship from 4 Sqn took off. We had arrived in the middle of Exercise Hazel Flute in which, for the first time ever, all three Harrier squadrons were deployed together – each independent on their own site, but all on Bentwaters airfield. The trucks, tents and hides were scattered amongst the many pine trees and, being in flat East Anglia, it looked like much of northern Germany. But since the collapse of the Warsaw Pact that is no longer a likely battle area. So, using commercial ferries, the squadrons from Germany had practised a more distant deployment by crossing the Channel. Even so, at Bentwaters they were still a long way from the 'front line', which was the Scottish, Welsh and Cornish borders. The 'enemy' occupied Jockland, Taffland and Tinland! Instead of quick half-hour sorties from close behind allied armies, they needed to plan hi-lo-hi flights of 1hr 40mins.

Being Thursday, there is no concert today! As we arrived the Site Commander, Sqn Ldr Nigel Wharmby, had declared a practice fire in the Ops. Caravan, so all planning boards etc. had been evacuated to a safe facility. All good preparations for the 'Mineval' due the following week! Sqn Adj Nick Prole doubles as Squadron Intelligence Officer and when all was back to normal he briefed us on the current situation. We saw the GLO's staff receive a new task, prepare maps for the pilots already in their cockpits and add details over the telebrief. Nick's assistant was Plt Off Vanessa Haven on summer detachment from her UAS [University Air Squadron]. I was surprised to learn that I knew her father, having done our flying training together in Canada in 1952/3 and having met occasionally since. The field kitchen was on site and Vanessa escorted us to an impressive lunch. With modern gas-fired ovens the cooks can offer a choice of good hot dishes within 1+ hours of pitching camp.

We watched the aircraft returning to a vertical landing on the specially laid mat in a clearing and then taxying to their hides for an OTR. We spent much time under the camouflage nets watching operations and even seeing FLIR and TV displays in the cockpit. The Squadron is in good hands! Before leaving Fred presented the CO, Wg Cdr Clive Loader, with a copy of Bee Beamont's latest book and Charlie Hale presented one of his Holly cartoons of a Harrier GR7. Further opportunities to come at Marham or Leeming.

Further visits during night training detachments took place in 1995:

The Harrier GR7 currently operated by the Squadron is equipped to enable a low level, night attack capability. Primarily this comprises a

Harrier GR.7 ZG511 on deployment to Bentwaters, May 1997. (Fred Dolman)

thermal imaging system – Forward Looking Infra Red [FLIR] – fitted in the aircraft's nose and Night Vision Goggles [NVGs] fitted just above the pilot's nose. The FLIR data is integrated with the aircraft's Nav/Attack System with pilot information being presented either by the Head Up Display [HUD] or on multipurpose cockpit display screens. The NVGs are principally light amplification devices which are mounted on the pilot's helmet and provide a near daylight image in conditions of very low ambient light. The requirement to become proficient in the use of this equipment up to Night Combat Ready status necessitated a concentrated programme to achieve. The restrictions imposed on low flying training in Germany, where the Squadron is normally based, resulted in a series of detachments to the UK over the period November 1994 to March 1995:

Wing Commander Clive Loader and 3 Squadron Harrier GR.7 ZG862/AI under 'Red Tint' camouflage, simulating an urban surrounding.

RAF Coltishall first, Marham in December; Leeming January and February, lastly West Freugh.

During each of these detachments a number of Association members were able to respond to the Squadron's invitation to visit and it would be fair to comment that those who did were made most welcome. Most aspects of their activities were shown and explained to us. This included an aircraft, with systems powered up, being available with air- and ground-crews in attendance to provide the technical talk. The capabilities of the NVGs were demonstrated with an opportunity to view the outside world through these very impressive pieces of equipment. Sitting in on pre-flight briefings and post-mission debriefings was encouraged, which included explanation of attack profile success – or lack of it! – using video tape record of the sortie.

A visit to Air Traffic Control during one of the Leeming visits included witnessing the unusual scenario of NVG equipped Harrier crews calling for runway lights 'out' during approaches with the Tornados in circuit wanting them back on!! At the end of flying we enjoyed a social gathering in the more relaxed atmosphere of a local hostelry for a pie and a pint. It was at the second Leeming detachment that the challenge – 'I defy you lot to turn up at West Freugh' – was issued by the Boss which resulted in six members, Ron [AFC] and Mary Ledwidge, Jack and June Long, Andy Anderson and Vic Lorriman doing just that. Two days were spent in

Portpatrick with visits to the Squadron by day [don't mention Yellow Boot Laces to Mary and June!] *and an entertaining dinner in the evening which included some very novel ways to raise funds for Comic Relief!!*

During the first Leeming detachment, Jim Nickson, a former 3[F] Sqdn pilot of the Tempest era, learned of the Squadron's presence in the UK from an article in his local newspaper. Being unaware of the existence of the Association, he later contacted the Squadron independently and was invited to visit them during the February detachment. With uncanny skill, the Adjutant at that time, Fg Off Nick Prole, arranged for Jim's visit to coincide with the now obligatory appearance of a group of Association members. Among that group was member Sam Merrikin who, on being introduced to Jim instantly recognised him and it was established that the last time they had met was during their service together on 3[F] Sqdn fifty years previously. Unfortunately for Jim, the Association Membership Secretary was also in the visiting group that day and he subsequently became member No. 294 [the total has now passed 350].

Now, here is an article by Bill Burchell, *Tomcat Neutered*! reproduced from British Aerospace magazine *Arrow* June 1999 by kind permission of the editor.

High above the Persian Gulf the American pilot of an F14 Tomcat was about to have a nice day. Like the identical fighter off his wing tip, he'd been launched from the aircraft carrier USS John Stennis *to engage in simulated air-to-air combat with two RAF Harrier GR7s. This was essential practice earlier this year, when there was a deteriorating situation in Iraq and the prospect of real combat.*

Spotting a Harrier on his radar, the F14 Pilot swept in for the kill. But having manoeuvred into a missile firing position, the Harrier he'd targetted suddenly seemed to stop in the air. Unable to brake, the F14 overshot the quarry – and the hunter suddenly became the hunted.

Now behind the Tomcat, the GR7 moved to attack, its weapon aiming systems quickly locking on to their target. Despite the American's evasive efforts, the simulated missile scored a computerised 'kill'. But as the US pilot came to terms with losing this fight, further embarrassment followed: instead of breaking off its attack the Harrier moved in closer, 'killing' the Tomcat a second time with a simulated burst from its guns.

To so comprehensively out-manoeuvre such a powerful adversary says much for the Harrier and its pilot, but the aircraft's ability to redirect its thrust, as the Tomcat found out, makes it a devil to catch in a dogfight.

As the Tomcat closed in, the Harrier had swivelled its jet nozzles from horizontally backwards to downwards and forwards – a manoeuvre known as 'viffing' [vectoring in forward flight] *which, as every Harrier pilot knows, can be highly effective in air combat.*

Flight Lieutenant Matt Vardy has flown Harriers for nearly three years, latterly with 3 [F] Squadron RAF, including a recent three-month tour in the Persian Gulf where he was able to hone his viffing skills.

'When you first start viffing it's quite exciting,' he explains. 'The most extraordinary feeling is when you vector thrust forwards in a steep dive. The braking effect is immense and, despite the dive, you don't accelerate. Any opposing aircraft attempting to follow you simply overshoots, leaving you in a position to attack it.

'That said, viffing has to be handled very carefully. In fact, in most combat situations we wouldn't viff, but it does provide another option in attack and defence. Generally speaking we only practise it in particular aircraft configurations, because the very nature of the manoeuvre takes you closer to the limits of control.'

Like all able people who make difficult things seem simple, this nonchalance masks considerable skills, for, according to its pilots, the British Aerospace Harrier is one of the most difficult aircraft to fly – thanks to its high cockpit workload during vertical take-off and landing.

Such are the qualities of its pilots that only 15 hand-picked candidates are taught to fly the aircraft each year. Selection for the seven-month conversion course at RAF Wittering in Cambridgeshire, however, is no guarantee of success, for even the best pilots can find the Harrier a handful. Those who master it are a rare breed indeed.

In addition to the 15 trainees, each year 14 operational Harrier pilots return to the training squadron for post-graduate courses. Four become weapons instructors – the most sought-after course in the Royal Air Force – another four become instrument rating examiners, and six progress as electronic warfare instructors.

Flight Lieutenant Vardy converted to Harriers in 1995, having been among the first to complete a demanding 10-month 'mirror image' course combining advanced flying training on the British Aerospace Hawk with tactics and weapons training. 'I chose the Harrier because of its challenging reputation,' he confides. 'Not only was it difficult to fly, but its suite of weapons gives it great flexibility. Add its amazing ability to take-off and land in so many different ways and, for a pilot, the combination is exceptional.'

The Harrier's attributes proved particularly useful when 3(F) Squadron were deployed aboard HMS *Illustrious* in the Gulf this year – the first time its pilots had operated from a ship.

'What makes ship operations different,' says Matt, 'is that once you've burned down below diversion fuel there's nowhere else to go. That said, the VSTOL [vertical and short take-off and landing] regime is tremendously rewarding, particularly when you're approaching a ship and you know there are eight aircraft behind you needing to land at 30 second intervals. Managing your fuel is critical. The Gulf's high temperatures also affected engine performance, so you had to be at the right weight at exactly the right time to ensure you didn't mess up someone else's approach.'

So is being a modern fighter pilot as exciting as it looks? 'Having done it *for some years many aspects become routine, but I guess it probably is,' he admits. 'Indeed I feel very privileged to have realised my ambition. Like any job, however, it still has its downsides – such as long days of planning in darkened rooms – but its rewards are unique.*

Flying very fast and low against all sorts of adversaries is spectacular – there's just nothing like it. Harriers also do a lot of air-to-air combat against a varied mix of types, from F-15s and F-16s to Tornado F3s, and fighting other very capable competitors adds an exhilarating edge. The professional incentive, however, is not to lose – and the Harrier takes some beating.

CHAPTER NINETEEN

The New Millennium

O N 15 JUNE 2000 the Association magazine published the following Commanding Officer's report:

Having just come to the end of another exciting episode in the history of 3 [Fighter] Squadron, *I thought you might appreciate the following update for inclusion in the next edition of* Three's Company.

The Squadron has been on the move again over the last eight weeks, both literally and continually. As I write, we find ourselves just north of the Canary Isles on the final leg of a remarkable trip which began as a NATO exercise, and turned into an adventure in equatorial latitudes, saving the UN and others from the unwelcome attentions of a particularly unsavoury group of individuals in Sierra Leone. As the good ship HMS Illustrious *steams homeward, there is time to reflect on recent events and put pen to paper before we disembark tomorrow afternoon for our return to Cottesmore.*

April began with a flurry of activity, as we completed preparations for what we thought would be a month afloat in the company of the Royal Navy. The whole Squadron would be deploying, pilots had already spent time at RNAS Yeovilton learning to launch themselves into the air from an inclined ramp, night sorties were being flown, VSTOL currencies regained, and the aircraft were being modified and readied for flying from the ship. I should add, however, that the prospect of a spell at sea had been dominating our activities since our return from the Christmas and New Year leave period; Three's Company, soon to be a ship's company, had spent the first few dark January days being burned, drowned, frozen, and told to plug holes in the Devil's own contraption, a sinking ship simulator. This was the Royal Navy's Basic Sea Survival Course, an excellent remedy for the excesses of the festive season and well worthwhile. The Squadron had a short respite before deploying to Italy in support of operations in the Balkans at the end of January; we returned in March, and began the workup for the shipboard Exercise LINKED SEAS in earnest. The first two weeks of the deployment were to begin in the benign waters of the Mediterranean, before sailing through the Straits of Gibraltar and northwards to Brest for a welcome weekend on terra firma. The Exercise would involve the combined forces of several NATO nations and a handful of 'partner' states, and would take place in the rather less forgiving environment of the Bay of Biscay at the beginning of May.

So much for the plan. We began as we intended, leaving the dreary weather of T.S. Elliot's 'cruellest month' for the clear skies of the central and eastern Mediterranean in spring. The majority of the Squadron flew to Malta to join the Ship, leaving a gallant, though apprehensive, team of pilots to fly the six Harriers on board two days later off the south coast of Sardinia. Not one of these pilots had flown from a Royal Navy aircraft carrier before and gale force winds and high seas on the day of the embarkation did little to quell their nerves. Delay after delay ensued, but Poseidon relented before nightfall and all six landed after a short but memorable trip, much to the delight of the BBC team that was aboard to cover the first deployment afloat of Harrier GR7s as part of the newly-formed Joint Force Harrier.

With all happily ensconced aboard, we set about exploring our new surroundings. A confusing rabbit warren of corridors, rooms and stairs with lids instead of landings, the Ship's innards were almost as mysterious as its workings. As the labyrinth of passages was kept secret by the complete absence of windows, so the organisation of the Ship was kept veiled by the use of unintelligible expressions, naval vernacular, and a working rhythm which would have been recognisable to the crew of the Victory. Before long, however, the Squadron had a useful knowledge of the Ship's layout, and had translated most of the alien jargon into something that could be understood. Thus began the process of integration that would continue throughout the deployment, and would prove so useful in its latter stages. In the air, workup sorties commenced and by the end of the month all 14 embarked pilots had attained carrier Combat Ready status.

Pleased at the way things were going, and overjoyed to be on dry land again, the Squadron left the ship in Brest for a welcome weekend break in France. As we reboarded on 1 May, however, how little we guessed that this would be the last time we would set foot on solid ground for over 40 days!

Exercise LINKED SEAS itself was, sadly, a disappointment. Poor weather, the positioning of the Ship far offshore and the lack of suitable diversions all combined to reduce the flying rate to much less than we had expected. Despite the efforts of HMS Illustrious' crew to sail to more suitable areas, very little training could be carried out in the conditions encountered. A number of Squadron personnel were disembarked, and all were relieved when the announcement came that the Ship was no longer taking part in the Exercise. The rest of the broadcast was hardly audible above the noise and vibration of the Ship's propulsion system, which was operating at full speed, but we ascertained that we were now on our way south to Sierra Leone. 'That's all,' said the 'pipe' or Tannoy, and four days of numbing rattling followed as we sailed south as fast as the ship was able.

During the transit, the skies cleared as we entered the Azores high pressure system and the flying rate improved, much to everyone's relief. Before long the water temperature had risen to nearly 30 deg C and a keen observer would spot shoals of flying fish, dolphins, and, later, sharks surrounding the Ship. Much planning was carried out as we steamed south. We were briefed on the situation in Sierra Leone, on the background to the problem, and on the UK government's intent to take action to provide support to the UN and to assist the Government of Sierra Leone in the implementation of the Lomé peace accord. The Operation was named PALLISER, and its immediate objectives were twofold: to conduct the evacuation of entitled persons, and to provide support to beleaguered UN forces in the country. It became apparent that we would provide a Close Air Support [CAS] capability should friendly UK forces come under attack. Besides the CAS role, we would be used, when approval was given, to fly 'presence' missions, which would show intent to use offensive air power.

The date of our arrival in theatre was kept a closely guarded secret, and, once in position, we were not permitted to fly into Sierra Leone for a few days until other ships were in theatre and political approval was granted. During this time we made use of the good weather to fly splash bombing and air combat training sorties, and to prepare for any operational flying that may have been tasked. While we waited, the aircraft were stripped of all non-essential equipment in the interest of retaining as much performance from the engines as possible in hot surroundings. This included flying without self-protection missiles, as there was deemed to be no air threat to the aircraft. The wait did not last long, however, and on 17 May the Squadron flew the first operational Joint Force Harrier mission, providing low level air presence over the heads of rebel forces. Operational sorties continued to be tasked over the following weeks, with the Navy's FA2 Harriers providing photographic reconnaissance of rebel positions, and our aircraft training for CAS missions with Forward Air Controllers on the ground as well as continuing to fly presence sorties 'over the beach' as the Royal Navy refers to it. [One should note that 'over the beach' actually means 'over and beyond the beach', i.e. the whole country, in the RN's terminology].

Reports from ashore soon began to indicate that the rebels were becoming demoralised, partly due to our efforts, certainly in part due to the establishment of an effective defence of Lungi airfield near the capital, Freetown, and not least the capture of the rebel leader, Foday Sankoh. Sporadic action continued; however, by early June, the situation ashore was stable enough that the Joint Task Force Commander could recommend that HMS Illustrious be released to voyage home. This coincided, by chance, with the arrival in earnest of the rains in Sierra Leone, and we were treated to some incredible displays of lightning in the evenings from the quarterdeck of the Ship as we awaited a decision on when we would be sent on our way home. Political approval for our releases was given on 7 June, and, as I write, we are slightly over 500 miles from a position where the aircraft could be launched directly to Cottesmore.

We have learned much from our deployment and the lessons will no doubt continue to be drawn from the experience during the forthcoming weeks. The new Joint Force Harrier has been used for the first time; if not exactly, as it turned out, in anger, at least in earnest, and I am pleased to report that 3 [Fighter] Squadron led Joint Force Harrier's first operational mission.

Tertius Primus Erit, as always!

Yours aye

Ashley Stevenson

In November 2003, *Three's Company* published Outgoing CO's Message – Wing Commander Stuart Atha wrote:

I write this missive sitting in an American tent in the desert 'somewhere in the Middle-East', whilst all around me there is much activity to ensure that we will be ready to send the aircraft back to the UK when permission is given. It does not feel correct to call what we have experienced over the past month a 'war', especially when one compares our experiences to those of Association members who flew in World War II*. However, on the night of 19 March we were not to know how the events of the following weeks would play out. It certainly is a relief to be taking back home the same number of people and aircraft I deployed with. As with any military conflict, the true picture of what we have achieved will take a long time to emerge, if 'truth' is a realistic aspiration. All I can comment on is what I saw from my cockpit and heard on the radio.*

Finally, and most importantly, I am proud of every member of No 3 [Fighter] Squadron regardless of whether they flew, fixed or supported. In very difficult circumstances they proved yet again that it is our people who are responsible for the high regard in which UK Forces are held by all. All tasks from cleaning portaloos to dropping bombs have been conducted with 100% professionalism. More often than not, it is the pilots who are feted as heroes; after all, they are the ones placed directly in harm's way and who deliver the bombs on the target. This time, however, it was different. Those searching for heroes need to visit the aircraft long after the pilots have left for the debriefing room, because our success depended upon the 'gingers' getting aircraft ready for the next sortie. For weeks on end the engineers worked without a break to ensure that we did not lose operational sorties needlessly. The results were exceptional. 290 sorties out of a possible 292 were flown. I am slightly embarrassed to admit that I was responsible for the 2 lost sorties. No matter how hard I tried, the aircraft would not start, which was one fault that even I could not take into the air!

I leave it to others to detail the number of bombs dropped and targets hit. However, before there is a rush to measure success by hit-rate [and I am confident that this was the most accurately conducted air campaign the Harrier Force has been involved in], *there are so many more reasons for us to take pride in our performance. Often it is the decision not to drop a bomb which is the most difficult. Moreover, when supporting our troops on the ground, it is not always the effect of a bomb going off that is required; simply being there providing eyes and the potential muscle is sufficient . . .*

It is now 6 weeks since I started writing this letter. I was interrupted by news of the decision to deploy the aircraft home via Cyprus the following day. As many of you may have seen on national TV news, we flew the aircraft into Cottesmore on Good Friday, appropriately – to be met by the C-in-C, a piper, the media and, most importantly, our families. Unfortunately, my imminent posting has left me little time for Caroline and the children, as I prepare to hand the Squadron over to Bruce Hedley. I am fortunate to have Bruce as my successor. This will be his third tour on 3 [F] Squadron; he is full of enthusiasm and will undoubtedly have many much-needed new ideas. Although I would love to do it all over again, the time has come to move on. At least I will take with me many happy memories, such as the 90th Anniversary Reunion, our 7-week deployment to Canada in 2001, and lastly our contribution to Operation TELIC [Iraqi Freedom].

Commanding the Fighting Third has been the highlight of my career and my experience as 'Boss' of the Squadron has reinforced my belief that 'the squadron' is the primary source of the ethos and the fighting spirit that are vital components of our operational capability. The Association has an important role to play in this process by promoting the sense of belonging and the esprit de corps *that flows from serving on a squadron. Therefore, I would like to close by thanking our Chairman, Alan East, for his immense contribution towards the Association. Without the efforts of both Alan and his wife Thelma, we would not have as active an Association as we currently enjoy and our Squadron would be all the weaker for it.*

Best wishes, Stuart Atha

Alan East was able to follow the above with a Stop Press:

Gulf Operational Honours

1. At the reunion last May, Stuart Atha said a little about long sorties during Operation TELIC. These involved several in-flight refuellings while strapped to the ejection seat for several hours, at night, wearing night vision goggles! The mid-November issue of RAF News reports that:

Wg Cdr Stuart Atha has been awarded the Distinguished Service Order for his 'conspicuous leadership, command and personal example' during the Squadron's detachment to the Gulf. His citation includes: 'As an example of his leadership from the front, he led a mission lasting 8 hours 50 mins on the night of 19/20th March to support UK forces, with whom he had trained so intensely. During his subsequent 14 missions, Atha was the model of professionalism, judgement, restraint, effectiveness and courage. He played a leading role in providing close air support to ground troops in repulsing enemy counter-attacks, personally attacking enemy firing locations, personnel and anti-aircraft artillery pieces.

'Following a 6-month work-up, Atha led his squadron in an exemplary fashion through an intense 28-day period of hostilities, during which his squadron flew an astounding total of 290 sorties and almost 1,250 flying hours without loss. He showed conspicuous leadership, command and personal example over a protracted period involving hostilities in extremely complex circumstances.'

2. Also honoured is FS Keith Prime, with Queen's Commendation for Valuable Service.

'On arrival in the area of operations, FS Prime's foresight, drive and intuitive managerial skills meant that the engineering site was very quickly established, ready to handle aircraft within hours of the main party arriving. When hostilities commenced, he continued to be at the hub of activities. Unstinting in his determination to look after his men, he was at pains to ensure that they were fed, rested and coping with the climate, while appearing to ignore his own fatigue.

'His matchless all round professionalism and determination to achieve the task, whatever the odds, gained him an enviable reputation across the whole deployed operating base. His inspirational leadership and effective management have resulted in a higher achievement from his squadron than could reasonably have been expected.'

It would be difficult, not to say unwise, to follow that so I institute a pause – not a conclusion – to these stories from the history of the Air Company as, at the time of writing, we approach the ninety-third Anniversary of its formation, 1 April 2004. We must all be proud of this latest chapter in our defence of freedom of thought, speech and action – too often needed to free the innocent from oppression.

I would like to close with the finest tribute I have found so far:

ODE WRITTEN IN 1746

HOW sleep the brave, who sink to rest,
By all their country's wishes blest!
When Spring, with dewy fingers cold,
Returns to deck their hallowed mould,
She there shall dress a sweeter sod
Than Fancy's feet have ever trod.

By fairy hands their knell is rung;
By forms unseen their dirge is sung;
There Honour comes, a pilgrim gray,
To bless the turf that wraps their clay;
And Freedom shall awhile repair
To dwell, a weeping hermit, there!

WILLIAM COLLINS

Bibliography

Arthur, Max. *There Shall Be Wings*. Hodder & Staughton, 1993

Ashworth, Chris. *Action Stations*, Vol. 5: Military Airfields of the South West. PSL, 1982

Baring, Maurice. *R.F.C. H.Q. 1914–1918*. G. Bell & Sons, 1920.

Bowyer, Chaz *The Sopwith Camel: King of Combat*. Aston Publications, 1978.

Bowyer, Chaz. *Fighter Command 1936–1968*. J M Dent & Sons Ltd, 1980. Reprint Book Club, Associates (also 1980).

Bowyer, Michael J.F. *Fighting Colours: RAF Fighter Camouflage and Markings 1937–1969*. Patrick Stephens, 1969.

Braybrook, Roy. *Harrier: The Vertical Reality*. RAFBF Enterprises, 1996.

Bruce, J.M. *The Aeroplanes of the Royal Flying Corps (Military Wing)*. Putnam, 1982.

Britain's First Warplanes. Arms and Armour Press Ltd, 1987.

Collyer, D.G. (compiler). *Buzz Bomb Diary*. Kent Aviation Historical Research Society, 1994.

Cull, Brian and Bruce Landers, with Heinrich Weiss. *Twelve Days in May*. Grub Street, 1995.

Dallas Brett, R. *British Aviation 1908-1916*, Aviation Book Club 2 Vols. 1933. Reprint single volume Air Research Publications, 1988.

Hart, Peter & Nigel Steel. *Tumult in the Clouds*. Hodder & Stoughton, 1997.

Dorman, Geoffrey. *Fifty Years Fly Past*. Forbes Robertson, 1951.

Driver, Hugh. *The Birth of Military Aviation*. RHS/The Boydell Press, 1977.

Flint, Peter. *RAF Kenley*. Terence Dalton, 1988.

Gelb, Norman. *Scramble: A Narrative History of the Battle of Britain*. Michael Joseph 1986.

Jackson, Robert. *F-86 Sabre: The Operational record*. Airlife, 1994.

James, Derek N. *Westland Aircraft Since 1915*. Putnam, 1991.

James, N.D.G. *Gunners at Larkhill: A History of the Royal School of Artillery*. Gresham Books, 1983.

Joubert de la Ferte, P.B. *The Fated Sky*. Hutchinison & Co Ltd. 1911-52. Reprint, White Lion, 1977.

Laffin, John. *Swifter Than Eagles*. Blackwood, 1964.

Loraine, Winifred (Widow). *Actor, Soldier, Airman*. Collins, 1938.

Luff, David. *The Bulldog Fighter*. Airlife, 1987.

Mason, Frank K. *The Gloster Gladiator*. Macdonald & Co. 1964.

Mason, Frank K. *The Hawker Hurricane*. Macdonald & Co. 1962.

McCudden, James Byford. *Five Years in the Royal Flying Corps*. The "Aeroplane" & General Publishing Co. Ltd. 1918. Plus numerous reprints

McInnes, I. and J.V. Webb. *A Contemptible Little Flying Corps*. London Stamp Exchange, 1991.

Milberry, Larry. *The Canadair Sabre*. Canav Books, 1986. (A.C.E. 7/9 2110A)

Moyes, Philip J.R. *Bomber Squadrons of the R.A.F and Their Aircraft.* Macdonald, 1964.

Pegg, Bill. *Sent Flying.* Macdonald, 1959.

Penrose, Harald. *British Aviation: The Pioneer Years.* Putnam, 1967.

Probert,Henry. *High Commanders of the RAF.* HMSO, 1991.

Raleigh, Walter. *The War in the Air. Vol. 1.* Oxford University Press, 1922. Reprinted by Hamish Hamilton, 1969.

Rawlings, John D.R. *Fighter Squadrons of the RAF and Their Aircraft.* Macdonald, 1969.

Rawlings, John D.R. *Coastal, Support and Special Squadrons of the R.A.F. and Their Aircraft.* Macdonald, 1982.

Robertson, Bruce. *British Aircraft Serials.* Ian Allan, 1971. Plus numerouus updated editions.

Shaw, Michael. *Twice Vertical.* Macdonald, 1971.

Shaw, Michael. *No. 1 Squadron.* Ian Allan, Macdonald, 1988.

Shirer, William L. *The Rise and Fall of the Third Reich.* Secker & Warburg, 1959.

Taylor, John W.R. and Maurice F. Allward. *Westland 50.* Ian Allan, 1965.

Wagner, Ray. *The North American Sabre.* Macdonald, 1963.

INDEX